FRENCH RAILWAYS
CHEMINS DE FER FRANÇAIS
LOCOMOTIVES AND RAILCARS
MATÉRIEL MOTEUR

SECOND EDITION/DEUXIÈME ÉDITION

The complete guide to Locomotives and
Railcars of the Railways of France

Le guide complet du Matériel Moteur
des Chemins de Fer Français

Brian Garvin, David Haydock and Peter Fox

Translation by/Traduction par Mr. et Mme D. Haydock

Published by /Publié par/ Platform 5 Publishing Ltd., Lydgate House, Lydgate Lane,
Sheffield S10 5FH, England.

Printed in England by/ Imprimé en Angleterre par/ Bayliss Printing Co., Turner Road,
Worksop, Notts and Finchmark Ltd., Bredbury, Stockport.

ISBN 1 872524 25-7

Distribué en France par David Haydock, 48 rue du Chemin Vert, F-59500 Douai, France.

TGV 113+TGV 112 'LAUSANNE'. 14.20 Paris–Lausanne. Between/entre Frasne and/et Vallorbe. 02/08/88.

G.B. Wise

CONTENTS/TABLE DES MATIÈRES

INTRODUCTION

FOREWORD TO SECOND EDITION

Welcome to the second edition of this book, which contains full details of all locomotives and multiple units of the Société Nationale des Chemins de Fer Français hereafter referred to as the SNCF. Details of the stock of certain minor railways are also included.

It is some five years since the first edition appeared and many changes have taken place in the intervening years. Beyond doubt the great SNCF success story is the TGV. The first edition of this book was published when TGV Sud Est was up and running and construction had been authorised for TGV Atlantique. TGV Atlantique is now with us and with it a new world speed record of 515.3 km/h (322 m.p.h.). Most of the TGV-A sets have now been delivered but soon to come are the Trans-Manche Super Train, TGV Nord, TGV Reseau and more!.

The changes on SNCF are continuing with the growth of local passenger services, especially around Paris but also elsewhere following contracts being signed with local authorities. On the freight sector, changes here will see many branch lines closed.

All these changes affect the traction scene and it is best appreciated by summarising what has happened in the last five years of so.

Classes extinct:

BB 900, BB 4100, 2D2 9100, CC 65000, BB 71000, X 2400, X 2701, X 3800, Z 3700, Z 4100, Y 2200.

Classes being withdrawn:

BB 9400, BB 13000 (1992), CC 14100 (1993), CC 40100 (1993) A1AA1A 62000 (1994), CC 65500 (1993), Y 6200, Y 6300, Y 6400, Z 5100(1997).

Additions:

26000, 62400, 64700, 64800, 66700, Y 8000, Y 8400, Z 8800, Z 11500, Z 20500, TGV-A.

In 1991 SNCF expects to receive more 26000s whilst rebuilding will be completed on two CC 1100s, seven 64700s, two 66700s and fourteeen 9600s. The last mentioned are 9400s converted for push-pull operation with RRR sets. Developments now taking place include modifying one 9200, and twelve 16000s for push-pull work on new RRR sets. They are expected to use the t.d.m. (time division multiplex) system which sends commands in digital form over the UIC cable on carriages. For freight trains a radio system is being developed to send the same signals to a locomotive in the middle or at the rear of a train which will thus be remotely controlled. The "Sybics" may be fitted with the same system to allow two locomotives to work in multiple on heavy freights. Then there are the TGV developments and that is a story all in itself. Perhaps the exciting development here is not TMST but the proposed double-deck TGV sets!. Yes the future is quite exciting!.

In this expanded edition details of museum lines have been included as in other recent titles in this series. Also provided are details of SNCF locomotives that have been sold out of service. The details are incomplete and the author welcomes sightings and and other fresh information on this subject.

Finally it is hoped that the arrival of this second edition will mean more interesting excursions over branch lines and private railways in France. I hope that you find the this book a useful companion.

Brian Garvin, David Haydock & Peter Fox

ROVER TICKETS

The "France Vacances Pass" Railrover ticket is available for the visitor to France. This gives the freedom of the SNCF for any 4 days in any 15 days and costs £78 (£39) 2nd class and £109.00 (£55) 1st class, or 9 days in any calendar month for £134 (£67) 2nd class and £195 (£98) 1st class. Prices in parentheses are for children aged 4–11. In addition to the freedom of the SNCF, the ticket also includes a one day Paris Metro rover, free transfers between Paris and the Airport plus reduced price travel on the Chemins de Fer de la Provence. The ticket includes TGV supplements where applicable. Please note that this ticket is only available for foreigners and is not available for French Nationals.

ABBREVIATIONS

Standard abbreviations used in this book are:

km/h   kilometres per hour
kN   kilonewtons
kW   kilowatts
BR   British Railways
DB   Deutsche Bundesbahn (German Federal Railway)
NS   Nederlandse Spoorwegen (Netherlands Railways)
RRR   Rames Réversibles Régionales (new regional push-pull hauled sets)
RATP   Regie Autonome des Transports Pariens (Paris Transport Authority)
SNCB   Société Nationale des Chemins de Fer Belgesi (Belgian Railways)
Length   Length over couplings or buffers
Power   One hour rating
T.E.   Tractive Effort

PASSENGER VEHICLE TYPE CODES

The vehicle type codes used in France are as follows:

T   Turbotrain driving motor.
TGV   TGV driving motor.
TGVZ   TGV vehicle with one power bogie.
X   Diesel railcar or multiple unit driving motor.
Z   Electric multiple unit driving motor.
R   indicates a trailer vehicle. (French=remorque).
A   1st Class
B   2nd Class
D   Luggage, i.e., vehicle with luggage space and guard's compartment
r   Catering vehicle.
P   Post, i.e., vehicle with compartment(s) for mail (and guard)
x   indicates a driving trailer.

Examples:

XBD   Second class DMU driving motor with luggage/guard's compartment.
ZRABx   Composite EMU driving trailer.

Note—The continental system does not differentiate between open and compartment stock, but all railcars and multiple unit vehicles are open.

Under 'accommodation' are shown the number of 1st and 2nd class seats, followed by the number of toilets, e.g. 24/49 1T indicates 24 first class seats, 49 second class seats and one toilet.

ACKNOWLEDGEMENTS

We would like to thank all who have helped with the preparation of this book, especially Jean-Paul Demoy, Messrs. C.R. Appleby, E. Dunkling, K. Dillon, E. White, L.Moore and other members of the LCGB and STARS, the photographers, and various officials and staff of the SNCF.

In addition to much research by the authors, the following magazines have proved useful:

La Vie du Rail, LCGB Bulletin, Voies Ferrées, Chemins de Fer régionaux et urbains, Le Train du Sud.

SNCF–GENERAL

SNCF was formed in 1937 when several private companies were nationalised. These formed the basis of the SNCF "Réseaux" or systems/networks. They were:

1. Est (East)–former CF de l'Est.
2. Nord (North)–former CF du Nord.
3. Ouest (West)–former CF d'État.
4. Sud Ouest (South West)–former PO-Midi.
5. Sud Est (South East)–former CF PLM.

Regions 1 and 2 have now been combined into a new region "Nord-Est" and 3 and 4 are now combined to form the new "Atlantique" region.

NUMBERING SYSTEM

The SNCF numbering system for steam locomotives was based on axle grouping so that a 4–6–2 became a 231 etc. Class letters then followed the axle details and then came the running number. eg 231 E 22. For tank locomotives an additional T followed the axle arrangement eg 141 TC 8.

No electric locomotives were renumbered on the formation of SNCF. Most locos came from the PO-Midi system with just a few others from the État and PLM. Those delivered to SNCF between 1938–50 continued the PO-Midi series. However from 1950 a new system was introduced bringing the locomotives somewhat into line with the steam system, but here the axle arrangement was shown by letters so that a BoBo became a BB.

Diesel locomotives were originally given a steam type number with an additional D in the number after the axle arrangement e.g. 040 DA 1 but in 1960 the whole fleet was renumbered into the present system.

SNCF traction is numbered in several different ways. eg BB 4750, CC 6505, A1AA1A 68001, T 2001, X 2101, Y 8101, Z 6101.

In this book locomotive numbers are listed without their prefix, but letter prefixes are used for multiple units or shunting tractors. (NB: not all locomotives carry their prefixes).

Electric locomotives are numbered as follows:

1– 9999	DC locomotives.
10000–19999	AC locomotives.
20000–29999	Dual voltage locomotives.
30000–39999	Triple voltage locomotives.
40000–49999	Quadruple voltage locomotives.

Examples: BB 8500, DC locomotive with BB axle arrangement; BB 17000, AC locomotive with BB axle arrangement; BB 25500 dual voltage locomotive of same type. (8500+17000=25500).

Diesel locomotives are numbered as follows:

50000–51999	Diesel locomoteurs (No longer in stock).
60000–79999	Diesel locomotives.

Shunting locos ("locotracteurs") are prefixed Y and numbered between 2201–9999.

Multiple units:

"T" denotes a turbotrain, power car numbers ranging between 1001 and 2082.
"X" denotes a DMU, power car numbers ranging between 2101 and 4999.
"Z" denotes an EMU, power car numbers ranging between 3711 and 9636.

Trains à Grande Vitesse:

TGV power cars are numbered as 2 or 3-voltage locomotives but they also carry a set number, e.g. TGV power cars 23001/2 are set 01 and can be referred to as TGV 01.

Note: Diesel and electric units owned or subsidised by local authorities or other "third parties" have their numbers prefixed by "9". eg XP 94750 is a DMU belonging to the Post Office and similar to SNCF X 4750 class.

There can be some confusion with the present numbering system. 7301 can be a BB electric locomotive, an EMU, or a tractor. SNCF have recognised this problem and a new numbering system has been devised to eliminate duplicate numbers. In future locomotives will be numbered up to 499 in a series and 500 upwards will be an m.u. of some description. e.g. 11001–499 would be a.c. electric locomotives, 11500–999 would be a.c. EMUs. It is not at present intended to renumber any existing stock.

INTRODUCTION

AVANT-PROPOS A LA DEUXIEME EDITION

Bienvenue à la deuxième édition de ce livre, qui contient des details de tout le matériel moteur de la SNCF et du matérial de certains chemins de fer privés. C'est aussi notre deuxième livre édité en français et en anglais. Europe oblige.

Il y a eu beaucoup de changements depuis la parution de la première édition il y a cinq ans. Sans doûte, le plus frappant est le succès du TGV. Lors de la première édition, le TGV Sud Est prenait son élan tandis que le TGV Atlantique était en construction. Le TGV Atlantique est maintenant en service et détient un nouveau record du monde de vitesse de 515.3 km/h. La plupart des rames TGV–A sont en service à la mi-1991 et elles seront suivies des TGV Réseau, Trans-Manche Super Trains et TGV-2N à deux niveaux, les deux dernières séries pour le projet TGV Nord.

Les autres changements à la SNCF sont liés au trafic croissant autour de Paris, aux contrats SNCF–Régions et à la rationalisation du service fret, où beaucoup de petites lignes seront fermées.

Voici un sommaire des changements du matériel moteur depuis la première édition.

Séries radiées:

BB 900, BB 4100, 2D2 9100, CC 65000, BB 71000, X 2400, X 2701, X 3800, Z 3700, Z 4100, Y 2200.

Séries à radier d'ici 10 ans:

BB 9400, BB 13000 (1992), CC 14100 (1993), CC 40100 (1996) A1AA1A 62000 (1994), CC 65500 (1993), Y 6200, Y 6300, Y 6400, Z 5100(1997).

Nouvelles Séries:

BB 9600, 26000, 62400, 64700, 64800, 66700, Y 8000, Y 8400, Z 8800, Z 11500, Z 20500, TGV-A.

En 1991, la SNCF compte recevoir une quarantaine de 26000, et transformera deux CC 1100, sept 64700/800, deux 66700 et quatorze 9600. Les modifications en cours incluent l'équipment d'une 9200 et douze 16000 du multiplexage pour utiliser avec des rames à deux niveaux appelées «Grand Couronne». En marchandises, la SNCF travaille sur un système pour commander une machine en milieu ou en queue d'un train par radio de la machine de tête. Le développement de nouvelles séries de TGV est une toute autre histoire. Qui osait râver d'un TGV à deux niveaux capable de 300 km/h il y a dix ans?

Comme dans les autres livres de «Platform 5» nous avons inclu un chapitre sur les lignes musées ainsi que quelques détails d'ancien matériel SNCF toujours en service sur d'autres résaux. Ces renseignements ont été recueillis à partir de plusieurs sources par des amateurs et nous serions heureux de recevoir vos propres observations.

Nous espérons que vous trouverez ce livre utile qu'il enrichira vos excursions ... par le train bien sur!

Brian Garvin, David Haydock & Peter Fox

TICKETS LIBRE CIRCULATION

Pour les visiteurs qui ne résident pas en France, il existe le ticket «France Vacances Pass». C'est un ticket qui donne libre circulation sur tout le réseau SNCF pour 4 jours, au choix, pendant une période de deux semaines ou 9 jours pendant un mois. En plus, ce ticket donne des transferts gratuits entre les aéroports et le centre de Paris, une journée de libre circulation sur le Métro de Paris et une réduction sur le prix du billet sur les Chemins de Fer de Provence. Avec le ticket on ne paye pas de supplément dans le TGV. Notez que les citoyens français n'ont pas le droit d'acheter ce ticket.

ABRÉVIATIONS

km/h	kilometres/heure
kN	kilonewtons
kW	kilowatts

BR	British Railways (Chemins de Fer britanniques)
DB	Deutsche Bundesbahn (Chemin de Fer federal allemand)
NS	Nederlandse Spoorwegen (Chemins de Fer des Pays-Bas)
RRR	Rames Réversibles Régionales
RATP	Regie Autonome des Transports Pariens
SNCB	Société Nationale des Chemins de Fer Belges
UM	Unité multiples
Longeur	Longeur hors tout
Puissance	Puissance horaire
E.T.	Effort de traction

CLASSIFICATION DES VOITURES VOYAGEURS

Les codes utilisés en France pour les voitures voyageurs sont comme suit:

T	Motrice turbotrain.
TGV	Motrice TGV.
TGVZ	Remorque TGV avec une bogie moteur.
X	Motrice autorail.
Z	Automotrice électrique.
R	Remorque.
A	Première classe.
B	Deuxième classe.
D	Compartiment à bagages.
r	Voiture restaurant ou buffet.
P	Voiture postale.
x	Remorque avec cabine de conduite.

Par exemple:

XBD	Motrice autorail de deuxième classe avec compartiment à bagages.
ZRABx	Remorque d'automotrice électrique avec cabine de conduite et sièges en première et deuxième classe.

Dans 'places' on indique le nombre de places assises en 1re et 2me classe suivi du nombre de toilettes, par exemple 24/49 1T indique 24 places en 1re, 49 places en 2me et un compartiment toilette.

REMERCIEMENTS

Nous remercions vivement tout ceux qui ont aidé à préparer ce livre, surtout Jean–Paul Demoy, Messrs C.R. Appleby, E. Dunkling, K. Dillon, P. White, L. Moore et d' autres membres du LCGB et STARS, les photographes et plusieurs membres du personnel de la SNCF.

Mis à part nos recherches personelles, nous avons consulté plusieurs livres et les magazines suivants:

La Vie du Rail, LCGB Bulletin, Voies Ferrées, Chemins de Fer régionaux et urbains, Le Train du Sud.

SNCF–GENERAL

La SNCF fut créee en 1937 à la suite de la mationalisation de compagnies privées. En général, les nouveaux réseaux SNCF correspondaient aux anciens réseaux des compagnies:

1. Est (East) – ex CF de l'Est.
2. Nord (North) – ex CF du Nord.
3. Ouest (West) – ex CF d'État.
4. Sud Ouest (South West) – ex PO-Midi.
5. Sud Est (South East) – ex CF PLM.

Ces réseaux sont restés tels quels pendant longtemps mais les 1 et 2 sont maintenant le «Nord-Est» tandis que les 3 et 4 formant le réseau «Atlantique».

SYSTEME DE NUMEROTATION

Le système SNCF de numérotation des locomotives à vapeur est basé sur le nombre d'essieux, suivi du lettres indiquant la série, suivi du numéro de série, par exemple 231 E 22. Pour les locomotives tender, un «T» suit le nombre d'essieux, par exemple 141 TC 8. A la formation de la SNCF les machines électriques ont gardé leur numéros d'origine. La plupart venaient du PO–Midi avec d'autres de l'Etat et du PLM. Les locomotives livrées à la SNCF de 1938 à 1950 furent numérotées avec celles du PO–Midi. Cependant, en 1950 un nouveau système fut introduit avec des lettres pour indiquer la disposition des essieux – par exemple, une BoBo devient BB.

A l'origine, les machines diesels avaient un numéro comme les machines à vapeur mais avec un D, par exemple 040DA. En 1960 le parc entier fut renuméroté dans le système actuel.

Le matériel de la SNCF est numéroté de différentes façons, par exemple BB 4750, CC 6505, A1AA1A 68001, T 2001, X 2101, Y 8101, Z 6101.

Dans ce livre, nous avons oté les préfixes dans le listes de numéros de série.

Les locomotives électriques sont numérotées comme suit:

1– 9999	Locomotives à courant continu.
10000–19999	Locomotives à courant monophasé.
20000–29999	Locomotives bi-courant.
30000–39999	Locomotives tri-courant.
40000–49999	Locomotives quadri-courant.

Par exemple: BB 8500 loco BB à courant continu; BB 17000 loco BB à courant monophasé; BB 25500 loco BB bi-courant.

Les locomotives diesel sont numérotées comme suit:

50000–51999	Locomoteurs (n'existant plus).
60000–79999	Locomotives.

Turbotrains: numérotés de 1001 à 2082 avec le préfixe T.
Autorails: numérotés de 2101 à 4999 avec le préfixe X.
Locotracteurs sont numérotés de 2201 à 9999 avec le préfixe Y.
Automotrices: numérotées de 5000 à 20599 avec le préfixe Z.

Nota: Les autorails et automotrices dont l'acquisition a été financée par un tiers, par exemple une des Régions, portent le préfixe 9. Par exemple, les X 94750 furent financés par La Poste.

Trains à Grande Vitesse:

Les motrices sont numérotées comme les locomotives bi– ou tri–courant mais chaque rame a aussi un numéro. Par exemple la rame TGV 01 a les motrices 23001/2.

La confusion est tout à fait possible avec le système actuel puisque que la SNCF supprime de plus en plus souvent les préfixes. Donc, 7301 peut être une BB électrique, un locotracteur ou une automotrice Z2. SNCF a reconnu ce problème et un nouveau système va éviter la duplication des numéros. Dans l'avenir, chaque tranche de numéros jusqu'à xx499 sera affectée aux locomotives et à partir de xx500 aux autorails ou automotrices. Par exemple 11001–499 seront des locomotives tandis que les 11500–999 seront des automotrices. Jusqu'à présent, la SNCF n'a pas l'intention de renuméroter le parc existant.

Disponible aussi chez Platform 5:

Des livres similaires sur le matériel de la Suisse, les Pays Benelux, l'Autriche, l'Allemagne et la Grande Bretagne.

Écrivez à David Haydock, 48 rue du Chemin Vert, F-59500 Douai, France.

SNCF MOTIVE POWER ORGANISATION
ORGANISATION DU MATERIEL

The main depots and the codes used for them are listed for convenience on page 176 of this book. Generally speaking the depots have large allocations but many locomotives and units stable at other places. A list of known stabling points is shown below with details of how many locos/multiple units might be found there on a typical Sunday. Where there are more than 10 a breakdown into types is given. (E = electric locomotives, D = diesel locomotives, X = DMUs, Y = tractors/locotracteurs, Z = EMUs).

Les dépôts titulaires et les codes correspondants sont marqués sur la page 176 du livre. L'affectation de chaque dépôt est grande mais le matériel est souvent stationné à d'autres dépôts dits «relais». Voici ci-dessous une liste de dépôts relais avec la nombre typique de machines qu'on peut trouver le dimanche. (E = locos électriques, D = locos diesels, X = autorails, Y = locotracteurs, Z = automotrices).

Réseau Nord–Est (North-East).

	Total	E	D	X	Y	Z		Total	E	D	X	Y	Z
Amiens	49	10	5	30	4		La Plaine	25		12	7	6	
Aulnoye	24	19	5				Lille Délivrance	17	8	8		1	
Belfort	24	6	3	9	3	3	Lilles Fives	44	24	11	6	2	1
Blainville	35	12	11		1		Longwy	17	10	7			
Bobigny	32	22	10				Mitry Claye	30					30
Boulogne Ville	20		9	8	3		Mulhouse Nord	10	3	3		1	
Calais Ville	21		13	5	3		Mulhouse Ville	34	21	6	4	3	
Châlons-sur-Marne	45	24	14	2	5		Nancy	29	10	10	6		3
Conflans Jarny	22	10	8	2	2		Persan Beaumont	24	4				20
Creil Petit Thérain	22	9	11		1		Pontoise	17	5			1	11
Creil Ville	11	2		2		7	Reims	42	6	14	10	7	5
Dunkerque Gr. Synthe	51	25	26				Somain	25	15	7		3	
Épinal	10		1	7	2		Tergnier	20	9	11			
Forbach	15	13		1		1	Vaires	22	17	5			
Hausbergen	50	28	20		2		Valenciennes	14	8	5		1	
Joncherolles	30	8			2	20	Woippy	24	16	7		1	

Other locations/autres endroits: Douai (7), Hazebrouck (8), Lauterbourg (6).

Réseau Atlantique (Atlantic).

	Total	E	D	X	Y	Z		Total	E	D	X	Y	Z
Angers	18	3	6	4	2	3	Mantes La Jolie	20	10	3	5	2	
Argentan	12		4	7	1		Massy Palaiseau	30					30
Bourges	12		3	4	5		Pau	10		4		2	4
Brest	16		6	9	1		Perigueux	12		8	4		
Brétigny	29	5	5		4	15	Poitiers	15		4	8	3	
Brive	17	3	2	7	2	3	St. Cloud	15					15
Étampes	16				3	13	Toulouse St. Jory	16		10	6		
La Rochelle Ville	14		10	2	2		Trappes	27		17	9	1	
Le Havre	20	11	8		1		Versailles	12					12
Le Mans Ville	34	7	15	3	6	3	Vierzon	33		18	9	3	3

Other locations/autres endroits: Auray (8), Batignolles (5), Chartres (5), Cherbourg (7), Dieppe (7), Mézidon (8), St. Brieuc (8), Saintes (6), Thouars (6), Quimper (9). Angoulême (6), Aurillac (8), Bayonne (6), Capdenac (6), Châteauroux (9), Juvisy (15), Rodez (6).

Reseau Sud Est (South East).

	Total	E	D	X	Y	Z		Total	E	D	X	Y	Z
Ambérieu	19	15	4				Laroche Migennes	20	10	10			
Besançon	17	1	2	9	3	2	Lyon Mouche	43	35			2	6
Cerbère	20	16	2	2			Marseille St.Charles	30	30				
Dijon Ville	19	4	1	12		2	Melun	16	2	2			12
Dôle	15	10	5				Miramas	71	32	29	7	3	
Grenoble	40	10	10	12	2	6	Modane	18	15	2		1	

	Total	E	D	X	Y	Z		Total	E	D	X	Y	Z
Nîmes	30	8	13	4		5	St. Germain des Fossés	10	1	7		2	
Nice St. Roche	24	10	10			4	St. Jean du Maurienne	13	12				1
Portes	15	10		3		2	Sibelin Triage	20	15	5			
Paris Charolais	25	23	1		1		Veynes	10			5	3	2
St. Etienne	33	8	18	4		3							

Other locations/autres endroits: Annemasse (5), Aix les Bains (6), Bellegarde (6), Culoz (10), Dijon Gevrey (8), Lyon Pérrache (6), Montargis (7), Neussargues (3), Perpignan (8), Roanne (8), Valenton (9).

WORKSHOPS/ATELIERS DIRECTEURS

The SNCF has no really large locomotive works, but has kept open many pre-nationalisation workshops. Each of these deals with specific classes for major overhauls. Bordeaux Workshops are expected to close 1993/4.

La SNCF a pluseurs ateliers de moyenne taille qui datent souvent de la période avant la nationalisation. Chaque atelier est directeur pour les séries suivantes. Bordeaux doit fermer en 1993/4. La Folie pourrait être fermé puisqu'il est prévu de transferer les X 6100 et X 6300 à Hellemmes.

Workshop Ateliers	Types overhauled Séries révisées
Béziers	BB 300, CC 1100, BB 4200, BB 4700, BB 8100, BB 8500, BB 9400, Z 100.
Bischheim (Strasbourg)	TGV 23000, TGV 24000, TGV 33000.
Bordeaux	X 2100, X 2200, X 2720, Trailers/remorques, T 2000.
Épernay	BB 12000, BB 16500.
Hellemmes (Lille)	BB 15000, BB 16000, BB 17000, BB 20200, BB 25100, BB 25150, BB 25200, BB 26000, CC 40100, Z 6100.
La Folie (Paris)	Z 6000, Z 6100, Z 6300, Z 6400.
Le Mans	X 4300, X 4500, X 4630, X 4750, X 4900, T 1000, T 1500.
Nevers	BB 63500, BB 64700, BB 66000, BB 66400, BB 66600, BB 66700, BB 67000, BB 67200, X 2800, XR 6000. Y 2400, Y 5100, Y 7100, Y 7400. Y 8000, Y 8400.
Oullins (Lyon)	CC 6500, CC 7100, BB 7200, BB 9200, BB 9300, CC 21000, BB 22200, BB 25500, Z 600, Z 7100, Z 7300, Z 7500, Z 9500, Z 9600, Z 11500.
Quatre Mares (Rouen)	BB 63000, BB 63400, BB 64800, BB 67300, BB 67400, A1AA1A 68000, A1AA1A 68500, CC 72000.
Vitry (Paris)	Z 5100, Z 5300, Z 5600, Z 8800, Z 20500.

Disponible aussi chez Platform 5:

Des livres similaires sur le matériel de la Suisse, les Pays Benelux, l'Autriche, l'Allemagne et la Grande Bretagne.

Écrivez à David Haydock, 48 rue du Chemin Vert, F-59500 Douai, France.

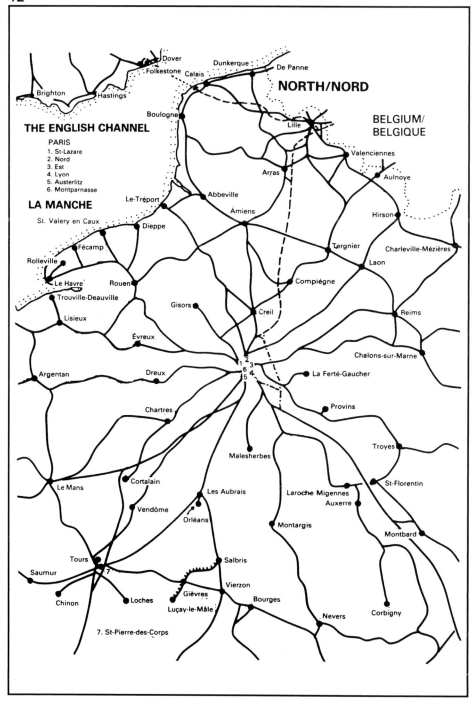

Dover
Folkestone Calais
Brighton   Hastings
Dunkerque   De Panne

NORTH/NORD

Boulogne

THE ENGLISH CHANNEL

PARIS
1. St-Lazare
2. Nord
3. Est
4. Lyon
5. Austerlitz
6. Montparnasse

Lille

**BELGIUM/
BELGIQUE**

Valenciennes

Arras

Aulnoye

LA MANCHE

Le-Tréport   Abbeville

St. Valery en Caux

Amiens

Hirson

Dieppe

Fécamp

Tergnier   Charleville-Mézières

Rolleville

Laon

Le Havre   Rouen

Trouville-Deauville

Compiégne

Lisieux

Gisors

Creil

Reims

Évreux

Argentan   Dreux

Chalons-sur-Marne

1
2
3
6
4
5

La Ferté-Gaucher

Chartres

Provins

Malesherbes

Troyes

Le Mans   Cortalain

Les Aubrais

Laroche Migennes
Auxerre

St-Florentin

Vendôme

Orléans

Montargis

Montbard

Tours

Saumur   7

Salbris

Chinon   Loches

Gièvres
Luçay-le-Mâle

Vierzon

Bourges

Nevers

Corbigny

7. St-Pierre-des-Corps

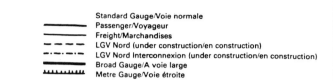

Standard Gauge/Voie normale
Passenger/Voyageur
Freight/Marchandises
LGV Nord (under construction/en construction)
LGV Nord Interconnexion (under construction/en construction)
Broad Gauge/A voie large
Metre Gauge/Voie étroite

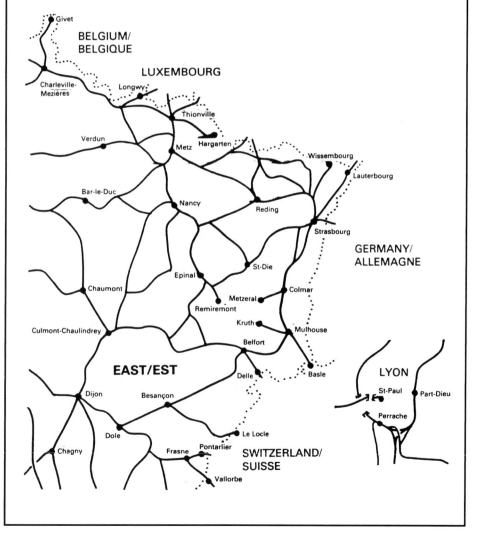

14

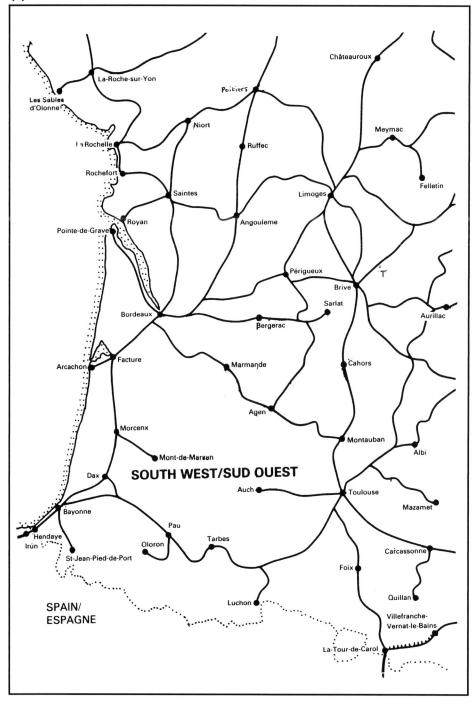

15

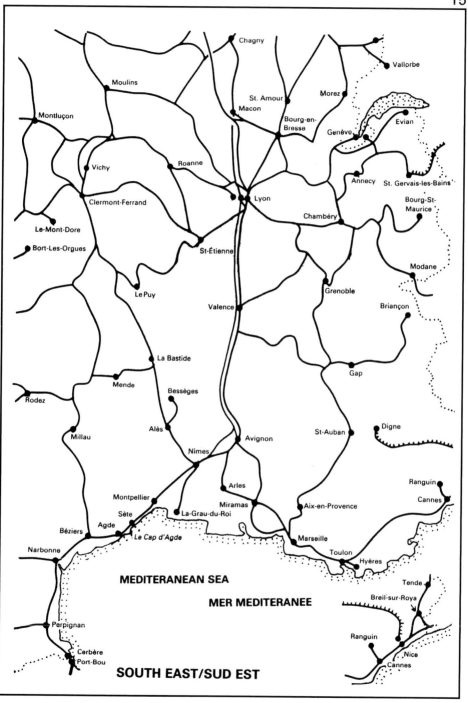

SOUTH EAST/SUD EST

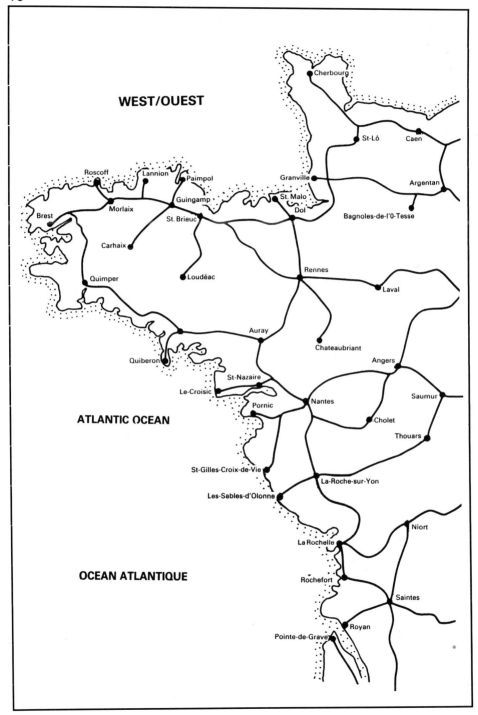

WEST/OUEST

ATLANTIC OCEAN

OCEAN ATLANTIQUE

TRAINS À GRANDE VITESSE

The TGV is a modern day success story for SNCF. It is the fastest service train in the world.
Le TGV – le train le plus rapide du monde – est devenu un très grand succès pour la SNCF.

TGV SUD-EST

Each TGV Sud-est set is a 10–car EMU with 1½ power cars at each end. It is not always appreciated that each TGV Sud-Est set has 6 motor bogies. There are two under each outer power car and the bogie next to the power car on the adjoining vehicles is also powered. The power cars are numbered as dual-voltage locomotives but with the prefix TGV. Each set also has a number – set 01 has power cars 23001/2 etc. Since their introduction, units have been fitted with new bogies with better suspension and some have received an improved interior. Normally the sets keep in formation but obviously changes take place following the discovery of defects etc. 23139 has been withdrawn after an accident and half the set remains in reserve. Set 88 became a TGV Atlantique prototype, but has now become triple-voltage set 118. The names of the TGV sets are carried on the non-driving motor car *(semi-motrice)*.

Electro-pneumatic brakes. Rheostatic brakes. Multiple working. Disc brakes on trailers in addition to blocks. Radio fitted. Cab signalling.

Chaque TGV est une automotrice à dix voitures avec une motrice et demie parce que les voitures d'extremité sont des semi-motrices. Les motrices sont numérotées comme des locomotives bi-courant – 23001 etc. – mais avec le préfixe TGV. Chaque rame a un numéro aussi – la rame 01 a les motrices 23001/2 etc. Depuis leur introduction, les rames ont reçu une suspension améliorée et certaines ont un intérieur modifié. En général, les rames sont indéformables mais des changements peuvent avoir lieu suite à des incidents. La motrice 23139 a été radiée suite à l'accident de Voiron et une demi-rame plus la motrice 23140 servent de reserve. la rame 88 a servi comme prototype du TGV-A mais est maintenant transformée en rame tri-courant 118. Les blasons portant des noms des villes sont portés sur la semi-motrice.

Équipées du frein électropneumatique et rhéostatique, de freins a disques sur les remorques, de la radio sol-train et de la signalisation en cabine. Couplables en UM.

TGV + TGVZRADr + TGVRAr + TGVRA + TGVRBr + 3TGVRB + TGVZRB + TGV.

* TGV + TGVZRADr + TGVRAr + TGVRA + TGVRAr + 2TGVRA + TGVZRA + TGV.

Systems/Systèmes: 1500 V d.c./continu + 25 kV a.c./monophasé.
Built/Date de mise en service: 1978–86.
Builders/Constructeurs: Alsthom/Francorail-MTE/De Dietrich.
Axle Arrangement/Disposition des essieux: BoBo + Bo2222222Bo + BoBo.
Traction Motors/Moteurs de traction: 12 x TAB676 per set/pro rame (525 kW each/chacun).
Accommodation/Places: 0 + 35/– 1T + 38/– 1T + 38/– 1T + –/35 1T + –/60 2T + –/60 1T + –/60 2T + –/60 1T + 0.
(0 + 35/– 1T + [2 x 38/– 1T] + 24/– 1T + [4 x 38/– 1T] + 0*).
Weight/Masse: 65 + 43 + [6 x 28] + 44 + 65 tonnes.
Length/Longeur: 22.15 + 21.845 + [6 x 18.70] + 21.845 + 22.15 m.
Max. Speed/Vitesse max.: 280 km/h.
Livery/Livrée: Orange with grey and white bands./Orange avec bandes grises et blanches.

Non-driving motors and trailer cars are numbered in the sequence as follows:
Les semi-motrices et remorques sont numérotées dans la sequence suivante:

Set/Rame *nnn*: 123*nnn*/223*nnn*/323*nnn*/423*nnn*/523*nnn*/623*nnn*/723*nnn*/823*nnn*.

01	TGV 23001	TGV 23002	PE	
02	TGV 23003	TGV 23004	PE	MARSEILLE
03	TGV 23005	TGV 23006	PE	BELFORT
04	TGV 23007	TGV 23008	PE	RAMBOUILLET
05	TGV 23009	TGV 23010	PE	RIS-ORANGIS
06	TGV 23011	TGV 23012	PE	FRASNE
07	TGV 23013	TGV 23014	PE	CONFLANS-SAINTE-HONORINE
08	TGV 23015	TGV 23016	PE	ROUEN
09	TGV 23017	TGV 23018	PE	VINCENNES
10	TGV 23019	TGV 23020	PE	HAYANGE
11	TGV 23021	TGV 23022	PE	NÎMES

12	TGV 23023	TGV 23024		PE	LE HAVRE
13	TGV 23025	TGV 23026		PE	ABLON-SUR-SEINE
14	TGV 23027	TGV 23028		PE	MONTPELLIER
15	TGV 23029	TGV 23030		PE	PAU
16	TGV 23031	TGV 23032		PE	LYON
17	TGV 23033	TGV 23034		PE	TERGNIER
18	TGV 23035	TGV 23036		PE	LE CREUSOT
19	TGV 23037	TGV 23038		PE	SAINT AMAND-LES-EAUX
20	TGV 23039	TGV 23040		PE	COLMAR
21	TGV 23041	TGV 23042		PE	DIJON
22	TGV 23043	TGV 23044		PE	VALENCIENNES
23	TGV 23045	TGV 23046		PE	MONTBARD
24	TGV 23047	TGV 23048		PE	ALFORTVILLE
25	TGV 23049	TGV 23050		PE	BESANÇON
26	TGV 23051	TGV 23052		PE	SAINT ETIENNE
27	TGV 23053	TGV 23054		PE	MÂCON
28	TGV 23055	TGV 23056		PE	MONTÉLIMAR
29	TGV 23057	TGV 23058		PE	VILLENEUVE-SAINT-GEORGES
30	TGV 23059	TGV 23060		PE	LILLE
31	TGV 23061	TGV 23062		PE	COMBS-LA-VILLE
32	TGV 23063	TGV 23064		PE	MAISONS-ALFORT
33	TGV 23065	TGV 23066	*	PE	FÉCAMP
34	TGV 23067	TGV 23068	*	PE	DUNKERQUE
35	TGV 23069	TGV 23070	*	PE	GRENOBLE
36	TGV 23071	TGV 23072	*	PE	SEINE SAINT-DENIS
37	TGV 23073	TGV 23074	*	PE	SAINT GERMAIN-EN-LAYE
38	TGV 23075	TGV 23076	*	PE	CANNES
39	TGV 23077	TGV 23078		PE	EVIAN + THONON-LES-BAINS
40	TGV 23079	TGV 23080		PE	VERSAILLES
41	TGV 23081	TGV 23082		PE	VILLIERS-LE-BEL
42	TGV 23083	TGV 23084		PE	CHAMBÉRY
43	TGV 23085	TGV 23086		PE	AIX-LES-BAINS
44	TGV 23087	TGV 23088		PE	CLERMONT-FERRAND
45	TGV 23089	TGV 23090		PE	VALENCE
46	TGV 23091	TGV 23092		PE	CONTREXÉVILLE
47	TGV 23093	TGV 23094		PE	NANCY
48	TGV 23095	TGV 23096		PE	COMTÉ-DE-NICE
49	TGV 23097	TGV 23098		PE	RENNES
50	TGV 23099	TGV 23100		PE	BEAUVAIS
51	TGV 23101	TGV 23102		PE	GIVORS + GRIGNY-BADAN
52	TGV 23103	TGV 23104		PE	GENÈVE
53	TGV 23105	TGV 23106		PE	LE PUY-EN-VELAY
54	TGV 23107	TGV 23108		PE	CHAGNY
55	TGV 23109	TGV 23110		PE	DENAIN
56	TGV 23111	TGV 23112		PE	ANNECY
57	TGV 23113	TGV 23114		PE	BOURG-EN-BRESSE
58	TGV 23115	TGV 23116		PE	OULLINS
59	TGV 23117	TGV 23118		PE	HAUTMONT
60	TGV 23119	TGV 23120		PE	LANGEAC
61	TGV 23121	TGV 23122		PE	FONTAINEBLEAU
62	TGV 23123	TGV 23124		PE	TOULOUSE
63	TGV 23125	TGV 23126		PE	VILLEURBANNE
64	TGV 23127	TGV 23128		PE	DOLE
65	TGV 23129	TGV 23130		PE	SÈTE
66	TGV 23131	TGV 23132		PE	AVIGNON
67	TGV 23133	TGV 23134		PE	BELLEGARDE-SUR-VALSERINE
68	TGV 23135	TGV 23136		PE	MODANE
69	TGV 23137	TGV 23138		PE	VICHY
71	TGV 23141	TGV 23142		PE	BRUNOY
72	TGV 23143	TGV 23144		PE	CAHORS
73	TGV 23145	TGV 23146		PE	CHARENTON-LE-PONT
74	TGV 23147	TGV 23148		PE	ARBOIS-MOUCHARD-PORT LESNEY
75	TGV 23149	TGV 23150		PE	VITTEL
76	TGV 23151	TGV 23152		PE	PONTARLIER
77	TGV 23153	TGV 23154		PE	NUITS-SAINT-GEORGES

```
 78  TGV 23155  TGV 23156      PE    CULOZ
 79  TGV 23157  TGV 23158      PE    ANNEMASSE
 80  TGV 23159  TGV 23160      PE    TOULON
 81  TGV 23161  TGV 23162      PE    TONNERRE
 82  TGV 23163  TGV 23164      PE    TRAPPES
 83  TGV 23165  TGV 23166      PE    MOISSY CRAMAYEL
 84  TGV 23167  TGV 23168      PE    DIEPPE
 85  TGV 23169  TGV 23170      PE    BEAUNE
 86  TGV 23171  TGV 23172      PE    MONTLUÇON
 87  TGV 23173  TGV 23174      PE    MONTCHANIN
 89  TGV 23175  TGV 23178      PE
 90  TGV 23179  TGV 23180      PE    EPINAL
 91  TGV 23181  TGV 23182      PE    MULHOUSE
 92  TGV 23183  TGV 23184      PE    NOYEN
 93  TGV 23185  TGV 23186      PE    SENS
 94  TGV 23187  TGV 23188      PE    LES ARCS EN PROVENCE
 95  TGV 23189  TGV 23190      PE    SAINT RAPHAEL
 96  TGV 23191  TGV 23192      PE    MONTE CARLO
 97  TGV 23193  TGV 23194      PE    CORBEIL-ESSONNE
 98  TGV 23195  TGV 23196      PE
100  TGV 23199  TGV 23200  *   PE    SAINT GERVAIS-LES-BAINS
101  TGV 23201  TGV 23202  *   PE    BOURG SAINT-MAURICE
102  TGV 23203  TGV 23204  *   PE    VIGNEUX-SUR-SEINE
Spare/Réserve.  TGV 23140      PE    MELUN
```

TGV SUD-EST (TRIPLE-VOLTAGE/TRICOURANT)

TGV 33000 are similar to TGV 23000 but fitted for triple-voltage selection for working into Switzerland. Details as for 23001 except:

Systems: 1500 V d.c./continu + 25 kV 50 Hz + 15 kV 16⅔ Hz a.c./monophasé.

Les rames 110–118 sont identiques aux autres TGV Sud-Est sauf qu'elles sont tri-courant pour des services jusqu'a Berne et lausanne en Suisse. Details comme pour 23001 sauf:

Systèmes: 1500 V continu/25 kV monophasé 50 Hz/15 kV monophasé 16⅔ Hz.

```
110  TGV 33001  TGV 33002      PE    PAYS DE VAUD
111  TGV 33003  TGV 33004      PE    SURESNES
112  TGV 33005  TGV 33006      PE    LAUSANNE
113  TGV 33007  TGV 33008      PE    NEUCHÂTEL
114  TGV 33009  TGV 33010      PE    CLUSES
115  TGV 33011  TGV 33012      PE
116  TGV 33013  TGV 33014      PE
117  TGV 33015  TGV 33016      PE    BERN/BERNE
118  TGV 33017  TGV 33018      PE    BISCHHEIM
     (23176)    (23177)
```

TGV POSTES

These sets have 8 trailers like the TGV Sud-Est sets, but the trailers are postal vans. There are five half-sets.

Ces rames ont 8 remorques comme les rames TGV Sud-Est, mais les remorques sont des fourgons postaux. Il existe 5 demi-rames.

Livery/Livrée: Yellow with grey and white bands./Jaune avec bandes grises et blanches.

Non-driving motors and trailer cars are numbered in the sequence as follows:
Les semi-motrices et remorques sont numérotées dans la sequence suivante:
Set/Rame *n*: 91230*n*/92230*n*/93230*n*/94230*n*.

```
1    923001     PE  | 3    923003     PE  | 5    923005     PE
2    923002     PE  | 4    923004     PE  |
```

TGV ATLANTIQUE

These sets are longer, more powerful and faster than the TGV Sud-Est sets. Trailer 2 has unidirectional seating with trailers 3 and 4 having facing seating including 6 "club" compartments with four seats in each. Trailer 1 has a wheelchair space and suitable toilet. Trailers 2,4 and 6 have a telephone. Trailers 8 and 9 include 4 family semi-compartments of 4 seats and trailer 9 also includes facilities for nursing mothers. Trailer 10 has a special 17 seat childrens compartment at the end. On 18th May 1990, set 325 attained a world record of 515.3 km/h.

Les rames Atlantiques représentent une grande avance, même par rapport aux TGV-Sud-Est. Elles sont plus puissantes avec deux bogies moteurs de moins, et incorporent 10 remorques au lieu de 8. Ce progrès est grâce aux moteurs synchrones. Les intérieurs sont aussi améliorés. La remorque 1 a des facilités pour handicapés, 2 remorques première classe ont des semi-partiments, les remorques 2,4 et 6 ont un téléphone et les remorques deuxième classe ont des facilités pour enfants et bébés. Certaines rames ont reçu des bandes de couleurs voyantes au-dessus de la cabine. La rame 325 a atteint la vitesse de 515,3 km.h le 18 mai 1990 et porte une bande diagonale en bleu sur le nez pour célébrer sa prouesse.

TGV + TGVRADr + TGVRAr + TGVRA + TGVRBr + 6TGVRB + TGV.

Systems/Systèmes: 1500 V d.c./continu + 25 kV a.c./monophasé.
Built/Date de mise en service: 1988–91.
Builders/Constructeurs: Alsthom/Francorail-MTE/De Dietrich.
Axle Arrangement/Disposition des essieux: BoBo + 22222222222 + BoBo.
Traction Motors/Moteurs de traction: 8 x 1100 kW per set/pro rame.
Accommodation/Places: 0 + 44/– 1T + 36/– 1T + 36/– 1T + Bar + –/60 2T + –/60S 1T + –/60S 2T + –/60S 1T + –/56S 1T + –/77S 2T + 0.
Weight/Masse:
Length/Longeur: 22.15 + 21.845 + [8 x 18.70] + 21.845 + 22.15 m.
Max. Speed/Vitesse max.: 300 km/h.
Livery/Livrée: Silver with a blue band./Argent avec bande bleu foncé.

Trailer cars are numbered in the following sequence.
Les semi-motrices et remorques sont numérotées dans la sequence suivante:
Set nnn: 241nnn/242nnn/243nnn/244nnn/245nnn/246nnn/247nnn/248nnn/249nnn/240nnn.

301	TGV 24001	TGV 24002	PC	
302	TGV 24003	TGV 24004	PC	
303	TGV 24005	TGV 24006	PC	
304	TGV 24007	TGV 24008	PC	LE MANS
305	TGV 24009	TGV 24010	PC	SAINT BRIEUC
306	TGV 24011	TGV 24012	PC	
307	TGV 24013	TGV 24014	PC	
308	TGV 24015	TGV 24016	PC	
309	TGV 24017	TGV 24018	PC	
310	TGV 24019	TGV 24020	PC	
311	TGV 24021	TGV 24022	PC	
312	TGV 24023	TGV 24024	PC	
313	TGV 24025	TGV 24026	PC	VILLEBON-SUR-YVETTE
314	TGV 24027	TGV 24028	PC	
315	TGV 24029	TGV 24030	PC	
316	TGV 24031	TGV 24032	PC	ANGOULEME
317	TGV 24033	TGV 24034	PC	
318	TGV 24035	TGV 24036	PC	
319	TGV 24037	TGV 24038	PC	MARCOUSSIS
320	TGV 24039	TGV 24040	PC	
321	TGV 24041	TGV 24042	PC	
322	TGV 24043	TGV 24044	PC	
323	TGV 24045	TGV 24046	PC	
324	TGV 24047	TGV 24048	PC	
325	TGV 24049	TGV 24050	PC	VENDÔME
326	TGV 24051	TGV 24052	PC	
327	TGV 24053	TGV 24054	PC	
328	TGV 24055	TGV 24056	PC	
329	TGV 24057	TGV 24058	PC	MORLAIX

330	TGV 24059	TGV 24060	PC	
331	TGV 24061	TGV 24062	PC	
332	TGV 24063	TGV 24064	PC	
333	TGV 24065	TGV 24066	PC	
334	TGV 24067	TGV 24068	PC	
335	TGV 24069	TGV 24070	PC	
336	TGV 24071	TGV 24072	PC	TOURS
337	TGV 24073	TGV 24074	PC	SAINT-PIERRE-DES-CORPS
338	TGV 24075	TGV 24076	PC	VOUVRAY
339	TGV 24077	TGV 24078	PC	MONT-LOUIS-SUR-LOIRE
340	TGV 24079	TGV 24080	PC	DOURDAN
341	TGV 24081	TGV 24082	PC	ANGERS
342	TGV 24083	TGV 24084	PC	
343	TGV 24085	TGV 24086	PC	SAINT-NAZAIRE
344	TGV 24087	TGV 24088	PC	NANTES
345	TGV 24089	TGV 24090	PC	REGION CENTRE
346	TGV 24091	TGV 24092	PC	
347	TGV 24093	TGV 24094	PC	
348	TGV 24095	TGV 24096	PC	POITIERS
349	TGV 24097	TGV 24098	PC	LA BAULE
350	TGV 24099	TGV 24100	PC	
351	TGV 24101	TGV 24102	PC	
352	TGV 24103	TGV 24104	PC	
353	TGV 24105	TGV 24106	PC	LAVAL
354	TGV 24107	TGV 24108	PC	
355	TGV 24109	TGV 24110	PC	LE CROISIC
356	TGV 24111	TGV 24112	PC	
357	TGV 24113	TGV 24114	PC	
358	TGV 24115	TGV 24116	PC	
359	TGV 24117	TGV 24118	PC	CHATELLERAULT
360	TGV 24119	TGV 24120	PC	
361	TGV 24121	TGV 24122	PC	
362	TGV 24123	TGV 24124	PC	
363	TGV 24125	TGV 24126	PC	
364	TGV 24127	TGV 24128	PC	
365	TGV 24129	TGV 24130	PC	
366	TGV 24131	TGV 24132	PC	
367	TGV 24133	TGV 24134	PC	
368	TGV 24135	TGV 24136	PC	
369	TGV 24137	TGV 24138	PC	LOURDES
370	TGV 24139	TGV 24140	PC	
371	TGV 24141	TGV 24142	PC	
372	TGV 24143	TGV 24144	PC	
373	TGV 24145	TGV 24146	PC	
374	TGV 24147	TGV 24148	PC	
375	TGV 24149	TGV 24150	PC	
376	TGV 24151	TGV 24152	PC	
377	TGV 24153	TGV 24154	PC	
378	TGV 24155	TGV 24156	PC	
379	TGV 24157	TGV 24158	PC	
380	TGV 24159	TGV 24160	PC	
381	TGV 24161	TGV 24162	PC	
382	TGV 24163	TGV 24164	PC	
383	TGV 24165	TGV 24166	PC	
384	TGV 24167	TGV 24168	PC	
385	TGV 24169	TGV 24170	PC	
386	TGV 24171	TGV 24172	PC	
387	TGV 24173	TGV 24174	PC	
388	TGV 24175	TGV 24176	PC	
389	TGV 24177	TGV 24178	PC	
390	TGV 24179	TGV 24180		
391	TGV 24181	TGV 24182		
392	TGV 24183	TGV 24184		
393	TGV 24185	TGV 24186		
394	TGV 24187	TGV 24188		

395	TGV 24189	TGV 24190
396	TGV 24191	TGV 24192
397	TGV 24193	TGV 24194
398	TGV 24195	TGV 24196
399	TGV 24197	TGV 24198
400	TGV 24199	TGV 24200
401	TGV 24201	TGV 24202
402	TGV 24203	TGV 24204
403	TGV 24205	TGV 24206
404	TGV 24207	TGV 24208
405	TGV 24209	TGV 24210

TGV RÉSEAU (TGV-R)

As soon as TGV-A production is finished at the end of 1991, TGV Réseau units will start to appear from Alsthom, Belfort. Réseau means network And these units are destined for services interconnecting the Sud–Est, Atlantique and Nord high speed lines. Based on TGV-A, they will only have eight trailers so as to be accommodated on the Sud–Est line, but seating will be lower density that TGV-A, reflecting longer distances passengers will travel. The first services operated will be Lyon–Rennes/Nantes. When LGV-Nord opens in 1993, they will operate Paris–Lille services before delivery of double-deck TGVs in 1994/5. Once the Paris 'Interconnexion' by-pass line opens in 1994, they will be fully exploited on Lille–Bordeaux and Lille–Marseille services, for example. 50 TGV-R dual-voltage rakes are on order with an option for 30 more. The triple-voltage batch of 30 units are destined for services penetrating Belgium such as Brussels–Marseille. A new depot is to be built in Lyon for TGV-R rakes.

Dès que la production des TGV-A sera terminée à la fin de 1991, les rames TGV Réseau commenceront à sortir de l'usine Alsthom à Belfort. Ces rames sont destinées aux services interconnectés entre les lignes à grande Vitesse Sud–Est, Atlantique et Nord. Basées sur les TGV-A, ces rames n'auront que 8 remorques, pour étre conforme avec les normes Sud–Est, avec moins de siéges que le TGV-A pour donner plus de place à chaque voyageur. Les premiers services assurés seront Rennes/Nantes–Lyon. À l'ouverture de la LGV Nord en 1993, les TGV-R assureront les Paris–Lille en attente des TGV-2N (2 niveaux) qui arriveront en 1994/5. Puis avec l'ouverture de l'Interconnexion parisien en 1994, elles assureront des services comme Lille–Bordeaux et Lille–Marseille. Il y a 50 TGV-R bi-courant en commande avec 30 en option. Une tranche de 30 rames tri-courant est destinée aux services penetranten Belgique tels que Bruxelles–Marseille Un nouveau dépôt TGV-R sera construit à Lyon.

TGV + TGVZRADr + TGVRAr + TGVRA + TGVRBr + 3TGVRB + TGVZRB + TGV.
Systems/Systèmes: 1500 V d.c./continu + 25 kV a.c./monophasé (+ 3000 V d.c./continu*).
Built/Date de mise en service: 1992–
Builders/Constructeurs: Alsthom/Francorail-MTE/De Dietrich.
Axle Arrangement/Disposition des essieux: BoBo + 222222222 + BoBo.
Traction Motors/Moteurs de traction: 8 per set/pro rame.
Accommodation/Places: 0 + 42/– 1T + 39/– 1T + 39/– 1T + –/16/bar + –/56 2T + –/56 2T + –/56 1T + –/73 (72*) 2T + 0.
Weight/Masse: 65 + 43 + [6 x 28] + 44 + 65 tonnes.
Length/Longeur: 22.15 + 21.845 + [6 x 18.70] + 21.845 + 22.15 m.
Max. Speed/Vitesse max.: 300 km/h.
Livery/Livrée: Silver with a blue band./Argent avec bande bleu foncé.

501	517	533	549		4515	*
502	518	534	550		4516	*
503	519	535	4501	*	4517	*
504	520	536	4502	*	4518	*
505	521	537	4503	*	4519	*
506	522	538	4504	*	4520	*
507	523	539	4505	*	4521	*
508	524	540	4506	*	4522	*
509	525	541	4507	*	4523	*
510	526	542	4508	*	4524	*
511	527	543	4509	*	4525	*
512	528	544	4510	*	4526	*
513	529	545	4511	*	4527	*
514	530	546	4512	*	4528	*
515	531	547	4513	*	4529	*
516	532	548	4514	*	4530	*

TRANS-MANCHE SUPER TRAINS (TMST)

A total of 30 TMSTs will be built for London–Paris/Brussels services via the Channel Tunnel starting in June 1993. They will be enormous trains, with two power cars and 18 trailers, measuring 393.48 m long. Each train will consist of two identical units, and can be split in the event of an emergency. Two pre-series trains will be delivered at the start of 1992. TMSTs will overhauled at Hellemmes (Lille).

Un total de 30 trains 'Trans-Manche' sera construit pour les services Londres–Paris/Bruxelles via le tunnel sous la Manche qui débuteront en juin 1993. Ce seront des trains énormes, avec deux motrices et 18 remorques, soit une longeur totale de 393.48 m. Chaque train consist de deux rames identiques et peut être scindées en deux moitiés en cas d'urgence. Les deux trains de pré-série seront livrées au début de 1992. L'atelier directeur des TMST sera Hellemmes.

TGV + TGVZBD + 4 TGVRB + TGVRr + 2TGVRA + TGVRAD.

Systems/Systèmes: 750 V (3rd/3me rail)/3000 V d.c./continu + 25 kV a.c./monophasé.
Built/Date de mise en service: 1992–93.
Builders/Constructeurs: GEC–Alsthom/Brush Electrical Machines/ANF/De Dietrich/BN Construction/ACEC.
Axle Arrangement/Disposition des essieux: BoBo + Bo222222222.
Traction Motors/Moteurs de traction: 6.
Accommodation/Places: 0 + –/52 1T + –/60 1T + –/60 2T + –/60 1T + –/60 2T + bar/kitchen/cuisine + –/56 2T + –/56 2T + 39/– 1T + 39/– 1T + 27/– 1T.
Weight/Masse: .
Length/Longeur: 22.15 + 21.845 + [7 x 18.70] + 21.845 m.
Max. Speed/Vitesse max.: 300 km/h.
Livery/Livrée: White with yellow window band/blanche avec une bande jaune.

Trailer cars will be numbered in the following sequence.
Les semi-motrices et remorques seront numérotées dans la séquence suivante:

Set *nnnn*: 7*nnnn*1/7*nnnn*2/7*nnnn*3/7*nnnn*4/7*nnnn*5/7*nnnn*6/7*nnnn*7/7*nnnn*8/7*nnnn*9.

3001–3028. BR Sets./Rames des BR.

3001 730010	3007 730070	3013 730130	3019 730190	3024 730240
3002 730020	3008 730080	3014 730140	3020 730200	3025 730250
3003 730030	3009 730090	3015 730150	3021 730210	3026 730260
3004 730040	3010 730100	3016 730160	3022 730220	3027 730270
3005 730050	3011 730110	3017 730170	3023 730230	3028 730280
3006 730060	3012 730120	3018 730180		

3101–3106. SNCB/NMBS Sets./Rames de la SNCB.

3101 731010	3103 731030	3104 731040	3105 731050	3106 731060
3102 731020				

3201–3226. SNCF Sets./Rames de la SNCF.

3201 732010	3207 732070	3212 732120	3217 732170	3222 732220
3202 732020	3208 732080	3213 732130	3218 732180	3223 732230
3203 732030	3209 732090	3214 732140	3219 732190	3224 732240
3204 732040	3210 732100	3215 732150	3220 732200	3225 732250
3205 732050	3211 732110	3216 732160	3221 732210	3226 732260
3206 732060				

Numbers 3301 upwards have been reserved for rakes to operate north of London.
Les numéros 3301–99 sont réservés aux rames prévues pour aller au delà de Londres.

TGV-2N

As this book went to press, SNCF ordered 45 double-deck TGV units with an option for 55 more. They will have two power cars and eight trailers and will be delivered in 1994/5. The first sets will go on Sud–Est services as the Sud–Est is desperately short of units. Later, they will take over Paris–Lille services. Set numbers will commence at 201.

A la mi-1991, la SNCF a commandé 45 TGV à deux niveaux (TGV-2N) avec une option pour 55 autres. Chaque rame aura deux motrices et huit remorques. La livraison débutera en 1994. Les premières rames seront utilisées sur Paris–Lyon où il existe des problèmes de capacité. Plus tard les TGV-2N seront mis sur Paris–Lille. Les numéros des rames commenceront à 201.

SNCF LIVERY CODES

The following codes for liveries are either used in number lists or in class introductory notes:

A. Red and cream. The classic DMU livery.
B. White with a blue window band. Adopted by the regions Centre, Basse Normandie, Champagne-Ardennes, Pays de la Loire, Midi-Pyrenées, franche-Comté and Provence-Alpes-Côte d'Azur.
C. Cement grey with orange bands. Standard 1980s/90s electric loco livery.
D. Blue and grey with white lining. Standard main-line diesel livery.
E. Blue-green with white lining or aluminium trim. The old standard livery for passenger or mixed traffic electrics.
G. White with green window band. Adopted by the regions Auvergne, Bretagne and Haute Normandie.
J. Orange with brown lining. Now the standard shunting loco livery.
M. "Massif Central". Blue with a white window band. This was the standard multiple unit/railcar livery in the 1970s/80s.
N. Non-standard. Refer to text.
O. Orange with white bands. Non-refurbished RGPs and Turbotrains.
P. White with a dark blue band plus red doors and front end. Modern Paris suburban EMUs.
R. White with red window band. Standard mid-80s DMU livery. Also adopted by the regions Alsace, Aquitaine, Limousin, Rhone-Alpes.
T. Pale grey with red band lined in orange. TEE or Grand Confort livery.
V. Dark green with yellow panels or lines.
W. All over white. Old Pays de la Loire livery.
Y. White with yellow window band. Adopted by the regions Bourgogne, Languedoc-Rousillon, Lorraine, Nord–Pas-de-Calais.
Z. Z2. Dark blue with red front end and doors. The original livery of Z2 EMUs.

LIVRÉES SNCF

Les lettres suivantes indique la livrée soit dans l'introduction de la série soit à côté du numéro de la machine.

A. Red and cream. La livrée «classique» des autorails.
B. Blanc avec une bande bleue. Adopté par régions Centre, Basse Normandie, Champagne-Ardennes, Pays de la Loire, Midi-Pyrenées, franche-Comté and Provence-Alpes-Côte d'Azur.
C. Gris béton avec bandes oranges. La livrée standard pour les électriques.
D. Gris-bleu avec bandes en blanc. La livrée standard des diesels de la ligne.
E. Vert-bleuté avec bandes en blanc ou enjoliveurs en aluminium. L'ancienne livrée standard pour les électriques.
G. Blanc avec une bande vert. Adopté par régions Auvergne, Bretagne and Haute Normandie.
J. Orange avec bandes marrons. Maintenant la livrée standard pour les machines de manoeuvre.
M. «Massif Central». Ce fut la livrée standard pour autorails pendant les années 70/80.
N. Autre livrée. Voir ci-dessus.
O. Orange avec bandes blanches. Les RGP non-modernisées et Turbotrains.
P. Blanc avec une bande bleu foncé et portes et faces frontales en rouge. Matériel modern pour la banlieu de Paris.
R. Blanc avec une bande rouge. La livrée standard dès le milieu des années 80. Adopté par les régions Alsace, Aquitaine, Limousin, Rhone-Alpes.
T. Gris pale avec bande rouge entouré d'orange. Livrée TEE ou Grand Confort.
V. Vert foncé avec bandes ou nez en jaune.
W. Blanc. L'ancienne livrée des Pays de la Loire.
Y. Blanc avec une bande jaune. Adopté par régions Bourgogne, Languedoc-Rousillon, Lorraine, Nord–Pas de-Calais.
Z. Z2. La livrée original des rames Z2.

SNCF ELECTRIC LOCOMOTIVES
LOCOMOTIVES ELECTRIQUES

Special Note: Many SNCF locos have monomotor bogies which can be regeared when the loco is at rest. An arrow on the bogie will be found pointing to the letter 'M' or 'V' denoting "marchandises" or "voyageurs" (freight/passenger) and this indicator is one of the items a driver must check when preparing a locomotive. In this publication, where two sets of figures are shown for max. speed, tractive effort, power etc., the first refers to the low gear ratio and the second to the high gear ratio.

Nota: Beaucoup de locomotives SNCF ont des bogies monomoteurs dont le rapport de réduction peut être changé quand la locomotive est immobilisée. Une flèche sur le bogie montre soit M (marchandises) soit V (voyageurs). Cette indication est vérifiée par le mécanicien lors de la préparation de la locomotive. Dans ce livre, lorsqu'il y a deux chiffres pour la vitesse maximale et l'effort de traction, le premier correspond à la réduction marchandises et la seconde à la réduction voyageurs.

CLASS/SERIE BB 300   BoBo

A pre-nationalisation design which was a development of the Midi E 4700 class. 301–324 were ordered by the PO–Midi but actually delivered to SNCF in 1938/9 as E 241–64. E 258 never became BB 318 as it was a war loss in 1944. The second batch was delivered to SNCF as 0325–55. Originally of similar appearance to the first batch, they were rebuilt without end doors in 1967–70. The two batches were renumbered BB 301–55 in 1950. Today all have been fitted with radio and downgraded to shunting duties and the maximum speed reduced to 75 km/h. The class will be found on station pilot and e.c.s. duties in their respective areas, and it is interesting to see them side by side with somewhat more modern TGV sets at both ends of the Sud–Est high-speed line.

Cette série fut développée à partir des E 4700 du Midi. Bien que commendées par le PO–Midi, les BB 301–24 furent livrées à la SNCF après la nationalisation et numérotées E 241–64. La E 258 fut détruite en 1944. La deuxième sous-série fut livrée à la SNCF, numérotée 0325–55. A l'origine elles étaient semblables aux E 241–64 mais furent modifiées sans portes d'intercirculation en 1967–70. Les deux sous-séries furent renumérotées BB 301–55 en 1950. Aujourd'hui toutes sont équipées de la radio et leur vitesse réduite à 75 km/h pour des manoeuvres de matériel vide et dans les triages. Il est intéressant de voir ces anciennes machines à côté des TGV ultra-modernes aux deux extremités de la Ligne à Grande Vitesse Sud–Est.

Built/Construction: 1938–48.
Builder-Mech. Parts/Constructeur-Partie mécanique: Alsthom/Schneider-Jeumont.
Builder-Elec. Parts/Constructeur-Partie électrique: Alsthom/Jeumont/Siemens.
Power/Puissance: 1240 kW.
Max. T.E./E.T. max.: kN.
Wheel Dia./Dia. des roues: 1350 mm.
Livery/Livrée: V.
System/Système: 1500 V d.c./continu.
Weight/Masse: 80 tonnes.
Length/Longeur: 12.93 m.
Max. Speed/Vitesse max.: 75 km/h.

301	PO	311	PO	319	PO	328	VE	340	VE	348	DP
302	CB	312	VG	320	VE	331	VE	342	VE	349	VG
304	PO	313	CB	321	PO	333	VG	343	VE	350	VE
305	PO	314	PO	322	PO	334	VE	344	VE	351	VE
307	VG	315	PO	323	PO	335	VE	345	AV	353	VG
308	PO	316	PO	324	PO	336	VG	346	AV	354	VG
309	CB	317	VE	327	AV	337	VE	347	VG	355	VG
310	PO								

CLASS/SERIE CC 1100   CC

This class was ordered by the PO–Midi with the first two being delivered in December 1937 as E 1001/2. Put into stock in 1938 they do not appear to have entered traffic until 1943. The remainder of the class was delivered in 1943–48 as E 1003–12. The whole class was renumbered in 1950 to CC 1101–12. They were built for heavy shunting duties, a task they still perform today. All are now radio fitted and can be remotely controlled. Those at Villeneuve St. Georges can often be found on shed on a Monday morning but at other times they are scattered around the extensive yards. Béziers Works is carrying out a refurbishment programme which sees the locos fitted with new cabs and repainted in the new standard orange and brown shunting livery.

Cette série fut commandée par le PO–midi et les deux premiéres, les E 1001/2, furent livrées en décembre 1937. Cependant il semble qu'elles ne furent pas mises en service avant 1943. Les autres locomotives livrées en 1943–48 furent numérotées E 1003–12. La série fut renumérotée en 1950. Les CC 1100 étaient conçues pour des manoeuvres lourdes, ce qui est toujours leur rôle. Toutes sont dotées de la radio et peuvent être telécommandées. Celles de VSG sont souvent dans le dépôt les lundis matins tandis qu'elles sont parpillées dans le vaste triage pendant la semaine. La série est en train d'être modernisée aux ateliers de Béziers. Elles seront dotées de nouvelles cabines de conduit et repeintes dans la livrée standard pour les machine de manoeuvres – orange et marron foncée.

Built/Construction: 1937–48. **System/Système:** 1500 V d.c./continu.
Builder-Mech. Parts/Constructeur-Partie mécanique: CGC.
Builder-Elec. Parts/Constructeur-Partie électrique: Oerlikon.
Power/Puissance: 400 kW. **Weight/Masse:** 91 tonnes.
Max. T.E./E.T. max.: 183 kN. **Length/Longeur:** 17.19 m.
Wheel Dia./Dia. des roues: 1400 mm. **Max. Speed/Vitesse max.:** 25 km/h.
Livery/Livrée: V (J r).

r Refurbished locos./locomotives modernisées.

1101 r	TL	1103	TP	1105 r	VG	1107	VG	1109 r	TL	1111	TP
1102	TP	1104	VG	1106 r	TL	1108	VG	1110	VG	1112 r	TL

CLASS/SERIE BB 4200 BoBo

This class has a complex history and has its origins in the electric locos built for the Newport–Shildon line of the North Eastern Railway in England. The class was built for the Midi railway, with 67 locos originally numbered E 4201–50, and E 4701–17. Four BB 4200s became BB 4718–21 in 1954 followed by ten BB 4700s becoming BB 4251–60 between 1973–5. BB 4227/35 were written off in march 1970 when they ran away on the Pau–Canfranc line demolishing the Estanguet bridge. (The line has been closed since this incident). This left 65 locos (54 BB 4200, 11 BB 4700). Then 37 BB 4200 and all BB 4700 were rebuilt to BB 4730 class in 1975–80 receiving wheels and traction motors from BB 4600s, most of the latter becoming BB 4152 onwards. Thus 17 BB 4200 were left which did not have parts from BB 4600 and these were downgraded to "MV" use in 1980–83.

Cette série, construite par le Midi, a une histoire trés complexe. A l'origine il y avait 67 locomotives numérotées E 4201–50 et E 4701–17. Quatre des 4200 sont devenues les BB 4718–21 en 1954 et puis dix BB 4700 sont devenues BB 4251–60 en 1973–75. Les BB 4227/35 furent radiées en mars 1970 suite à l'accident sur la ligne Pau–Canfranc dans lequel elles avaient endommagé le pont d'Estanguet (la ligne est fermée depuis). Il restait 65 machines (54 BB 4200 et 11 BB 4700 dont 37 BB 4200 et toutes les BB 4700 sont devenues BB 4730 en 1975–80. Pour cette modification les machines ont reçues les roues et moteurs de traction des BB 4600. Les 17 BB 4200 qui restent ont été modifiées pour les manoeuvres en 1980–83.

Built/Construction: 1933–35. **System/Système:** 1500 V d.c./continu.
Builder-Mech. Parts/Constructeur-Partie mécanique: CEF.
Builder-Elec. Parts/Constructeur-Partie électrique: Alsthom.
Power/Puissance: 1160 kW. **Weight/Masse:** 75 tonnes.
Max. T.E./E.T. max.: kN. **Length/Longeur:** 12.87 m.
Wheel Dia./Dia. des roues: 1400 mm. **Max. Speed/Vitesse max.:** 75 km/h.
Livery/Livrée: V.

Multiple working within class and with BB 4730. Radio fitted.
Couplables en UM et avec la série BB 4730. Équipées de la radio manoeuvre.

4206	PO	4211	PO	4226	TL	4234	PO	4242	TL	4246	TP
4208	TL	4221	TL	4228	TL	4239	PO	4245	PO	4249	TL
4209	TL	4224	PO	4231	TP	4240	TP				

CLASS/SERIE BB 4730 BoBo

This is another former Midi Railway type. All were rebuilt from BB 4200/4700 with parts from BB 4600 in 1975–80. Found as station pilots and also as hump shunters. Radio fitted.

Encore une série ex Midi. Toutes furent modifiées en 1975–80 à partir des séries BB 4200 et BB 4700 avec des organes des BB 4600. Toutes sont équipées de la radio et sont utilisées pour des manoeuvres dans les gares et triages.

Built/Construction: 1933–35.
Builders/Constructeurs: Alsthom.
Power/Puissance: 1160 kW.
Max. T.E./E.T. max.:   kN.
Wheel Dia./Dia. des roues: 1400 mm.
Livery/Livrée: V.

System/Système: 1500 V d.c./continu.
Weight/Masse: 75 tonnes.
Length/Longeur: 12.87 m.
Max. Speed/Vitesse max.: 90 km/h.

4730 (4204)	TA	4747 (4220)	PO	4760 (4243)	PO
4732 (4216)	TP	4748 (4257)	LA	4761 (4233)	TP
4733 (4218)	BD	4749 (4205)	LA	4762 (4223)	LA
4734 (4201)	BD	4750 (4225)	LA	4763 (4255)	TP
4735 (4213)	BD	4752 (4256)	TP	4764 (4219)	PO
4736 (4202)	TA	4753 (4260)	TP	4765 (4248)	TA
4737 (4222)	TA	4754 (4254)	PO	4767 (4250)	LA
4738 (4252)	TA	4755 (4238)	PO	4769 (4701)	MR
4740 (4207)	LA	4756 (4251)	LA	4770 (4714)	MR
4741 (4703)	TP	4757 (4253)	PO	4773 (4712)	MR
4743 (4243)	TP	4758 (4214)	LA	4774 (4715)	LA
4745 (4258)	LA	4759 (4210)	PO	4775 (4717)	MR

CLASS/SERIE CC 6500   CC

This class, together with the similar dual-voltage locos of class CC 21000 are the most powerful on the SNCF. There are three sub series: 6501–38, 6539–59 and 6560–74. with different body side grills. The second batch is of particular interest as these locos were originally fitted out for working off third-rail supply on the Chambéry–Modane "Maurienne" route. They were all converted to standard some years ago but some still carry their original light green livery. Some have been repainted in the standard red and grey livery which was designed to blend with TEE and Grand Confort liveries. The class is fitted with monomotor bogies with two gear ratios. Their use at 200 km/h is causing maintenance problems and replacement by 'Sybics' on Paris–Toulouse is a priority. 6541 is being cannibalised at Oullins after a serious accident.

Avec leurs équivalents bi-courant, les CC 21000, ces locomotives sont les plus puissantes de la SNCF. Il existe trois sous-séries – 6501–38, 6539–59 et 6560–74 – avec des persiennes latérales différentes. Les 6539–59 sont particuliérement intéressantes car elles furent dotées à l'origine de frotteurs pour l'utilisation sur la «ligne de Maurienne» de Chambéry à Modane qui était dotée d'un troisiéme rail. La ligne fut réélectrifiée et la sous-Série est revenue au type. Bien que certaines gardent toujours leur livrée verte, les autres ont été repeintes dans la livrée gris, rouge et orange qui s'harmonise avec les voitures Grand Confort et TEE. L'utilisation des CC 6500 à 200 km/h entrainent des problémes d'entretien et leur remplacement par des «Sybics» aur Paris–Toulouse est une priorité. Accidentée, la 6541 sert comme réserve de pièces détachées à Oullins.

Built/Construction: 1969–75.
Builders/Constructeurs: Alsthom/MTE.
Power/Puissance: 5900 kW.
Max. T.E./E.T. max.: 288/131 kN.
Wheel Dia./Dia. des roues: 1140 mm.
Livery/Livrée: See below./Voir ci-dessus. N = Maurienne green/vert maurienne.

System/Système: 1500 V d.c./continu.
Weight/Masse: 116 (110 t) tonnes.
Length/Longeur: 20.19 m.
Max. Speed/Vitesse max.: 100 /220 km/h.

Fitted with rheostatic braking, electro-pneumatic braking, driver-guard communication and cab to shore radio.
Équipées de frein rhéostatique, commande électropneumatique du frein, liaison train-engin moteur et radio sol-train.

c Fitted with 'préannonce' cab signalling./équipées de 'préannonce' signalisation en cabine.
e Fitted with snowploughs./dotées d'éperons chasse neige.

6501 T		VE		6538 T	c	PO		
6502 T	c	PO	IVRY-SUR-SEINE	6539 N		PO		
6503 T	c	PO		6540 N		VE		
6504 T	c	PO	VITRY-SUR-SEINE	6541 T		VE		
6505 T	c	PO	CASTELNAUDARY	6542 N		VE		
6506 T	c	PO	VIERZON	6543 N		VE		
6507 T	c	PO	SAINTE-FOY-LA-GRANDE	6544 N	e	VE		
6508 T	c	PO	MONTAUBAN	6545 N	e	VE		
6509 T	c	PO	AGEN	6546 N	e	VE		
6510 T	c	PO	CARCASSONNE	6547 T	e	VE		
6511 T	c	PO	PAMIERS	6548 N	e	VE		
6512 C	c	PO	NARBONNE	6549 N	e	VE		
6513 T	c	PO	COGNAC	6550 N	e	VE		
6514 T	c	PO	POITIERS	6551 N	e	VE		
6515 T	c	PO	BLOIS	6552 T	e	VE		
6516 T	c	PO	CHÂTELLERAULT	6553 T	e	VE		
6517 T	c	PO	ARCACHON	6554 T	e	VE		
6518 T	c	PO	ORLÉANS	6555 T	e	VE		
6519 T	c	PO	ANGOULÊME	6556 T	e	VE		
6520 T	c	PO	RUFFEC	6557 T	e	VE		
6521 T	c	PO	SAINTES	6558 T	e	VE		
6522 T	c	PO	LIMOGES	6559 T	e	VE		
6523 T	c	PO	BRIVE	6560 T		VE	OULLINS	
6524 T	c	PO	TOULOUSE	6561 T		VE		
6525 T	c	PO	CHÂTEAUROUX	6562 T		VE		
6526 T	c	PO	CHOISY-LE-ROI	6563 T		VE	LAVAL	
6527 T	c	PO	AMBOISE	6564 T		VE	BEAUNE	
6528 T	c	PO	LUCHON	6565 T		VE		
6529 T	c	PO	ISSOUDUN	6566 T		VE	MAUBEUGE	
6530 T	c	PO	CAHORS	6567 T		VE	BREST	
6531 T	c	PO	SAINT-PIERRE-DES-CORPS	6568 C		VE		
6532 T	c	PO		6569 T		VE	LA MULATIÈRE	
6533 T	c	PO	BEAUTIRAN	6570 T		VE	ARMENTIERES	
6534 T	c	PO	BÉZIERS	6571 T		VE	JEUMONT	
6535 T	c	PO	SAINT-CHAMOND	6572 T		VE	RÉSISTANCE-FER	
6536 T	c	PO	ANNECY	6573 T	c	PO	LIBOURNE	
6537 T	c	PO	SALON-DE-PROVENCE	6574 T	c	PO	DOLE	

CLASSES/SERIES CC 7000/7100   CoCo

The outline of these locomotives will be familiar to visitors to The Netherlands and Spain where examples exist as class 1300 and class 276 respectively. The two prototypes 7001/2 were the first big CoCo locomotives on the SNCF that were designed for express passenger use, previous ones being 2D2s. The class has moved around somewhat over the years but is now seeing out its days based at Avignon but still operating over a large area from the Pyrenees to Paris. The advent of TGVs has reduced their workload but they still turn up in Paris on overnight trains from the south and have fill in turns on e.c.s. trips at Paris Lyon. This class is now being withdrawn but 7107 will be preserved as it is joint holder of the 331 km/h speed record attained in 1955. It is already a favourite locomotive for attending special events such as open days etc.

Les deux prototypes de cette série, les CC 7001/2, furent les premières CoCo françaises pour des services voyageurs à grande vitesse, la SNCF ayant utilisée des 2D2 auparavant. Alsthom a aussi vendu des versions de cette série aus Pays Bas (série 1300), et à l'Espagne (série 276). Bien que les CC 7100 ont changé plusieurs fois d'affectation, elles finiront leur carrière à Avignon, tout en continuant de sillonner le réseau Sud–Est de Paris (où elles remorquent souvent des rames vides à la Gare de Lyon) jusqu'aux Pyrénées avec des percées à Toulouse et Bordeaux. La série subit maintenant un amortissement lent mais sûr. Cependant, la CC 7107 sera gardée pour le musée de Mulhouse puisqu'elle est co-détentrice du record de vitesse du monde – 331 km/h atteint en 1955. C'est déjà une locomotive populaire pour des journées portes ouvertes et autres manifestations ferroviaires.

Built/Construction: 1949*/1952–55.   **System/Système:** 1500 V d.c./continu.
Builder-Mech. Parts/Constructeur-Partie mécanique: Alsthom/Fives-Lille.
Builder-Elec. Parts/Constructeur-Partie électrique: Alsthom/MTE.
Power/Puissance: 3490 (2770*, 3240†) kW.

Weight/Masse: 107 (104*, 106†) tonnes
Max. T.E./E.T. max.: 260 kN.
Wheel Dia./Dia. des roues: 1250 mm.
Livery/Livrée: E with turquoise band/E avec bande turquoise.

Fitted with cab to shore radio./Équipées de radio sol-train.

7001	* AV	7110	AV	7120	AV	7130	AV	7139	AV	7149	† AV
7002	* AV	7111	AV	7121	AV	7131	AV	7140	AV	7151	† AV
7101	AV	7112	AV	7122	AV	7132	AV	7141	AV	7152	† AV
7102	AV	7113	AV	7123	AV	7134	AV	7142	AV	7153	† AV
7103	AV	7115	AV	7124	AV	7135	AV	7143	AV	7154	† AV
7105	AV	7116	AV	7125	AV	7136	AV	7144	† AV	7155	† AV
7106	AV	7117	AV	7126	AV	7137	AV	7145	† AV	7157	† AV
7107	AV	7118	AV	7128	AV	7138	AV	7146	† AV	7158	† AV
7109	AV	7119	AV						

CLASS/SERIE BB 7200   BB

This mixed traffic class is part of a large family of locomotives, BB 7200 is the d.c. version, BB 15000 the ac version and BB 22200 the dual-voltage version. (7200 + 15000 = 22200). Unlike most monomotor-bogied locomotives class 7200 has fixed gearing for freight or passenger use, certain locos being limited to 100 km/h with the remainder having the higher rating of 160 km/h. 7411–40 also have modern microprocessor controls and regenerative braking. The introduction of TGV Atlantique has seen Limoges losing 7201–35 to Bordeaux, allowing 9400s to move to Avignon.

Cette grande série pour services mixtes est la version 1500 V continu de la famille qui comprend les BB 15000 (version 25 kV monophasé) et les BB 22200 (bi-courant). Bien que dotées de bogies monomoteurs, on ne peut pas change la réduction sur les BB 7200 comme, par exemple, sur les CC 6500. Certaines BB 7200 ont un rapport de réduction pour les marchandises (100 km/h max) bien que d'autres ont un rapport voyageurs (160 km/h). La dernière sous-série, BB 7411–7440, est dotée du contrôle par microprocesseur ainsi que du freinage à récupération. Les 7201–35 ont été transférées récemment de Limoges à Bordeaux qui a permi le transfert des BB 9400 à Avignon.

Built/Construction: 1976–85.   **System/Système:** 1500 V d.c./continu.
Builders/Constructeurs: Alsthom/MTE.
Power/Puissance: 4360 kW.
Max. T.E./E.T. max.: 288 (3xx*†) kN.   **Weight/Masse:** 84 tonnes.
Wheel Dia./Dia. des roues: 1250 mm.   **Length/Longeur:** 17.48 m.
Max. Speed/Vitesse max.: 160 (100*†, 200‡) km/h.
Livery/Livrée: C.

Fitted with cowcatchers, rheostatic brakes, electro-pneumatic brakes, driver-guard communication. Cab to shore radio.

Équipées d'éperons chasse-obstacle, frein rhéostatique, commande électropneumatique du frein, liaison train-engin moteur et radio sol-train.

c Modified for working the 'Catalan Talgo'/Apte à la remorque des rames 'Catalan Talgo'
† Fitted for multiple working over the Maurienne line./Couplable en UM pour la ligne du Maurienne.
‡ Fitted with "préannonce" cab signalling./Dotées de «préannonce» signalisation en cabine.

7201	* BD	7216	* BD	7230	* BD	7244	PO	7258	PO	7272	VG
7202	* BD	7217	* BD	7231	* BD	7245	PO	7259	PO	7273	VG
7203	* BD	7218	* BD	7232	* BD	7246	PO	7260	PO	7274	VG
7204	* BD	7219	* BD	7233	* BD	7247	PO	7261	‡ PO	7275	VG
7205	* BD	7220	* BD	7234	* BD	7248	PO	7262	‡ PO	7276	VG
7206	* BD	7221	* BD	7235	* BD	7249	PO	7263	‡ PO	7277	VG
7207	* BD	7222	* BD	7236	PO	7250	PO	7264	VG	7278	VG
7208	* BD	7223	* BD	7237	PO	7251	PO	7265	VG	7279	VG
7210	* BD	7224	* BD	7238	PO	7252	PO	7266	VG	7280	VG
7211	* BD	7225	* BD	7239	PO	7253	PO	7267	VG	7281	c VG
7212	* BD	7226	* BD	7240	PO	7254	PO	7268	VG	7282	c VG
7213	* BD	7227	* BD	7241	PO	7255	PO	7269	VG	7283	c VG
7214	* BD	7228	* BD	7242	PO	7256	PO	7270	VG	7284	c VG
7215	* BD	7229	* BD	7243	PO	7257	PO	7271	VG	7285	c VG

7286 c VG	7312	VG	7338	VG	7364 † CB	7390	VG	7416 † CB
7287 c VG	7313	VG	7339	VG	7365 † CB	7391	VG	7417 † CB
7288 c VG	7314	VG	7340	VG	7366 † CB	7392	VG	7418 † CB
7289 c VG	7315	VG	7341	VG	7367 † CB	7393	VG	7419 † CB
7290 c VG	7316	VG	7342	VG	7368 † CB	7394	VG	7420 † CB
7291 c VG	7317	VG	7343 † CB	7369 † CB	7395	VG	7421 † CB
7292 c VG	7318	VG	7344 † CB	7370 † CB	7396	VG	7422 † CB
7293 c VG	7319	VG	7345 † CB	7371 † CB	7397	VG	7423 † CB
7294 c VG	7320	VG	7346 † CB	7372 † CB	7398	VG	7424 † CB
7295 c VG	7321	VG	7347 † CB	7373 † CB	7399	VG	7425 † CB
7296 c VG	7322	VG	7348 † CB	7374 † CB	7400	VG	7426 † CB
7297 VG	7323	VG	7349 † CB	7375 † CB	7401	VG	7427 † CB
7298 VG	7324	VG	7350 † CB	7376 † CB	7402	VG	7428 † CB
7299 VG	7325	VG	7351 † CB	7377 † CB	7403	VG	7429 † CB
7300 VG	7326	VG	7352 † CB	7378 † CB	7404	VG	7430 † CB
7301 VG	7327	VG	7353 † CB	7379 † CB	7405	VG	7431 † CB
7302 VG	7328	VG	7354 † CB	7380 † CB	7406	VG	7432 † CB
7303 VG	7329	VG	7355 † CB	7381	VG	7407	VG	7433 † CB
7304 VG	7330	VG	7356 † CB	7382	VG	7408	VG	7434 † CB
7305 VG	7331	VG	7357 † CB	7383	VG	7409	VG	7435 † CB
7306 VG	7332	VG	7358 † CB	7384	VG	7410	VG	7436 † CB
7307 VG	7333	VG	7359 † CB	7385	VG	7411 † CB	7437 † CB
7308 VG	7334	VG	7360 † CB	7386	VG	7412 † CB	7438 † CB
7309 VG	7335	VG	7361 † CB	7387	VG	7413 † CB	7439 † CB
7310 VG	7336	VG	7362 † CB	7388	VG	7414 † CB	7440 † CB
7311 VG	7337	VG	7363 † CB	7389	VG	7415 † CB	

Names/Noms:

7203	SAINT-FLOUR	7241	VILLEURBANNE
7221	SAINT-AMAND-MONTROND	7242	VIENNE
7223	LA SOUTERRAINE	7243	VILLENEUVE-SAINT-GEORGES
7232	SOUILLAC	7244	VERNOU-LA CELLE-SUR-SEINE
7236	CHAMBÉRY	7253	MONTRÉJEAU
7237	PIERRELATTE	7256	VALENTON
7238	THONON-LES-BAINS	7410	FONTENAY-SOUS-BOIS
7239	SAINT-PIERRE-D'ALBIGNY	7411	LAMURE-SUR-AZERGUES
7240	SAINT-ETIENNE		

CLASS/SERIE BB 8100   BoBo

A post-war development of BB 300 and exported to other countries (the NS Railway has some as class 1100). Although only based at two depots the class sees general use on freight trains all over the Sud Est area and examples often turn up at Paris Gare de Lyon on e.c.s duties. Locos from the 8237–71 batch can only be used in multiple at 80 km/h as they do not have modified suspension and are being withdrawn.

La séries est un développement d'après-guerre des BB 300 qui fut vendu à plusieurs autres pays y compris les Pays Bas – série 1100. Bien que basée à deux dépôts, la série est utilisée partout sur le réseau Sud-Est et jusqu'a Toulouse et Bordeaux via Narbonne. Les BB 8237 à 8271, qui ne sont pas utilisables en UM à 100 km/h, seront radiées quand elles arriveront en fin de parcours.

Built/Construction: 1947–55   **System/Système:** 1500 V d.c./continu.
Builder-Mech. Parts/Constructeur-Partie mécanique: Alsthom/Schneider-Jeumont/CGC.
Builder-Elec. Parts/Constructeur-Partie électrique: Alsthom/Siemens/Jeumont/Oerlikon.
Power/Puissance: 2100 kW.   **Weight/Masse:** 92 tonnes.
Max. T.E./E.T. max.: 152 kN.   **Length/Longeur:** 12.93 m.
Wheel Dia./Dia. des roues: 1400 mm.   **Max. Speed/Vitesse max.:** 105 km/h.
Livery/Livrée: V or/ou C.

Multiple working fitted. Cab to shore radio.
Couplables en UM. Dotées de la radio sol-train.

8001	AV	8104	AV	8108	AV	8112	AV	8116	AV	8120	AV
8101	AV	8105	AV	8109	AV	8113	AV	8117	AV	8121	AV
8102	AV	8106	AV	8110	AV	8114	AV	8118	AV	8122	DP
8103	AV	8107	AV	8111	AV	8115	AV	8119	AV	8123	AV

8124	AV	8148	DP	8171	DP	8194	AV	8217	DP	8240	AV
8125	DP	8149	AV	8172	DP	8195	DP	8218	DP	8241	DP
8126	AV	8150	AV	8173	DP	8196	DP	8219	AV	8242	AV
8127	DP	8151	AV	8174	DP	8197	DP	8220	DP	8245	DP
8128	AV	8152	AV	8175	DP	8198	DP	8221	AV	8246	DP
8129	AV	8153	DP	8176	DP	8199	DP	8222	AV	8247	AV
8130	DP	8154	AV	8177	AV	8200	AV	8223	DP	8248	AV
8131	DP	8155	DP	8178	DP	8201	DP	8224	DP	8249	DP
8132	DP	8156	DP	8179	AV	8202	DP	8225	DP	8250	DP
8133	DP	8157	DP	8180	DP	8203	DP	8226	DP	8251	AV
8134	DP	8158	AV	8181	AV	8204	DP	8227	DP	8252	AV
8135	DP	8159	DP	8182	AV	8205	AV	8228	AV	8253	DP
8136	DP	8160	DP	8183	AV	8206	AV	8229	DP	8257	DP
8137	DP	8161	AV	8184	AV	8207	DP	8230	AV	8258	AV
8138	DP	8162	AV	8185	DP	8208	DP	8231	DP	8259	AV
8139	AV	8163	AV	8186	DP	8209	DP	8232	DP	8263	DP
8140	AV	8164	DP	8187	DP	8210	DP	8233	DP	8264	DP
8141	AV	8165	AV	8188	DP	8211	DP	8234	AV	8265	DP
8142	DP	8166	AV	8189	AV	8212	DP	8235	DP	8266	AV
8143	DP	8167	DP	8190	DP	8213	DP	8236	DP	8267	DP
8144	AV	8168	DP	8191	DP	8214	DP	8237	DP	8269	AV
8145	DP	8169	AV	8192	DP	8215	DP	8238	DP	8270	DP
8146	AV	8170	AV	8193	DP	8216	DP	8239	DP	8271	DP
8147	AV										

CLASS/SERIE BB 8500   BB

A mixed traffic loco being a d.c. version of BB 17000. Monomotor bogies with two gear ratios. Being such a large class there are detail variations between batches. They are often used in multiple for freight on the difficult Paris–Toulouse line and on push-pull suburban trains out of Paris Montparnasse and Lyon. On local push-pull they will be replaced by Class BB 9600 so that they can take over further heavy freight work.

Une série pour services mixtes qui est la version 1500 V continu de la famille qui inclut les BB 17000 (25 kV monophasé) et BB 25500 (bi-courant). Plusieurs différences de détail existent entre les sous-séries. Elles sont souvent utilisées en UM sur des trains de marchandises sur la ligne Toulouse–Paris et sur des trains de banlieue à Paris Montparnasse et Gare de Lyon. Sur des rames TER elles seront remplacées par des BB 9600, et utilisés encore plus sur des marchandises lourds.

Built/Construction: 1964–74
Builder/Constructeur: Alsthom.
Power/Puissance: 2610 (2940*†) kW.
Max. T.E./E.T. max.: 323 /197 kN.
Wheel Dia./Dia. des roues: 1100 mm.
Livery/Livrée: E or/ou C.

System/Système: 1500 V d.c./continu.
Weight/Masse: 78 (79*, 80†) tonnes.
Length/Longeur: 14.70 (14.94*, 15.57†) m.
Max. Speed/Vitesse max.: 100/140 km/h.

Multiple working fitted. Rheostatic braking. Cab to shore radio.
Couplables en UM. Dotées du freinage rhéostatique, et radio sol-train.

*† Push-pull fitted./Dotées de la reversabilité.

8501	LG		8516	LG		8531		LG		8546	* MR		8561	* VG		8576	* TL
8502	LG		8517	LG		8532		LG		8547	* MR		8562	* MR		8577	* VE
8503	LG		8518	LG		8533		PO		8548	* MR		8563	* VG		8578	* VE
8504	LG		8519	LG		8534		PO		8549	* TL		8564	* VG		8579	* VE
8505	LG		8520	LG		8535		PO		8550	* VG		8565	* VE		8580	* TL
8506	LG		8521	LG		8536		PO		8551	* TL		8566	* VG		8581	* MR
8507	LG		8522	LG		8537	*	PO		8552	* MR		8567	* VE		8582	* VE
8508	LG		8523	LG		8538	*	PO		8553	* MR		8568	* MR		8583	* TL
8509	LG		8524	LG		8539	*	PO		8554	* MR		8569	* MR		8584	* TL
8510	LG		8525	LG		8540	*	TL		8555	* VG		8570	* VE		8585	* MB
8511	LG		8526	LG		8541	*	PO		8556	* MR		8571	* VE		8586	* TL
8512	LG		8527	LG		8542	*	PO		8557	* MR		8572	* TL		8587	* TL
8513	LG		8528	LG		8543	*	PO		8558	* MR		8573	* VE		8588	† MR
8514	LG		8529	LG		8544	*	TL		8559	* MR		8574	* VE		8589	† MR
8515	LG		8530	LG		8545	*	VG		8560	* VG		8575	* TL		8590	† MR

8591 † MR	8601 † TL	8611 † TL	8620 † TL	8629 † TL	8638 † TL
8592 † MR	8602 † TL	8612 † TL	8621 † TL	8630 † TL	8639 † TL
8593 † MR	8603 † TL	8613 † TL	8622 † TL	8631 † TL	8640 † TL
8594 † MR	8604 † TL	8614 † TL	8623 † TL	8632 † TL	8641 † TL
8595 † MR	8605 † TL	8615 † TL	8624 † TL	8633 † TL	8642 † TL
8596 † MR	8606 † TL	8616 † TL	8625 † TL	8634 † TL	8643 † MR
8597 † MR	8607 † TL	8617 † TL	8626 † TL	8635 † TL	8644 † TL
8598 † MR	8608 † TL	8618 † TL	8627 † TL	8636 † TL	8645 † MR
8599 † TL	8609 † TL	8619 † TL	8628 † TL	8637 † TL	8646 † MR
8600 † TL	8610 † TL				

Names/Noms:

8600	FLEURY-LES-AUBRAIS	8603	LANNEMEZAN
8601	AX-LES-THERMES	8604	CERDAGNE
8602	FOIX	8605	SAINT-GAUDENS

CLASS/SERIE BB 9200   BoBo

This class was the first of the SNCF standard types of the late 1950s. The same styling is also found on BB 9300, 9400, 16000, 25100, 25150, 25200. Class BB 9200 was originally scattered over the d.c. network south of Paris but now they are concentrated at Bordeaux and Paris Sud Ouest and are used on mixed traffic all over the Sud–Ouest network.

Les BB 9200 furent les première des séries standards introduites dans les années 50 par la SNCF. Les BB 9300, 9400, 16000, 25100, 25150 et 25200 ont la même silhouette. Bien qu'affectées à plusieurs dépôts du réseau 1500 V continu dans le passé, la série est maintenant concentrée à Bordeaux et Paris Sud Ouest mais utilisée sur des services mixtes sur tout le réseau Sud–Ouest.

Built/Construction: 1957–64   **System/Système:** 1500 V d.c./continu.
Builders/Constructeurs: Schneider-Jeumont/CEM.
Power/Puissance: 3850 kW.   **Weight/Masse:** 82 tonnes.
Max. T.E./E.T. max.: 260 kN.   **Length/Longeur:** 16.20 m.
Wheel Dia./Dia. des roues: 1250 mm.   **Max. Speed/Vitesse max.:** 160 km/h.
Livery/Livrée: E or/ou C.

Cab to shore radio. 9263–9292 are fitted with rheostatic braking.
Équipées de radio sol-train. Les 9263 à 9292 sont dotées de freins rhéostatiques.

p Modified for push-pull operation with Corail stock/.
Dotées de la réversabilité 'Intervilles' pour matériel Corail
t TDM push-pull fitted./Équipées du multiplexage
† Special buffers for Talgo trains./Tampons spéciaux pour trains «Talgo».
v 200 km/h gear ratio./Couple 200 km/h.

9201	BD	9217	BD	9232	BD	9247	BD	9263	tv PO	9278	† PO
9202	BD	9218	BD	9233	BD	9248	BD	9264	t PO	9279	† PO
9203	BD	9219	BD	9234	BD	9250	PO	9265	t PO	9280	tv PO
9204	BD	9220	BD	9235	BD	9251	PO	9266	PO	9281	p PO
9205	BD	9221	BD	9236	BD	9252	PO	9267	t PO	9282	p PO
9206	BD	9222	BD	9237	BD	9253	BD	9268	t PO	9283	PO
9207	BD	9223	BD	9238	BD	9254	PO	9269	PO	9284	PO
9208	BD	9224	BD	9239	BD	9255	PO	9270	PO	9285	PO
9209	BD	9225	BD	9240	BD	9256	BD	9271	PO	9286	PO
9210	BD	9226	BD	9241	BD	9257	PO	9272	PO	9287	tv PO
9211	BD	9227	BD	9242	BD	9258	PO	9273	t PO	9288	p PO
9212	BD	9228	BD	9243	BD	9259	PO	9274	† PO	9289	t PO
9213	BD	9229	BD	9244	BD	9260	PO	9275	† PO	9290	tv PO
9214	BD	9230	BD	9245	BD	9261	PO	9276	† PO	9291	p PO
9215	BD	9231	BD	9246	BD	9262	PO	9277	† PO	9292	p PO
9216	BD										

Names/Noms:

9248	LA-TESTE-DE-BUCH	9280	ARPAJON

▲ TGV 32 'MAISONS-ALFORT'. La Napoule Plage. ECS/Matériel vide Marseille–Nice. 19/08/89.
Peter Fox

▼ CC 1106. Toulouse depot./Dépôt de Toulouse. 25/06/90. *S.C. Falcus*

▲BB 335. Lyon Perrache. 15/04/89.　　　　　　　　　　　　　　T.N. Hall
▼BB 4762. Vierzon Yard/Vierzon Triage. 15/07/89.　　　　　　S.C. Falcus

▲CC 6518. 'ORLEANS'. Les Aubrais depot./Dépot des Aubrais. 27/06/90. *S.C. Falcus*

▼CC 6543. Vénissieux depot./Dépôt de Vénissieux. Livery/livrée: Maurienne. 28/06/90.
S.C. Falcus

▲CC 7158. Southbound car-carrier train near Vias airport./Un train à voitures vide près de l'Aéroport de Vias. 24/04/91. *Peter Fox*

▼BB 7286. Leaving Perpignan with the southbound 'Catalan-Talgo'/Quittant Perpignan vers Barcelona avec le «Catalan-Talgo». *Paul Russenberger*

▲BB 8555. Paris Gare de Lyon. Double-decker push-pull set/Rame réversible à deux niveaux.
26/05/90.   *Adrian Norton*

▼BB 9208. Béziers. Eastbound freight./Train de marchandises vers l'est. 03/06/90.
                                                                         David Haydock

38

BB 9461 + BB 9405. Westbound mixed freight near Vias Airport./Marchandises près de l'Aeroport de Vias. 24/04/91.

Peter Fox

▲BB 9601. Toulouse depot./Dépôt de Toulouse. 13/04/91.   *Peter Heppenstall*

▼BB 10003. Belfort. 18/10/90.   *David Haydock*

Peter Fox

BB 12137. Paris-bound freight./Train de marchandises vers Paris. Aulnay-sous-Bois. 26/04/91.

▲BB 15008 'NANCY'. Strasbourg depot./Dépôt de Strasbourg. 26/04/90.   *Peter Moody*
▼BB 16049. La Chapelle depot./Dépôt de La Chapelle. 11/09/90. Livery/livrée 'E'.
Adrian Norton

▲BB 16677. La Villette depot./Dépôt de La Villette. 12/07/90.

S.C. Falcus

▼BB 17034. Paris Gare de St. Lazare. 09/76.

Paul Russenberger

▲CC 21002. Charolais depot./Dépôt de Charolais. 14/07/89.　　　　　*S.C. Falcus*
▼BB 25221. Villeneuve St. Georges. 06/09/89.　　　　　*Peter Moody*

David Haydock

BB 25180. La Roche sur Foron. Lille—St. Gervais. 02/85.

▲BB 25608. Achères depot./Dépôt d'Achères. 14/07/89. *S.C. Falcus*
▼CC 40103 'BRIOUDE'. La Chapelle depot./Dépôt de La Chapelle. 11/09/90. *Adrian Norton*

46

Sybic 26030 leaves Conflans-Jarny with a Somain–Dijon freight on 25/04/91.
Sybic 26030 quitte Conflans-Jarny avec un train de marchandises Somain–Dijon. 25/04/91.

David Haydock
David Haydock

▲A1AA1A 62030. Dunkerque West/Ouest. Shunting the train ferry 'Nord–Pas de Calais'./Faisant des manoeuvres du ferry-boat 'Nord-Pas de Calais'. *Paul Russenberger*

▼62513 + 62458. Longueau depot./Dépôt de Longueau. Livery/Livrée: NS. 30/05/91.
David Haydock

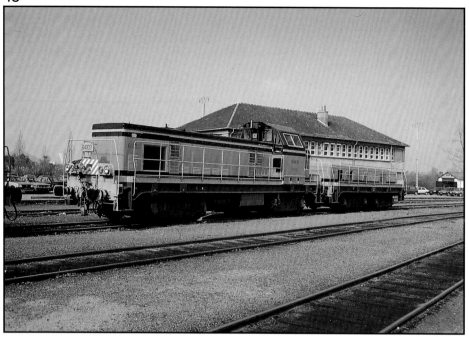

▲BB 64702 + TBB 64802 Lens depot./Dépôt de Lens. 09/04/91.   *David Haydock*
▼CC 65530. Tours St. Pierre depot./Dépôt de Tours St.Pierre. 15/07/89.   *S.C. Falcus*

CLASS/SERIE BB 9300   BoBo

An updated version of BB 9200. All are now grouped at Toulouse but see widespread use on the Paris–Sud Ouest main lines and the Toulouse–Marseille route. 9302 is being cannibalised at Oullins after a serious accident.

Une version moderniseé des BB 9200. Toutes sont basées à Toulouse mais sillonnent tout le réseau Sud–Ouest ainsi que la ligne Toulouse–Marseille. Accidentée, la 9302 sert comme réserve de piéces détachées à Oullins.

Built/Construction: 1967–69   **System/Système:** 1500 V d.c./continu.
Builders/Constructeurs: Schneider-Jeumont, MTE, CEM.
Power/Puissance: 3850 kW.   **Weight/Masse:** 84 tonnes.
Max. T.E./E.T. max.: 260 kN.   **Length/Longeur:** 16.20 m.
Wheel Dia./Dia. des roues: 1250 mm.   **Max. Speed/Vitesse max.:** 160 km/h.
Livery/Livrée: E or/ou C.

Fitted with rheostatic braking, electro-pneumatic brakes, cab to shore radio and driver-guard communication.
Dotées du frein rhéostatique et frein électropneumatique, radio sol-train et liaison train-engin moteur.

9301	TL	9308	TL	9315	TL	9322	TL	9329	TL	9335	TL
9302	TL	9309	TL	9316	TL	9323	TL	9330	TL	9336	TL
9303	TL	9310	TL	9317	TL	9324	TL	9331	TL	9337	TL
9304	TL	9311	TL	9318	TL	9325	TL	9332	TL	9338	TL
9305	TL	9312	TL	9319	TL	9326	TL	9333	TL	9339	TL
9306	TL	9313	TL	9320	TL	9327	TL	9334	TL	9340	TL
9307	TL	9314	TL	9321	TL	9328	TL				

Names/Noms:

9329 CASTRES   9326 MONTRABÉ

CLASS/SERIE BB 9400   BB

Although classed as a mixed traffic locomotive their main duties are on freight trains, often in multiple. The low weight of the locomotive however has proved to be a problem and is the main reason why the class has had mixed success. A decision has been taken to modernise or rebuild some locos and gradually withdraw the remainder. The 9400s also have the monopoly of passenger trains on the Béziers–Neussargues line. The remaining locos at Bordeaux will be transferred to Avignon in 09/91. 9429 is push-pull fitted and served as the prototype for class BB 9600.

Bien que considerérées comme des machines pour services mixtes, les BB 9400 sont utilisées sur tout le réseau Sud–Est principalement sur les trains de marchandises et souvent en UM. La seule utilisation programmée en voyageurs est sur les deux trains de la «ligne des Causses» de Béziers à Neussargues. Leur poids peu élevé n'a pas aidé au succés mitigée de cette série, et la SNCF a décidé de moderniser 42 machines (qui deviendront BB 9600) et de radier les autres des que possible. La 9429 est équipe de la reversabilité et a servi comme prototype des BB 9600.

Built/Construction: 1959–64   **System/Système:** 1500 V d.c./continu.
Builder-Mech. Parts/Constructeur-Partie mécanique: Fives/MTE.
Builder-Elec. Parts/Constructeur-Partie électrique: CEM/MTE.
Power/Puissance: 2210 kW.   **Weight/Masse:** 60 tonnes.
Max. T.E./E.T. max.: 270 kN.   **Length/Longeur:** 14.40 m.
Wheel Dia./Dia. des roues: 1020 mm.   **Max. Speed/Vitesse max.:** 130 km/h.
Livery: Most in pale grey with chocolate brown bands. Rest E or C.
Livrée: La plupart sont en gris clair avec des bandes marrons. Les autres E ou C.

Multiple working fitted. Cab to shore radio./Couplables en UM. Dotées de radio sol-train.

9401	BD	9406	BD	9411	BD	9419	BD	9425	AV	9434	AV
9403	BD	9408	BD	9413	BD	9421	BD	9426	AV	9435	AV
9404	BD	9409	BD	9415	BD	9423	BD	9429	TP	9436	AV
9405	AV	9410	BD	9416	BD	9424	AV	9433	AV	9437	AV

9438	AV	9450	AV	9471	AV	9493	AV	9507	AV	9520	AV
9439	AV	9451	AV	9474	AV	9495	AV	9508	AV	9521	AV
9440	AV	9454	BD	9478	AV	9496	AV	9509	AV	9522	AV
9442	AV	9455	BD	9480	AV	9497	AV	9510	AV	9524	AV
9443	AV	9456	BD	9481	AV	9498	AV	9511	AV	9526	AV
9444	AV	9459	AV	9482	AV	9500	AV	9512	AV	9529	AV
9445	AV	9464	AV	9485	AV	9503	AV	9513	AV	9530	AV
9446	AV	9466	AV	9487	AV	9504	AV	9514	AV	9532	AV
9447	AV	9467	AV	9489	AV	9505	AV	9515	AV	9533	AV
9448	AV	9468	AV	9490	AV	9506	AV	9518	AV	9535	AV
9449	AV								

CLASS/SERIE BB 9600 BB

Béziers Works is rebuilding 42 9400s for push-pull work. They will be used with the new RRR sets. They wil replace the BB 8500s on local services in the Lyon, Marseille, Montpellier and Toulouse areas. BB 9641/2 are used on the Tours–St. Pierre des Corps shuttle and have a similar livery to TGV-Atlantique.

Les ateliers de Béziers viennent de commencer la conversion de 42 BB 9400 pour itilisation avec des rames reversibles régionales (RRR). Les BB 9600 remplaceront des BB 8500 autour de Lyon, Marseille, Montpellier et Toulouse. Les BB 9641/2 sont utilisées sur les navettes Tours–St Pierre des Corps et portent une livrée proche de celle du TGV-Atlantique.

Details as BB 9400 except:/détails comme les BB 9400 sauf:

Max. Speed/Vitesse max.: 140 km/h. **Livery/Livrée:** C.
Multiple working (not with BB 9400) and push-pull fitted.
Couplables en UM (mais pas avec les BB 9400) et équipées pour la reversabilité.

9601 (9477)	TP	9615 (9	)	9629 (9	)
9602 (9	)	9616 (9	)	9630 (9	)
9603 (9	)	9617 (9	)	9631 (9	)
9604 (9	)	9618 (9	)	9632 (9	)
9605 (9	)	9619 (9	)	9633 (9	)
9606 (9	)	9620 (9	)	9634 (9	)
9607 (9	)	9621 (9	)	9635 (9	)
9608 (9	)	9622 (9	)	9636 (9	)
9609 (9	)	9623 (9	)	9637 (9	)
9610 (9	)	9624 (9	)	9638 (9	)
9611 (9	)	9625 (9	)	9639 (9	)
9612 (9	)	9626 (9	)	9640 (9	)
9613 (9	)	9627 (9	)	9641 (9452)	TP
9614 (9	)	9628 (9	)	9642 (9470)	TP

CLASS/SERIE BB 10000 Bo2

The SNCF numbers its experimental locomotives at the beginning of a series so that the experimental a.c. locos are in the 10000 series. This particular locomotive is a modified BB 15000 and is fitted with GTO asynchronous drive and is a test-bed for the Trans-Manche Super Trains. One bogie is fitted with two 1020 kW Brush motors whilst the other is unpowered. Apart from SNCF 25 kV, it can operate under standard Belgian 3000 V dc and BR Southern Region 750 V dc, albeit via the pantograph! It can often be found around Belfort, where the Alsthom factory is located. The other prototype, 10004 has regained its original identity of 15055. For dimensions see Class BB 15000.

Cette machine est une BB 15000 modifiée en profondeur avec la chaîne de traction prévue pour les Trans-Manche Super Trains (TMST). Une bogie est équipée de deux moteurs asynchrones Brush de 1020 kW chacun tandis que l'autre n'est pas motorisée. La 10003 marche sous les 25 kV de la SNCF mais aussi sous 3000 V continu belge et même sous 750 V continu (par pantographe). Cette dernière tension est alimenté par un troisième rail entre le tunnel sous la Manche (Folkestone) et Londres. La 10003 est souvent à Belfort où se trouve l'usine GEC-Alsthom qui organise les essais de traction. L'autre prototype, la BB 10004, a repris son identité original de BB 15055. Détails comme la série BB 15000.

Livery/Livrée: Pale grey with red and orange lining./Gris clair embelli en rouge et orange/

10003 (15007) SB

CLASS/SERIE BB 12000 BoBo

Called "Monocabines" or even "flat irons" this class was built for the newly electrified Valenciennes–Thionville line and was the first 25 kV ac type to go into series production. Considered to be a mixed traffic locomotive they rarely appear on passenger work being concentrated now on freight trains all over the Nord-Est region as well as Amiens–Rouen. and Rouen–Paris. Withdrawals have slowed down due to late deliveries of the 26000s.

Connues sous le nom de «monocabines» ou «fers à repasser», ces machines furent les premières locomotives monophasées commandées par la SNCF et construites pour l'electrification de la ligne Valenciennes–Thionville. Bien que considérées comme locomotives pour services mixtes, elles remorquent très peu de trains de voyageurs. Sur des marchandises elles sillonnent tout le réseau Nord–Est ainsi que Amiens–Rouen et Rouen–Paris. Leur amortissement a été freiné par les livraisons tardives des «Sybics».

Most are fitted with cab-shore radio.
La plupart sont équipées de radio sol-train.

Built/Construction: 1954–61. **System/Système:** 25 kV a.c./monophasé.
Builders-Mech. Parts/Constructeurs-Partie mécanique: Alsthom/Schneider.
Builders-Elec. Parts/Constructeurs-Partie électrique: MTE/Alsthom.
Power/Puissance: 2470 kW. **Weight/Masse:** 82–86 tonnes.
Max. T.E./E.T. max.: 353 kN. **Length/Longeur:** 15.20 m.
Wheel Dia./Dia. des roues: 1250 mm. **Max. Speed/Vitesse max.:** 120 km/h.
Livery/Livrée: V.

12002	LE	12025	MN	12048	LE	12076	LE	12103	MN	12126	LE
12003	MN	12026	LE	12049	MN	12077	MN	12104	LE	12127	LE
12004	MN	12027	LE	12050	MN	12078	MN	12105	LE	12128	LE
12005	MN	12028	LE	12051	MN	12080	MN	12106	MN	12129	LE
12006	LE	12029	MN	12053	LE	12081	LE	12107	MN	12130	LE
12007	MN	12030	MN	12054	MN	12082	MN	12108	LE	12131	LE
12008	MN	12031	LE	12055	MN	12083	MN	12109	MN	12132	MN
12009	MN	12032	LE	12056	LE	12084	LE	12110	MN	12133	LE
12010	MN	12033	MN	12059	MN	12085	LE	12111	MN	12134	MN
12011	MN	12034	MN	12060	MN	12086	LE	12112	LE	12136	MN
12012	LE	12035	LE	12061	MN	12087	MN	12113	MN	12137	LE
12013	MN	12036	MN	12062	MN	12088	MN	12114	MN	12138	LE
12014	MN	12037	MN	12063	MN	12090	LE	12115	LE	12139	LE
12015	LE	12038	MN	12064	MN	12091	MN	12116	MN	12140	MN
12016	MN	12039	MN	12065	LE	12092	MN	12117	MN	12141	MN
12017	MN	12040	MN	12067	MN	12094	MN	12118	MN	12142	LE
12018	MN	12041	MN	12068	MN	12095	LE	12119	MN	12143	LE
12019	LE	12042	LE	12069	MN	12096	MN	12120	LE	12144	MN
12020	MN	12043	LE	12070	MN	12097	MN	12121	MN	12145	MN
12021	MN	12044	LE	12071	MN	12098	MN	12122	MN	12146	LE
12022	LE	12045	MN	12073	LE	12099	MN	12123	MN	12147	MN
12023	LE	12046	MN	12074	MN	12100	MN	12124	MN	12148	LE
12024	LE	12047	MN	12075	MN	12101	LE	12125	MN		

CLASS/SERIE BB 13000 BoBo

A mixed traffic locomotive of similar appearance to BB 12000 but with technical differences. Deliveries of 'Sybics' have brought a drastic reduction in activity and all are likely to go by 1994. In mid-1991 many were stored although conditional freight activity continued. Some passenger work remained around Nancy, Metz amd Longwy, particularly Fridays–Sundays.

Une série pour trafic mixte avec un profil très semblable à celui des BB 12000 mais avec des différences techniques. Cette série connait une baisse sensible d'activité dûe à l'introduction des 'Sybics' et sera vraisemblablement éliminée avant 1994. En 1991, beaucoup de BB 13000 étaient garées en bon état mais la série avait conservé quelques prestations voyageurs autour de Nancy, Metz et Longwy, surtout du vendredi au dimanche, ainsi que des marchandises en service facultatif.

Built/Construction: 1954–57. **System/Système:** 25 kV a.c./monophasé.
Builder-Mech. Parts/Constructeur-Partie mécanique: MTE/Fives-Lille/SLM.

BB 13053. Longwy. 17.59 to/à Paris. 09/09/89. *Eric Dunkling*
CC 14133. Somain. 17/04/87. *Eric Dunkling*

Builder-Elec. Parts/Constructeur-Partie électrique: Jeumont/Oerlikon/Brown Boveri/Séchéron.
Power/Puissance: 2130 (2000*) kW.　　**Weight/Masse:** 84 tonnes.
Max. T.E./E.T. max.: 255 kN.　　**Length/Longeur:** 15.20 m.
Wheel Dia./Dia. des roues: 1250 mm.　　**Max. Speed/Vitesse max.:** 120 (105*) km/h.
Livery/Livrée: V.

13003 * SB	13011 * SB	13027 SB	13038 SB	13043 SB	13051 SB
13005 * SB	13017 SB	13029 SB	13039 SB	13044 SB	13052 SB
13006 * SB	13018 SB	13031 SB	13041 SB	13045 SB	13053 SB
13009 * SB	13020 SB	13034 SB			

CLASS/SERIE CC 14100　　CoCo

A heavy freight locomotive that is now on the way out. Its slow speed and heavy pulling power was useful 30 years ago when steam was replaced. Today however wagon speeds have increased as have the speeds of most trains so no more overhauls are being done and the locomotives will be withdrawn as they reach overhaul time or need major repairs. Late deliveries of 26000s have given this class a new lease of life, but withdrawals are starting again and all are likely to be withdrawn in the next few years.

Des locomotives conçues pour remorquer des trains de marchandises lourds. Leur capacité de traction est toujours appréciée mais l'augmentation de la vitesse des convois fret rend les CC 14100 complètement obsolètes. La livraison tardive des «Sybics» avait donné un sursis mais les radiations recommencement et les CC 14100 vont vivre leurs derniers jours en 1992/3.

Built/Construction: 1954–58.　　**System/Système:** 25 kV a.c./monophasé.
Builder-Mech. Parts/Constructeur-Partie mécanique: Alsthom/Fives.
Builder-Elec. Parts/Constructeur-Partie électrique: Alsthom/CEM.
Power/Puissance: 1860 kW.　　**Weight/Masse:** 127 tonnes.
Max. T.E./E.T. max.: 422 kN.　　**Length/Longeur:** 18.89 m.
Wheel Dia./Dia. des roues: 1100 mm.　　**Max. Speed/Vitesse max.:** 60 km/h.
Livery/Livrée: V.

14101 TV	14125 TV	14148 TV	14155 TV	14169 TV	14187 TV
14102 TV	14126 TV	14151 TV	14156 TV	14174 TV	14188 TV
14104 TV	14129 TV	14152 TV	14161 TV	14181 TV	14195 TV
14109 TV	14131 TV	14153 TV	14162 TV	14182 TV	14200 TV
14113 TV	14133 TV	14154 TV	14167 TV	14183 TV	14201 TV
14123 TV	14146 TV				

CLASS/SERIE BB 15000　　BB

The first of the 1970 generation of locomotives. They work mainly passenger from Paris Est to Basel, Luxembourg and Longwy as well as from Mulhouse to Besançon. 15007 became prototype 7003 later becoming 10003. 15055 became prototype 10004, but has since reverted to its original identity.

La première série de la «famille» des années 70 qui inclut les BB 7200 et BB 22200. Elles remorquent surtout des trains de voyageurs de Paris Est à Bâle, Luxembourg et Longwy ainsi que de Mulhouse à Besançon. La 15007 est devenue la 7003, prototype des BB 7200, et plus tard la BB 10003. La 15055 est devenu 10002 mais a repris son identité originale en 1989.

Built/Construction: 1971–78.　　**System/Système:** 25 kV a.c./monophasé.
Builders/Constructeurs: Alsthom/MTE.
Power/Puissance: 4620 kW.　　**Weight/Masse:** 87–90 tonnes.
Max. T.E./E.T. max.: 294 kN.　　**Length/Longeur:** 17.48 m.
Wheel Dia./Dia. des roues: 1250 mm.　　**Max. Speed/Vitesse max.:** 160 km/h.

Rheostatic braking./Freinage rhéostatique.

15001 T SB	GRETZ-ARMAINVILLIERS	15006 T SB	METZ
15002 T SB	LONGWY	15008 T SB	NANCY
15003 T SB	SARREGUEMINES	15009 T SB	REIMS
15004 T SB	SEDAN	15010 T SB	STRASBOURG
15005 T SB	SAINT-LOUIS	15012 T SB	CHÂLONS-SUR-MARNE

15013	T	SB	LONGUYON	15039	T	SB	ROSNY-SOUS-BOIS
15014	T	SB	THIONVILLE	15040	C	SB	LIVRY GARGAN
15015	T	SB	BIARRITZ	15041	T	SB	SAINTE MENEHOULD
15016	T	SB	CHARLEVILLE-MÉZIÈRES	15042	T	SB	ETIVAL-CLAIREFONTAINE
15017	T	SB	SAINT-AVOLD	15043	T	SB	MAIZIÈRES-LES-METZ
15018	T	SB	BONDY	15044	T	SB	SUIPPES
15019	T	SB	MONTIGNY-LÈS-METZ	15045	T	SB	RAON L'ÉTAPE
15020	T	SB	PAU	15046	T	SB	
15021	T	SB	CHÂTEAU-THIERRY	15047	T	SB	CHELLES
15022	T	SB	PANTIN	15048	T	SB	HAGUENAU
15023	T	SB	MEAUX	15049	T	SB	
15024	T	SB	LUNÉVILLE	15050	T	SB	VITRY-LE-FRANÇOIS
15025	T	SB	TOUL	15051	T	SB	AULNOYE-AYMERIES
15026	T	SB	ÉPERNAY	15052	T	SB	CAMBRAI
15027	T	SB	CREUTZWALD	15053	T	SB	TROUVILLE-SUR-MER
15028	T	SB	VILLIERS-LE-BEL	15054	T	SB	
15029	T	SB	AURILLAC	15055	T	SB	
15030	T	SB	FORBACH	15056	T	SB	VANNES
15031	T	SB	MOYEUVRE-GRANDE	15058	T	SB	ÉPINAL
15032	T	SB	CHAMBLY	15059	T	SB	TOURCOING
15033	T	SB	GAGNY	15060	T	SB	CREIL
15034	C	SB	SÈTE	15061	T	SB	SARREBOURG
15035	T	SB	NOGENT-SUR-MARNE	15062	T	SB	MONTMÉDY
15036	T	SB	LE PERREUX-SUR-MARNE	15063	T	SB	VERDUN
15037	T	SB	LA FERTÉ-SOUS-JOUARRE	15064	T	SB	SAVERNE
15038	T	SB	ARS SUR MOSELLE	15065	T	SB	VAIRES-SUR-MARNE

CLASS/SERIE BB 16000   BoBo

This is an ac version of BB 9200. At one time split between La Chapelle and Strasbourg the delivery of new BB 15000 allowed all BB 16000 to be concentrated at La Chapelle. After many years of working the principal expresses from Paris Nord 10 locomotives now see use on trains from Paris St.Lazare to Le Havre for which duties they were fitted with Corail type push-pull equipment. 16028 spent some time converted to dual-voltage prototype BB 20005 from which classes 25100, 25200 were developed. In 1991, three locos will be fitted with TDM and will become Class BB 16100.

Une version en 25 kV monophasé de la série BB 9200. Auparavant scindée entre La Chapelle et Strasbourg, la série fut concentré à La Chapelle après la livraison de BB 15000. Les BB 16000 remorquent la plupart des express sur Paris–Amiens–Lille et Paris–St. Quentin–Maubeuge depuis plusieurs années. En plus, celles dotées de la reversabilité Corail prennent en charge des express sur Paris–Rouen–Le Havre. La 16028 fut la prototype bi-courant des 25100 et 25150, sous le numéro BB 20005, au début des années 60. En 1991, trois membres de la série seront dotés du multiplexage at deviendront les BB 16100.

Built/Construction: 1958–63.   **System/Système:** 25 kV a.c./monophasé.
Builder/Constructeur: MTE.
Power/Puissance: 4130 kW.   **Weight/Masse:** 88 tonnes.
Max. T.E./E.T. max.: 309 kN.   **Length/Longeur:** 16.20 m.
Wheel Dia./Dia. des roues: 1250 mm.   **Max. Speed/Vitesse max.:** 160 km/h.
Livery/Livrée: E or/ou C.

p Push-pull fitted./Dotées de la reversabilité.

16001		PL	16012		PL	16022		PL	16033		PL	16044	p	PL	16054		PL
16002		PL	16013		PL	16023		PL	16034		PL	16046		PL	16055		PL
16003	p	PL	16014		PL	16024		PL	16035		PL	16047	p	PL	16056	p	PL
16005		PL	16015		PL	16026		PL	16036		PL	16048		PL	16057		PL
16006	p	PL	16016		PL	16027		PL	16037		PL	16049		PL	16058		PL
16007	p	PL	16017		PL	16028		PL	16039	p	PL	16050	p	PL	16059		PL
16008	p	PL	16018	p	PL	16029		PL	16040		PL	16051		PL	16060		PL
16009		PL	16019		PL	16030		PL	16041		PL	16052		PL	16061		PL
16010		PL	16020		PL	16031		PL	16042		PL	16053	p	PL	16062		PL
16011		PL	16021		PL	16032	p	PL	16043		PL						

Names/Noms:

16001 NEUILLY-SUR-MARNE	16008 DRANCY
16007 MANTES-LA-JOLIE	16062 DOL-DE-BRETAGNE

CLASS/SERIE BB 16100   BoBo

A conversion of fifteen BB 16000 for TDM working of push-pull double-decker sets between Paris and Amiens.

Une conversion de quinze BB 16000 qui seront dotées de multiplexage pour des rames réversibles à deux niveaux «Grande Couronne» sur Paris–Amiens.

Livery/Livrée: C.

16101 (16004)	PL	16106 (160)		16111 (160)	
16102 (160)		16107 (160)		16112 (160)	
16103 (160)		16108 (160)		16113 (160)	
16104 (160)		16109 (160)		16114 (160)	
16105 (160)		16110 (160)		16115 (160)	

CLASS/SERIE BB 16500   BB

The monomotor bogie originated with this class and with it the idea of providing alternative gear ratios to create true mixed traffic locomotives. With such a large class there are many detail variations. The most interesting is 16700 which has modified cab front end panels. 16540 became the prototype of the 25500s and was numbered 20004 in the 60s. Recently Strasbourg has regained an allocation of this class after many years when they were only based at two depots, Lens and la Villette. However their work is unchanged – freight, often in multiple, and suburban passenger all over the Nord-Est region as well as to Le Havre. 16600 onwards are now modified for 100 km/h in low gear.

Cette série fut la première avec des bogies monomoteurs à deux réductions – pour voyageurs et marchandises – ce qui donne une vraie machine à utilisation mixte. Dans une si grande série il y a plusieurs différences de détails. La plus intéressante est la 16700 qui à des cabines et traverse renforcées, prévues à l'origine pour des attelages automatiques. La 16540 fut le prototype des BB 25500, sous le numéro BB 20004, dans les années 60. Après avoir été partagée pendant plusieurs années entre Lens et La Villette, une partie de la série fut transférée à Strasbourg en 1990. Cependant, leur tâches n'ont pas changé – fret, souvent en UM, et trains de banlieue sur tout le réseau Nord–Est et jusqu'au Havre sur l'Atlantique. Les 16501–99 qui n'ont pas été modifiées pour rouler à 100 km/h sur les frets sont limitées à des trains de banlieue autour de Lille et Paris Est. Celles de PV ont leurs numéros entre deux traits jaunes.

Built/Construction: 1958–64.
Builder/Constructeur: Alsthom.
Power/Puissance: 2580 kW.
Max. T.E./E.T. max.: 324/192 kN.
Wheel Dia./Dia. des roues: 1100 mm.
Livery/Livrée: E or/ou C.

System/Système: 25 kV a.c./monophasé.
Weight/Masse: 71–74 (81*) tonnes.
Length/Longeur: 14.00 (15.27*) m.
Max. Speed/Vitesse max.: 100 (90†)/140 km/h.

Multiple working and push-pull fitted./Couplable en UM. Dotées de la reversibilité.
t TDM fitted for working 3600 tonne Dunkerque–Dieulouard iron ore trains.
t Dotées du multiplexage pour des trains de minarais de 3600 t de Dunkerque à Dieulouard.

16501 † LE	16514 † LE	16527 † LE	16540 † LE	16553 † PV	16566 † PV
16502 † LE	16515 † LE	16528 † LE	16541 † LE	16554 † PV	16567 † PV
16503 † LE	16516 † LE	16529 † LE	16542 † LE	16555 † PV	16568 † PV
16504 † LE	16517 † LE	16530 † LE	16543 † LE	16556 † PV	16569 † PV
16505 † LE	16518 † LE	16531 † LE	16544 † LE	16557 † PV	16570 † PV
16506 † LE	16519 † LE	16532 † LE	16545 † LE	16558 † PV	16571 † PV
16507 † LE	16520 † LE	16533 † LE	16546 † LE	16559 † PV	16572 † PV
16508 † LE	16521 † LE	16534 † LE	16547 † LE	16560 † PV	16573 † PV
16509 † LE	16522 † LE	16535 † LE	16548 † LE	16561 † PV	16574 † PV
16510 † LE	16523 † LE	16536 † LE	16549 † LE	16562 † PV	16575 † PV
16511 † LE	16524 † LE	16537 † LE	16550 † LE	16563 † PV	16576 † PV
16512 † LE	16525 † LE	16538 † LE	16551 † PV	16564 † PV	16577 † PV
16513 † LE	16526 † LE	16539 † LE	16552 † PV	16565 † PV	16578 † PV

16579 †	PV	16615	PV	16651	PV	16687	PV	16723	SB	16759	LE
16580 †	PV	16616	PV	16652	PV	16688	PV	16724	SB	16760	LE
16581 †	PV	16617	PV	16653	PV	16689	PV	16725	SB	16761	LE
16582 †	PV	16618	PV	16654	PV	16690	PV	16726	SB	16762	LE
16583 †	PV	16619	PV	16655	PV	16691	PV	16727	SB	16763	LE
16584 †	PV	16620	PV	16656	PV	16692	PV	16728	SB	16764	LE
16585 †	PV	16621	PV	16657	PV	16693	PV	16729	SB	16765	LE
16586 †	PV	16622	PV	16658	PV	16694	PV	16730	SB	16766	LE
16587 †	PV	16623	PV	16659	PV	16695	PV	16731	SB	16767	LE
16588 †	PV	16624	PV	16660	PV	16696	PV	16732	SB	16768	LE
16589 †	PV	16625	PV	16661	PV	16697	PV	16733	SB	16769	LE
16590 †	PV	16626	PV	16662	PV	16698	PV	16734	SB	16770	LE
16591 †	PV	16627	PV	16663	PV	16699	PV	16735	SB	16771	LE
16592 †	PV	16628	PV	16664	PV	16700 *	PV	16736	SB	16772	LE
16593 †	PV	16629	PV	16665	PV	16701	PV	16737	SB	16773	LE
16594 †	PV	16630	PV	16666	PV	16702	PV	16738	SB	16774	LE
16595 †	PV	16631	PV	16667	PV	16703	PV	16739	SB	16775	LE
16596 †	PV	16632	PV	16668	PV	16704	PV	16740	SB	16776	LE
16597 †	PV	16633	PV	16669	PV	16705	PV	16741	SB	16777	LE
16598 †	PV	16634	PV	16670	PV	16706	PV	16742	SB	16778	LE
16599 †	PV	16635	PV	16671	PV	16707	PV	16743	SB	16779	LE
16600	PV	16636	PV	16672	PV	16708	PV	16744	SB	16780	LE
16601	PV	16637	PV	16673	PV	16709	PV	16745	LE	16781 t	LE
16602	PV	16638	PV	16674	PV	16710	SB	16746	LE	16782 t	LE
16603	PV	16639	PV	16675	PV	16711	SB	16747	LE	16783 t	LE
16604	PV	16640	PV	16676	PV	16712	SB	16748	LE	16784 t	LE
16605	PV	16641	PV	16677	PV	16713	SB	16749	LE	16785 t	LE
16606	PV	16642	PV	16678	PV	16714	SB	16750	LE	16786 t	LE
16607	PV	16643	PV	16679	PV	16715	SB	16751	LE	16787	LE
16608	PV	16644	PV	16680	PV	16716	SB	16752	LE	16788	LE
16609	PV	16645	PV	16681	PV	16717	SB	16753	LE	16789	LE
16610	PV	16646	PV	16682	PV	16718	SB	16754	LE	16790	LE
16611	PV	16647	PV	16683	PV	16719	SB	16755	LE	16791	LE
16612	PV	16648	PV	16684	PV	16720	SB	16756	LE	16792	LE
16613	PV	16649	PV	16685	PV	16721	SB	16757	LE	16793	LE
16614	PV	16650	PV	16686	PV	16722	SB	16758	LE	16794	LE

CLASS/SERIE BB 17000   BB

Similar in outline to BB 16500, their main use is on suburban trains from Paris Nord and St Lazare. They also fill in on freight mainly on the Paris–Le Havre route although the class has not been upgraded for 100 km/h freights. 17005 has a similar outline to BB 16700. Certain Achères locos have their numbers between two blue lines, indicating a v.d.u. in the cab for one-person operation.

Extérieur semblable à celui des BB 16500, leur utilisation principale est sur des trains de banlieue de Paris Nord et St. Lazare. Elles remorquent aussi des marchandises sur la ligne Paris–Le Havre tandis que la série n'a pas été modifée pour les marchandises à 100 km/h. La 17005 à des cabines renforcées comme la BB 16700. Certaines machines d'Achères ont leur numéros entre deux traits bleus. Ceci indique leur dotation d'une télévision en cabine pour exploitation par un agent seul.

Built/Construction: 1965-68.
Builder/Constructeur: Alsthom.
Power/Puissance: 2940 kW.
Max. T.E./E.T. max.: 323/197 kN.
Wheel Dia./Dia. des roues: 1100 mm.
Livery/Livrée: C.

System/Système: 25 kV a.c./monophasé.
Weight/Masse: 78 tonnes.
Length/Longeur: 14.70 (15.57*) m.
Max. Speed/Vitesse max.: 90/140 km/h.

Multiple working and push-pull fitted./Couplables en UM. Équipées de la réversibilité

17001	AC	17007	AC	17013	AC	17019	AC	17025	AC	17031	AC
17002	AC	17008	AC	17014	AC	17020	AC	17026	AC	17032	AC
17003	AC	17009	AC	17015	AC	17021	AC	17027	AC	17033	AC
17004	AC	17010	AC	17016	AC	17022	AC	17028	AC	17034	AC
17005 *	AC	17011	AC	17017	AC	17023	AC	17029	AC	17035	AC
17006	AC	17012	AC	17018	AC	17024	AC	17030	AC	17036	AC

17037	AC	17049	AC	17061	AC	17073	PL	17084	PL	17095	PL
17038	AC	17050	AC	17062	AC	17074	PL	17085	PL	17096	PL
17039	AC	17051	AC	17063	AC	17075	PL	17086	PL	17097	PL
17040	AC	17052	AC	17064	AC	17076	PL	17087	PL	17098	PL
17041	AC	17053	AC	17065	AC	17077	PL	17088	PL	17099	PL
17042	AC	17054	AC	17066	PL	17078	PL	17089	PL	17100	PL
17043	AC	17055	AC	17067	PL	17079	PL	17090	PL	17101	PL
17044	AC	17056	AC	17068	PL	17080	AC	17091	PL	17102	PL
17045	AC	17057	AC	17069	PL	17081	PL	17092	PL	17103	PL
17046	AC	17058	AC	17070	PL	17082	PL	17093	PL	17104	PL
17047	AC	17059	AC	17071	PL	17083	PL	17094	PL	17105	PL
17048	AC	17060	AC	17072	PL						

Names/Noms:

17042 CHAUMONT-EN-VEXIN |17051 CORMEILLES-EN-PARISIS

CLASS/SERIE BB 20011   BB

Originally ordered as BB 22379/80 these two locomotives were never delivered as such but their body shells used to become the synchronous dual voltage prototypes for class BB 26000. They may be rebuilt to 22379/80.

Deux prototypes bi-courant à moteurs synchrones des 'Sybics' qui furent construites à partir des caisses des BB 22379/80 avant leur livraison. Avec la fin des essais il est possible que les 20011/2 soient remises au type.

Built/Construction: 1986. .
Systems: 1500 V d.c./continu/25 kV a.c./monophasé.
Builders/Constructeurs: Alsthom/MTE.
Power/Puissance: kW. **Weight/Masse:** 90 tonnes.
Max. T.E./E.T. max.: kN. **Length/Longeur:** 17.48 m.
Wheel Dia./Dia. des roues: 1250 mm. **Max. Speed/Vitesse max.:** 200 km/h.
Livery/Livrée: White, blue and yellow./Blanc, bleu foncé et jaune.

20011 SB |20012 SB |

CLASS/SERIE BB 20200   BB

This small class which is a dual-voltage version of the BB 17000 class is allocated to Strasbourg for working into the West German and Swiss systems which use 15 kV a.c. They are highly concentrated on the Mulhouse–Basel line. They rarely stray from these duties.

Une version bi-courant des BB 17000 qui sont utilisées sur des trains qui pénètrent en Allemagne et en Suisse, surtout sur Mulhouse–Bâle.

Built/Construction: 1970.
Systems/Systèmes: 25 kV 50 Hz/15 kV 16⅔ Hz.a.c./monophasé.
Builder/Constructeur: Alsthom. **Weight/Masse:** 80 tonnes.
Max. T.E./E.T. max.: 324/197 kN. **Length/Longeur:** 14.94 m.
Wheel Dia./Dia. des roues: 1100 mm. **Max. Speed/Vitesse max.:** 100/140 km/h.
Power/Puissance: 1660 kW (15 kV)/2940 kW (25 kV).
Livery/Livrée: E or/ou C.

20201	SB	20204	SB	20206	SB	20208	SB	20210	SB	20212	SB
20202	SB	20205	SB	20207	SB	20209	SB	20211	SB	20213	SB
20203	SB										

CLASS/SERIE CC 21000   CC

These are dual-voltage CC 6500s. The class now has no regular diagrams. 21001/2 are used for tests on the LGV Sud-Est as they are fitted with cab signalling for that line. Others are used on freight around Dole. 21003 was tested by Amtrak in the USA in 1976 and was numbered X 996. 21001–2 have bodysides as for CC 6501–39 whilst 2↓003/4 are like CC 6560–74.

Une version bi-courant des CC 6500. Les 21001/2 sont équipées de la signalisation en cabine pour la ligne à grande vitesse (LGV) Sud–Est et sont parfois utilisées sur des trains d'essais. Les autres sont souvent à Dole sur des services marchandises. La CC 21003 a été testée par Amtrak aux USA en 1976 sous le numéro X 996. Les 21001/2 ont des persiennes comme les CC 6501–38, tandis que les 21003/4 sont dans le même style que les CC 6560–74.

Built/Construction: 1969/1974*.
Systems: 1500 V d.c./continu/25 kV a.c./monophasé.
Builders/Constructeurs: Alsthom/MTE.
Power/Puissance: 5900 kW.
Max. T.E./E.T. max.: 288/131 kN.
Wheel Dia./Dia. des roues: 1140 mm.
Livery/Livrée: T.

Weight/Masse: 124 (128*) tonnes.
Length/Longeur: 20.19 m.
Max. Speed/Vitesse max.: 100/200 km/h.

Fitted with rheostatic braking, snowploughs, electro-pneumatic brakes, driver-guard communication, cab to shore radio.

Dotées d'éperons chasse-neige, freins électro-pneumatiques, radio sol-train, frein rhéostatique et communication engin moteur-train.

| 21001 | DP | 21002 | DP | 21003 * | DP | 21004 * | DP | |

CLASS/SERIE BB 22200   BB

This dual-voltage version of BB 7200/15000 started off working in the Marseille area but can be found virtually over the whole electrified network on through trains from or over routes with different voltages. They even turn up at Amiens to work the VSOE! Dijon locos now work to Le Havre and also have a turn between Paris Est and Luxembourg. 10 locos will be transferred from Dijon to Rennes in 1991 when Rennes–Lorient is electrified. 22278 has for some years worked on d.c. only between Paris and Bordeaux as a test locomotive for high speed running on 1500 V d.c. As such it was a prototype for the other locos of the class which are now allowed to run at 200 km/h. 22379/80 have not existed as such being delivered as experimental locos 20011/2. These locos may be converted to standard. 22351/2 are equipped with cab signalling for the LGV Atlantique.

Une version bi-courant des BB 7200/15000. Les BB 22200 ont commencé leur carrière sur la Côte d'Azur mais sont maintenant utilisées presque partout sur le réseau électrifié sauf dans l'extrême sud–ouest. La 22278 fut utilisé pendant plusieurs années entre Austerlitz et Bordeaux pour des essais à 200 km/h sous 1500 V continu. Les 22379/80 n'ont jamais existé puisqu'elles sont sorties de l'usine en tant que 20011/12. Il est possible qu'elles soient remises au type. Les 22351/2 sont équipées de la signalisation en cabine pour la LGV Atlantique. 10 unités seront transférées de Dijon à Rennes en 1991 pour l'électrification Rennes–Lorient.

Built/Construction: 1976–1986.
Systems: 1500 V d.c./continu/25 kV a.c./monophasé.
Builders/Constructeurs: Alsthom/MTE.
Power/Puissance: 4360 kW.
Max. T.E./E.T. max.: 294 kN.
Wheel Dia./Dia. des roues: 1250 mm.
Livery/Livrée: C.

Weight/Masse: 89 tonnes.
Length/Longeur: 17.48 m.
Max. Speed/Vitesse max.: 160 (200*) km/h.

Fitted with rheostatic braking, electro-pneumatic brakes, cowcatchers and driver-guard communication and cab to shore radio.

Équipées de freins rhéostatiques et électro-pneumatiques, éperons chasse-obstacle, communication engin moteur-train et radio sol-train.

22201	DP	22214	DP	22227	DP	22240	DP	22252	MB	22264	MB
22202	DP	22215	DP	22228	DP	22241	DP	22253	MB	22265	MB
22203	DP	22216	DP	22229	DP	22242	DP	22254	MB	22266	MB
22204	DP	22217	DP	22230	DP	22243	DP	22255	MB	22267	MB
22205	DP	22218	DP	22231	DP	22244	DP	22256	MB	22268	MB
22206	DP	22219	DP	22232	DP	22245	MB	22257	MB	22269	MB
22207	DP	22220	DP	22233	DP	22246	MB	22258	MB	22270	MB
22208	DP	22221	DP	22234	DP	22247	MB	22259	MB	22271	MB
22209	DP	22222	DP	22235	DP	22248	MB	22260	MB	22272	MB
22210	DP	22223	DP	22236	DP	22249	MB	22261	MB	22273	MB
22211	DP	22224	DP	22237	DP	22250	MB	22262	MB	22274	MB
22212	DP	22225	DP	22238	DP	22251	MB	22263	MB	22275	MB
22213	DP	22226	DP	22239	DP								

Names/Noms:

22202 OYONNAX
22218 FOURMIES

22219 ALBERTVILLE
22239 LONS LE SAUNIER

22276	MB	DIJON		22342	MB	CARNOULES
22277	MB	IS-SUR TILLE		22343	MB	
22278	* RS			22344	MB	
22280	MB	HAZEBROUCK		22345	MB	
22281	MB			22346	MB	AUBAGNE
22282	MB			22347	MB	
22283	MB			22348	MB	SAINT-MARTIN-DE-CRAU
22284	MB	GEVRY-CHAMBERTIN		22349	MB	
22285	MB	CHANTILLY		22350	MB	
22286	DP	BÉTHUNE		22351	* RS	VALOGNES
22287	DP	SAINT-JEAN-DE-MAURIENNE		22352	* RS	SABLÉ-SUR-SARTHE
22288	DP	LOUHANS		22353	* RS	PLAISIR
22289	DP			22354	* RS	ANCENIS
22290	DP			22355	* RS	SÈVRES
22291	DP	LA FERTÉ-ALAIS		22356	* RS	LORIENT
22292	DP			22357	* RS	
22293	DP			22358	RS	
22294	DP			22359	RS	
22295	DP			22360	RS	
22296	DP			22361	RS	
22297	DP			22362	RS	
22298	DP			22363	RS	
22299	DP			22364	RS	
22300	DP	CHALON-SUR-SAÔNE		22365	RS	
22301	DP	VILLENEUVE-D'ASCQ		22366	RS	MALAKOFF
22302	DP	RIVE-DE-GIER		22367	RS	5ème Regiment Du Génie
22303	DP	CROIX		22368	RS	
22304	DP			22369	RS	
22305	DP	ST-RAMBERT-D'ALBON		22370	RS	THOUARS
22306	DP			22371	RS	LADOIX-SERRIGNY
22307	DP	LE TEIL		22372	RS	MAURIAC
22308	DP	GISORS		22373	RS	AULNAY-SOUS-BOIS
22309	DP			22374	RS	NOYON
22310	DP			22375	RS	MÉRICOURT
22311	DP	PIERREFITTE		22376	RS	DOUAI
22312	MB	ANTIBES-JUAN-LES-PINS		22377	RS	ROUBAIX
22313	MB	DIGNE-LES-BAINS		22378	RS	LE QUESNOY
22314	MB	TAIN-L'HERMITAGE		22379		
22315	MB	MIRAMAS		22380		
22316	MB	LOMME		22381	RS	LE BOURGET
22317	MB	LA-TOUR-DU-PIN		22382	RS	CLERMONT DE L'OISE
22318	MB	CARPENTRAS		22383	DP	BULLY-LES-MINES
22319	MB	SORGUES-SUR OUVÈZE		22384	DP	SAINT-ANDRÉ-LÈS-LILLE
22320	MB	ISTRES		22385	DP	LONGUEAU
22321	MB	BELLEVILLE		22386	DP	BAILLEUL
22322	MB	BOLLÈNE		22387	DP	LIÉVIN
22323	MB	CAGNES-SUR-MER		22388	DP	SOMAIN
22324	MB	LANNION		22389	DP	COMINES
22325	MB	CHAMPIGNY-SUR-MARNE		22390	DP	LESQUIN
22326	MB			22391	DP	HIRSON
22327	MB			22392	DP	CHARLES TELLIER PÈRE DU FROID
22328	MB			22393	DP	PONT-À-VENDIN
22329	MB	QUIMPER		22394	DP	JOINVILLE-LE-PONT
22330	MB			22395	DP	NEUILLY-PLAISANCE
22331	MB			22396	DP	BAIE-DE-SOMME
22332	MB			22397	DP	PAGNY-SUR-MEUSE
22333	MB			22398	DP	COUDEKERQUE-BRANCHE
22334	MB			22399	DP	MORMANT
22335	MB			22400	DP	MONTIGNY-EN-OSTREVENT
22336	MB			22401	DP	MOULINS
22337	MB			22402	DP	SAINT-DIE-DES-VOSGES
22338	MB			22403	DP	NEUVES-MAISONS
22339	MB			22404	DP	PAVILLONS-SOUS-BOIS
22340	MB	CAVAILLON		22405	DP	
22341	MB					

CLASS/SERIE BB 25100   BoBo

An early dual-voltage locomotive based at Chalindrey. Until 1988, the class rarely strayed from the Dijon–Thionville route but now they share a diagram with Chalindrey's 25150s and on freight get to Dunkerque via Charleville and to Paris via Châlons-sur-Marne. However, very little remains of their passenger work on Metz–Dijon.

Une version bi-courant de BB 16000. Jusqu'en 1988, la série fut quasiment limitée à l'axe Dijon–Metz–Thionville mais maintenant elles partagent un roulement avec les BB 25150 de Chalindrey et sont envoyées jusqu'a à Dunkerque via Lumes et à Paris via Chalons-sur-Marne en service marchandises. Elles gardent très peu de prestation voyageurs.

Built/Construction: 1964–1965.
Systems: 1500 V d.c./continu/25 kV a.c./monophasé.
Builder/Constructeur: MTE.
Power/Puissance: 3400 kW (1500 V)/4130 kW (25 kV).
Weight/Masse: 85 tonnes.
Max. T.E./E.T. max.: 367 kN.   **Length/Longeur:** 16.20 m.
Wheel Dia./Dia. des roues: 1250 mm.   **Max. Speed/Vitesse max.:** 130 km/h.
Livery/Livrée: E or/ou C.

25101	CY	25106	CY	25110	CY	25114	CY	25118	CY	25122	CY
25102	CY	25107	CY	25111	CY	25115	CY	25119	CY	25123	CY
25103	CY	25108	CY	25112	CY	25116	CY	25120	CY	25124	CY
25104	CY	25109	CY	25113	CY	25117	CY	25121	CY	25125	CY
25105	CY								

CLASS/SERIE BB 25150   BoBo

Similar to BB 25100 from which it was developed. Chalindrey locos share a diagram with Class BB 25100 whilst Chambéry engines work over all the Alpine lines. The class has three different designs of lateral grilles.

Une version plus moderne des BB 25100. Celles de Chalindrey partagent un roulement avec les BB 25100 tandis que les engins de Chambéry sillonnent les lignes des Alpes du nord. Il y a trois sous-séries avec de persiennes latérales différentes.

Built/Construction: 1967–69/1974*/1976–77†.
Systems: 1500 V d.c./continu/25 kV a.c./monophasé.
Builder/Constructeur: MTE.
Power/Puissance: 3400 kW (1500 V)/4130 kW (25 kV).
Weight/Masse: 85 (89*†) tonnes.
Max. T.E./E.T. max.: 367 kN.   **Length/Longeur:** 16.20 (16.68*,16.73†) m.
Wheel Dia./Dia. des roues: 1250 mm.   **Max. Speed/Vitesse max.:** 130 km/h.
Livery/Livrée: E or/ou C.

Fitted with rheostatic braking and cab to shore radio. 25186–95 are fitted with snowploughs.
Équipées du frein rhéostatique et de la radio sol-train. Les 25186–95 sont équipées d'éperons chasse-neige.

25151	CY	25159	CY	25167	CY	25175 *	CB	25182 †	CB	25189 †	CB
25152	CY	25160	CY	25168	CY	25176 †	CB	25183 †	CB	25190 †	CB
25153	CY	25161	CY	25169	CY	25177 †	CB	25184 †	CB	25191 †	CB
25154	CY	25162	CY	25170	CB	25178 †	CB	25185 †	CB	25192 †	CB
25155	CY	25163	CY	25171 *	CB	25179 †	CB	25186 †	CB	25193 †	CB
25156	CY	25164	CY	25172 *	CB	25180 †	CB	25187 †	CB	25194 †	CB
25157	CY	25165	CY	25173 *	CB	25181 †	CB	25188 †	CB	25195 †	CB
25158	CY	25166	CY	25174 *	CB						

Name: 25175 LE CREUSOT

CLASS/SERIE BB 25200   BoBo

A faster version of the preceding two classes, being a dual voltage version of BB 9200 and BB 16000. For many years all have been used on services between Paris and Le Mans/Rennes. However delivery of BB 22351–70 to Rennes has meant the loss of most of their high speed work and their operating area has spread to include freight duties as far as Aulnoye, Le Havre, Poitiers and Laroche-Migennes. Some are fitted with TDM equipment for push-pull trains in the Alps and Montparnasse–Brittany.

Une autre version bi-courant des BB 16000 conçue pour les trains de voyageurs. Pendant de longues années, la série avait le quasi-monopole des trains sur Paris–Rennes. Cependant, avec l'arrivée des BB 22200 et puis celle des TGV-A, leur utilisation sur les trains de voyageurs a été réduite mais leur champ d'action s'est agrandi. En service marchandises celles de Rennes atteignent Aulnoye, Le Havre, Poitiers et Laroche-Migennes. Certaines machines sont équipées du multiplexage pour l'utilisation avec des rames réversibles dans les Alpes et sur Paris–Bretagne.

Built/Construction: 1965–67/1974*.
Systems: 1500 V d.c./continu/25 kV a.c./monophasé.
Builder/Constructeur: MTE.
Power/Puissance: 3400 kW (1500 V)/4130 kW (25 kV).
Weight/Masse: 85 (89*) tonnes.

Max. T.E./E.T. max.: 304 kN.	**Length/Longeur:** 16.20 (16.68*) m.
Wheel Dia./Dia. des roues: 1250 mm.	**Max. Speed/Vitesse max.:** 160 km/h.
Livery/Livrée: E or C.	

t TDM push-pull fitted.

25201 t	RS	25210	RS	25219	RS	25228	RS	25236	CB	25244	CB
25202 t	RS	25211	RS	25220	RS	25229	RS	25237	CB	25245	CB
25203	RS	25212	RS	25221	RS	25230	RS	25238	CB	25246 t	RS
25204	RS	25213	RS	25222	RS	25231	RS	25239	CB	25247 *t	RS
25205	RS	25214	RS	25223	RS	25232	RS	25240	CB	25248 *t	RS
25206	RS	25215	RS	25224	RS	25233	RS	25241	CB	25249 *t	RS
25207	RS	25216	RS	25225	RS	25234	RS	25242	CB	25250 *t	RS
25208	RS	25217	RS	25226	RS	25235	RS	25243	CB	25251 *t	RS
25209	RS	25218	RS	25227	RS							

Names/Noms:

25201 LE MANS	25250 VITRÉ
25247 COMBOURG	25251 VERSAILLES

CLASS/SERIE BB 25500   BB

A dual voltage version of BB 8500 and BB 17000 and built in three batches with detail variations in styling and cabs. Mostly used on freight especially on the Paris Grande Ceinture. On push-pull passenger they are used out of Montparnasse, Rennes, Dijon, Lyon and on the Côte d'Azur. The Les Aubrais locos are likely to be transferred away, mostly to Tours, but also to Achères.

Une version bi-courant des BB 8500/BB 17000. Il existe trois sous-séries avec des persiennes latérales et cabines de conduites différentes. Elles sont utilisées sur des marchandises sur une grande partie du réseau mais surtout sur la Grande Ceinture de Paris. En voyageurs, elles sont utilisées avec des rames réversibles autour de Paris Montparnasse, Rennes, Dijon, Lyon et sur la Côte d'Azur. Celles affectées aux Aubrais seront transférées à Tours et Achères en 1991.

Built/Construction: 1964–76.
Systems: 1500 V d.c./continu/25 kV a.c./monophasé.
Builder/Constructeur: Alsthom.
Power/Puissance: 2940 (2610*) kW.

Max. T.E./E.T. max.: 330/197 kN.	**Weight/Masse:** 81 (79*,77§,80†) tonnes.
Wheel Dia./Dia. des roues: 1100 mm.	**Length/Longeur:** 15.57 (14.70*, 14.94†§) m.
Livery/Livrée: E or/ou C.	**Max. Speed/Vitesse max.:** 100/140 km/h.

Rheostatic braking. Multiple working and push-pull fitted. Dijon locos are fitted with snowploughs.
Équipées du frein rhéostatique. Couplables en UM. Les engins affectées à Dijon sont équipées d'éperons chasse-neige.

25501 *	LA	25509 *	TP	25517 *	AC	25525 *	AC	25533 *	LA	25542 *	TP
25502 *	LA	25510 *	LA	25518 *	AC	25526 *	AC	25534 *	TP	25543 *	TP
25503 *	DP	25511 *	LA	25519 *	AC	25527 *	AC	25535 *	TP	25544 *	TP
25504 *	TP	25512 *	AC	25520 *	AC	25528 *	AC	25536 *	TP	25545 †	TP
25505 *	LA	25513 *	AC	25521 *	AC	25529 *	AC	25537 *	LA	25546 †	TP
25506 *	TP	25514 *	AC	25522 *	AC	25530 *	AC	25538 *	LA	25547 †	TP
25507 *	LA	25515 *	AC	25523 *	AC	25531 *	AC	25540 *	LA	25548 †	TP
25508 *	LA	25516 *	AC	25524 *	AC	25532 *	LA	25541 *	TP	25549 †	TP

25550	† TP	25575	§ AC	25599	AC	25623	MB	25647	MB	25671	DP
25551	† TP	25576	§ AC	25600	AC	25624	MB	25648	MB	25672	DP
25552	† TP	25577	§ AC	25601	AC	25625	MB	25649	VE	25673	DP
25553	† TP	25578	§ AC	25602	AC	25626	MB	25650	DP	25674	DP
25554	† TP	25579	§ AC	25603	AC	25627	MB	25651	MB	25675	DP
25555	† TP	25580	§ AC	25604	AC	25628	MB	25652	MB	25676	DP
25556	§ DP	25581	§ AC	25605	AC	25629	MB	25653	VE	25677	DP
25557	§ DP	25582	§ AC	25606	AC	25630	MB	25654	VE	25678	DP
25558	§ AC	25583	§ AC	25607	AC	25631	MB	25655	DP	25679	DP
25559	§ DP	25584	§ AC	25608	AC	25632	VE	25656	VE	25680	DP
25560	§ AC	25585	§ AC	25609	AC	25633	MB	25657	VE	25681	DP
25561	§ AC	25586	§ AC	25610	AC	25634	VE	25658	MB	25682	DP
25562	§ AC	25587	§ AC	25611	AC	25635	MB	25659	VE	25683	DP
25563	§ AC	25588	AC	25612	AC	25636	MB	25660	AC	25684	DP
25564	§ AC	25589	AC	25613	AC	25637	VE	25661	AC	25685	DP
25565	§ AC	25590	AC	25614	AC	25638	VE	25662	AC	25686	DP
25566	§ AC	25591	AC	25615	AC	25639	DP	25663	MB	25687	DP
25567	§ AC	25592	AC	25616	AC	25640	VE	25664	VE	25688	DP
25568	§ AC	25593	AC	25617	AC	25641	VE	25665	DP	25689	DP
25569	§ AC	25594	AC	25618	AC	25642	VE	25666	MB	25690	DP
25570	§ AC	25595	AC	25619	AC	25643	VE	25667	MB	25691	DP
25571	§ AC	25596	AC	25620	MB	25644	MB	25668	MB	25692	DP
25572	§ AC	25597	AC	25621	MB	25645	MB	25669	MB	25693	DP
25573	§ AC	25598	AC	25622	MB	25646	MB	25670	MB	25694	DP
25574	§ AC										

Name: 25544 PARTHENAY

CLASS/SERIE BB 26000   BB

These new dual voltage locomotives feature synchronous motors and are known as "Sybics" (Synchronous-bicourant). Although introduced in 1988, the class is only now coming on stream. There have been numerous teething problems which have all now been resolved. In the next few years, the introduction of this class will bring about big changes over large areas of the SNCF. The first locos were allocated to Dijon and took over certain trains on the Paris–Vallorbe route. A growing number are employed on freight over the Dijon–Metz–Lille route which is bringing about withdrawals of BB 12000, BB 13000 and CC 14100. From June 1991, two locos have been working passenger on Paris–Clermont Ferrand and from September 1991. Sybics will be used on the 'Capitole' between Paris and Brive and on Strasbourg–Basel Corail services at 200 km/h. Lens depot is expected to receive Sybics in 1992.

Cette série nouvelle de locomotives bi-courant à moteurs synchrones est connue sous le nom de «Sybics» (synchrone/bi-courant). Bien que leur livraison a débuté en 1988, plusieurs difficultés de jeunesse et des problèmes chez Alsthom ont retardé leur introduction. Cependant, leur nombre croît rapidement et leur introduction est en train de produire des changements profonde sur une grande partie de la SNCF. Les premières machines furent affectées à Dijon et prirent en charge des trains sur Paris–Vallorbe. Un nombre croissant est employé en service marchandises sur Dijon–Metz–Lille, ce qui entraine le remplacement et la radiation des 12000, 13000 et 14100. Depuis juin 1991, deux machines roulent sur Paris–Clermont Ferrand et dès septembre 1991, les Sybic seront utilisées entre Austerlitz et Brive sur le «Capitole» et sur des TER à 200 km/h entre Strasbourg et Bâle. Il est prévu que Lens recoive le deuxieme tranche de Sybics en 1992.

Built/Construction: 1988–.
Systems: 1500 V d.c./continu/25 kV a.c./monophasé.
Builder/Constructeur: Alsthom.
Power/Puissance: 6400 kW.   **Weight/Masse:** 91 tonnes.
Max. T.E./E.T. max.: 320 kN.   **Length/Longeur:** 17.48 m.
Wheel Dia./Dia. des roues: 1250 mm.   **Max. Speed/Vitesse max.:** 200 km/h.
Livery: Two tone grey with orange front end.
Livrée: Gris clair et foncé aves faces frontales orange.

c Fitted with préannonce cab signalling/équipées de préannonce signalisation en cabine.

26001	c DP		26005	c DP		
26002	c DP		26006	c DP		MUSÉE FRANCAIS
26003	c DP	FONTVIELLE				DU CHEMIN DE FER
26004	c DP	CERNAY	26007	c DP		BÉNING-LJES-SAINT-AVOLD

26008	c	DP		26073
26009	c	DP	LONGVIC-EN-BOURGOGNE	26074
26010	c	DP	VALLORBE	26075
26011	c	DP		26076
26012	c	DP		26077
26013	c	DP		26078
26014	c	DP		26079
26015	c	DP		26080
26016	c	DP		26081
26017	c	DP		26082
26018	c	DP		26083
26019	c	DP		26084
26020	c	DP		26085
26021	c	DP		26086
26022	c	DP		26087
26023	c	DP		26088
26024	c	DP		26089
26025	c	DP		26090
26026	c	DP		26091
26027	c	DP		26092
26028	c	DP		26093
26029	c	DP		26094
26030	c	DP		26095
26031	c	DP		26096
26032	c	DP		26097
26033	c	DP		26098
26034	c	DP		26099
26035	c	DP		26100
26036	c	DP		26101
26037	c	DP		26102
26038	c	DP		26103
26039	c	DP		26104
26040	c	DP		26105
26041	c	DP		26106
26042	c			26107
26043	c			26108
26044	c			26109
26045				26110
26046				26111
26047				26112
26048				26113
26049				26114
26050				26115
26051				26116
26052				26117
26053				26118
26054				26119
26055				26120
26056				26121
26057				26122
26058				26123
26059				26124
26060				26125
26061				26126
26062				26127
26063				26128
26064				26129
26065				26130
26066				26131
26067				26132
26068				26133
26069				26134
26070				26135
26071				26136
26072				26137

26138	26167	26196	26225	26253	26281
26139	26168	26197	26226	26254	26282
26140	26169	26198	26227	26255	26283
26141	26170	26199	26228	26256	26284
26142	26171	26200	26229	26257	26285
26143	26172	26201	26230	26258	26286
26144	26173	26202	26231	26259	26287
26145	26174	26203	26232	26260	26288
26146	26175	26204	26233	26261	26289
26147	26176	26205	26234	26262	26290
26148	26177	26206	26235	26263	26291
26149	26178	26207	26236	26264	26292
26150	26179	26208	26237	26265	26293
26151	26180	26209	26238	26266	26294
26152	26181	26210	26239	26267	26295
26153	26182	26211	26240	26268	26296
26154	26183	26212	26241	26269	26297
26155	26184	26213	26242	26270	26298
26156	26185	26214	26243	26271	26299
26157	26186	26215	26244	26272	26300
26158	26187	26216	26245	26273	26301
26159	26188	26217	26246	26274	26302
26160	26189	26218	26247	26275	26303
26161	26190	26219	26248	26276	26304
26162	26191	26220	26249	26277	26305
26163	26192	26221	26250	26278	26306
26164	26193	26222	26251	26279	26307
26165	26194	26223	26252	26280	26308
26166	26195	26224			

CLASS/SERIE CC 40100   CC

A small class for working under 4 different voltages. There is now no need for the 1500 V d.c. and 15 kV ac capabilities as for many years now they have worked only between Paris and Brussels/Liège. They share these duties with SNCB classes 15 & 18. At one time it was intended CC 40100 would work through to Amsterdam and Köln on trains from Paris Nord. They were finished off in stainless steel to match the TEE stock used on these services. 40106 was a virtual write-off after an accident near Brussels circa 1970. It was reconstructed (almost new) when SNCB class 1800 was being built as an extra loco after this batch and re-entered service in 1974. This class is likely to be withdrawn when the TGV Nord service commences.

Une petite série de machines qui fonctionnaient sous 4 systèmes différents à l'origine. Il était prévu que les CC 40100 remorquent des trains de Paris Nord jusqu' Amsterdam et Cologne. Cependant elles sont limitées à Bruxelles et Liège depuis plusieurs années et leur équipement pour 1500 V et 15 kV est isolé. Elles partagent ces taches avec les séries 15 et 18 des chemins de fer belges (SNCB). Les CC 40100 ont des caisses en inox, emballies en rouge, comme les voitures TEE qui sont toujours en service sur Paris–Bruxelles. La 40106 fut très endommagée en 1970 dans un accident près de Bruxelles. Elle fut reconstruite à l'epoque où les 18 de la SNCB (qui sont très proches des 40100) furent introduites et reprirent le service en 1974. Cette série sera radiée dès que les TGV seront introduits sur Paris–Bruxelles.

Built/Construction: 1964/1969–1970.
Systems: 1500/3000 V d.c./continu/25 kV 50 Hz/15 kV 16⅔ Hz a.c./monophasé.
Builder/Constructeur: Alsthom.
Power/Puissance: 5410 (4480*) kW.   **Weight/Masse:** 109 tonnes.
Max. T.E./E.T. max.: 198/142 kN.   **Length/Longeur:** 22.03 m.
Wheel Dia./Dia. des roues: 1100 mm.   **Max. Speed/Vitesse max.:** 160 km/h.
Livery/Livrée: Stainless steel and red/acier inox avec bandes rouges.

40101	* PL	PERPIGNAN		40106	PL	COMPIÉGNE
40102	* PL	MENTON		40107	PL	BAYONNE
40103	* PL	BRIOUDE		40108	PL	HENDAYE
40104	* PL	ST-JEAN-DE-LUZ		40109	PL	CANNES
40105	PL	HYÉRES		40110	PL	NICE

BB 20206. Strasbourg Hausbergen. 10/09/89.   *Eric Dunkling*
26006. Dijon Perrigny depot/Dépôt de Dijon Perrigny. 15/07/90.   *Eric Dunkling*

SNCF DIESEL LOCOMOTIVES
LOCOMOTIVES DIESEL

CLASS/SERIE A1AA1A 62000   A1AA1A

These are typical American hood units of the immediate post war period and continue to be known as "Baldwins" after the USA constructor. They have spent most of their life along the Eastern corridor on heavy shunting duties in large yards between Dunkerque and Mulhouse. The class is no longer receiving overhauls and as locomotives come up for main overhaul they will be withdrawn. Two have already been preserved.

Ce sont machines de manoeuvres américaines typiques de la période après-guerre et connues sous le nom «Baldwins» – le nom du constructeur américain. Elles ont été utilisées pour des manouevres lourdes pendant toute leur carrière dans les différents triages de l'artère nord–est entre Dunkerque et Mulhouse. Elles ne reçoivent plus de grandes révisions et seront toutes radiées avant 1995. Il y a déjà trois unités préservées.

Built/Construction: 1946–47.
Engine/Moteur: Baldwin 606NA (560 kW).
Transmission: Electric/Electrique.
Heating/Chauffage: None/aucun.
Max. T.E./E.T. max.: 143 kN.
Wheel Dia./Dia. des roues: 1100 mm.
Livery/Livrée: V.

Builder/Constructeur: Baldwin.

Weight/Masse: 110 tonnes.
Length/Longeur: 17.70 m.
Max. Speed/Vitesse max.: 96 km/h.

62001	LE	62019	TV	62043	TV	62071	TV	62082	LE	62091	TV
62006	SB	62026	LE	62051	LE	62072	TV	62083	TV	62092	SB
62007	LE	62028	LE	62061	LE	62076	TV	62084	TV	62094	LE
62011	LE	62029	LE	62062	TV	62078	LE	62088	TV	62095	TV
62012	LE	62030	LE	62065	SB	62081	TV	62090	SB	62099	TV
62016	LE	62033	LE								

CLASS/SERIE BB 62400   BoBo

A surprise in the latter part of 1990 was to learn that the SNCF was seriously short of diesel locos! This has come about because of the large number of construction projects. In the north of France, TGV and Channel Tunnel works have resulted in a big demand for diesel locos. to work construction trains etc. As this was an urgent problem, the SNCF decided to buy second-hand locos from the NS which was just receiving a big fleet of new diesels. In addition, the SNCF is hiring SNCB 5900 Class diesels which return to Belgium for maintence. Note: The SNCF number of this class is the former NS number with a '6' prefix. SNCF will operate 44 BB 62400 but has also bought six other NS 2400 for spares which will be kept at Nevers works. 62501 is in maroon livery and is reserved for Utrecht museum on completion of SNCF service.

Une surprise de 1990 fut de constater que la SNCF n'avait pas assez de locos diesels. Ce problème est dû au nombre élevé de grand projets. Dans le nord de la France les travaux de LGV–Nord et tunnel sous la Manche demandent beaucoup de machines diesels pour les trains de travaux. SNCF à décidé d'acheter des diesels de la série 2400 des chemins de fer néerlandais (NS). La SNCF va exploiter 44 BB 62400 mais à acheté six autres 2400 qui seront gardées aux ateliers de Nevers pour fournir des pièces détachées. La 62501 est en livrée rouge bordeaux et est réservée pour le musée d'Utrecht après son service en France. Pour le LGV–Nord, la SNCF va louer des diesels de la série 59 des chemins de fer belges qui seront entretenus en Belgique.

Built/Construction: 1954–56.
Engine/Moteur: SACM V12 SHR (625 kW).
Transmission: Electric/Electrique.
Heating/Chauffage: None/aucun.
Max. T.E./E.T. max.: 161 kN.
Wheel Dia./Dia. des roues: 1000 mm.
Livery/Livrée: NS. Grey with yellow cabs and front panels/gris avec des cabines et faces frontales en jaune.

Builder/Constructeur: Alsthom.

Weight/Masse: 60 tonnes.
Length/Longeur: 12.52 m.
Max. Speed/Vitesse max.: 80 km/h.

62403	LN	62412	LN	62425	LN	62439	LN	62453	LN	62467	LN
62406	LN	62414	LN	62429	LN	62443	LN	62458	LN	62477	LN
62407	LN	62419	LN	62432	LN	62449	LN	62465	LN	62501	LN

62504	LN	62	62	62	62	62
62506	LN	62	62	62	62	62
62513	LN	62	62	62	62	62
62		62	62	62	62	62
62		62				

CLASS/SERIE BB 63000   BoBo

BB 63000, 63400, 63500 are all virtually identical and form a large family of over 800 locomotives. These low powered locomotives are found on station pilot duties, freight trips and general shunting duties and appear all over France. Those assigned to big yards invariably have radios fitted whilst some also have BSI automatic couplings. This type of locomotive will also be found in Spain (class 307), Portugal (class 1200), Luxembourg (class 850/900), Yugoslavia (class 642/643) and Chile (Class D 700). Some locos are being withdrawn and converted into mate units of Class TBB 64800.

Les BB 63000, 63400 et 63500 constituent une grande famille de plus de 800 locomotives avec seulement quelques petites différences qui les séparent. Ces machines sont utilisées partout en France sur des manoeuvres et trains de marchandises légers. Celles utilisées dans les triages on la radio tandis que certaines sont équipées d'attelages BSI. Ce type existe aussi en Espagne (série 307), au Portugal (série 1200), au Luxembourg (séries 850 et 900), en Yougoslavie (séries 642/3) et même au Chili. Quelques machines sont en train d'être transformées en truck moteurs de la série TBB 64800.

Built/Construction: 1953–64.   **Builder/Constructeur:** Brissonneau & Lotz.
Engine/Moteur: Sulzer 6LDA22B of 440 kW [Sulzer 6LDA22B (440 kW)*, Sulzer 6LDA22C (535 kW)†, Sulzer 6LDA22D of 535 kW§, Sulzer 6LDA22E of 550 kW‡].
Transmission: Electric/Electrique.
Heating/Chauffage: None/aucun.   **Weight/Masse:** 64–69 tonnes.
Max. T.E./T.E. max.: 167 kN.   **Length/Longeur:** 14.68 m.
Wheel Dia./Dia. des roues: 1050 mm.   **Max. Speed/Vitesse max.:** 80 km/h.
Livery/Livrée: V or/ou J.

63002	VG	63037	PO	63075 *	CB	63109 †	CY	63142 §	LE	63175 §	LE
63003	TP	63038	TP	63076 *	CB	63110 †	NV	63143 §	LE	63176 §	LE
63004	TP	63039	MB	63077 *	CB	63111 †	CB	63144 §	LE	63177 §	PV
63005	TP	63040	NV	63078 *	CB	63112 †	LE	63145 §	LE	63178 §	LE
63006	TP	63041	MB	63079 *	CB	63113 †	PV	63146 §	LE	63179 §	LE
63007	TP	63042	MB	63081 *	CB	63114 †	NV	63147 §	LE	63180 §	PV
63008	TP	63044	MB	63082 *	PO	63115 †	NV	63148 §	VG	63181 §	PV
63009	TP	63045	MB	63083 *	PO	63116 †	LE	63149 §	LE	63182 §	LE
63010	TP	63046	MB	63084 *	CB	63117 †	CB	63150 §	LE	63183 §	LE
63011	TP	63047	MB	63085 *	DP	63118 †	CB	63151 §	LA	63184 §	LE
63012	TP	63048	MB	63086 *	DP	63119 †	NV	63152 §	LA	63185 §	LE
63013	TP	63049	MB	63087 *	PO	63120 †	CY	63153 §	LE	63186 §	LE
63015	VG	63050	MB	63088 *	CB	63121 †	LE	63154 §	LE	63187 §	CB
63016	MB	63052	MB	63089 *	CB	63122 †	LE	63155 §	LA	63188 §	LE
63017	MB	63053	VG	63090 *	CB	63123 †	MB	63156 §	LA	63189 §	PV
63018	MB	63054	VG	63091 *	CB	63124 †	CY	63157 §	LA	63190 §	PV
63019	MB	63055	DP	63092 *	LA	63125 †	CB	63158 §	LA	63191 §	PV
63020	MB	63056	VG	63093 *	PO	63126 †	CB	63159 §	PV	63192 §	LE
63021	MB	63058	VG	63094 *	DP	63127 †	CB	63160 §	PV	63193 §	DP
63022	NV	63060	PO	63095 *	CB	63128 †	LE	63161 §	PV	63194 §	LE
63023	MB	63061	PO	63096 *	DP	63129 §	CY	63162 §	LE	63195 §	PV
63025	VG	63062	NV	63097 *	DP	63130 §	VG	63163 §	MB	63196 ‡	CY
63026	VG	63063	NV	63098 *	DP	63131 §	PV	63164 §	PV	63197 ‡	LE
63027	VG	63064	NV	63099 *	DP	63132 §	LE	63165 §	PV	63198 ‡	LE
63028	VG	63065	NV	63100 *	DP	63133 §	LE	63166 §	PV	63199 ‡	LE
63029	VG	63066	MB	63101 *	TP	63134 §	PV	63167 §	LE	63200 ‡	DP
63030	VG	63067	NV	63102 *	DP	63135 §	PV	63168 §	LE	63201 ‡	PV
63031	VG	63068	VG	63103 *	NV	63136 §	PV	63169 §	LE	63202 ‡	CY
63032	VG	63069	MB	63104 *	DP	63137 §	LE	63170 §	PV	63203 ‡	LA
63033	NV	63071	MB	63105 *	TP	63138 §	LE	63171 §	PV	63204 ‡	LE
63034	VG	63072	NV	63106 *	TP	63139 §	CY	63172 §	LE	63205 ‡	DP
63035	TP	63073 *	LA	63107 *	TP	63140 §	LE	63173 §	LE	63206 ‡	PV
63036	TP	63074 *	CB	63108 *	PO	63141 §	LE	63174 §	LE	63207 ‡	LE

63208 ‡ LA	63216 ‡ CY	63223 ‡ LE	63230 ‡ LE	63237 ‡ DP	63244 ‡ VG
63209 ‡ LE	63217 ‡ CY	63224 ‡ LE	63231 ‡ DP	63238 ‡ CY	63245 ‡ LE
63210 ‡ DP	63218 ‡ LE	63225 ‡ CY	63232 ‡ DP	63239 ‡ LE	63246 ‡ CB
63211 ‡ CY	63219 ‡ LE	63226 ‡ DP	63233 ‡ DP	63240 ‡ CY	63247 ‡ LE
63212 ‡ PV	63220 ‡ LE	63227 ‡ DP	63234 ‡ LE	63241 ‡ LE	63248 ‡ LE
63213 ‡ LE	63221 ‡ CY	63228 ‡ DP	63235 ‡ PV	63242 ‡ LE	63249 ‡ LA
63214 ‡ PV	63222 ‡ LE	63229 ‡ CY	63236 ‡ DP	63243 ‡ LA	63250 ‡ LA
63215 ‡ LE					

CLASS/SERIE BB 63400 — BoBo

These locomotives were financed under the Eurofima arrangements and are similar to BB 63500. For many years all were based at Nantes but the spread of electrification and changing requirements has meant some transferring to other areas. Mostly used as yard pilots.

Une série presque identiques au BB 63500 qui fut financée par Eurofima. Toutes furent basées à Nantes pendant longtemps. Maintenant affectes à plusieurs dépôts du réseau Atlantique. Utilisation commes les BB 63000.

Built/Construction: 1959–60.
Engine/Moteur: MGO V12SH (605 kW).
Transmission: Electric/Electrique.
Heating/Chauffage: None/aucun.
Max. T.E./T.E. max.: 167 kN.
Wheel Dia./Dia. des roues: 1050 mm.
Livery/Livrée: V or/ou J.

Builder/Constructeur: Brissonneau & Lotz.

Weight/Masse: 68 tonnes.
Length/Longeur: 14.68 m.
Max. Speed/Vitesse max.: 80 km/h.

63401 NB	63405 NB	63409 NB	63413 NB	63417 NB	63421 NB
63402 SO	63406 NB	63410 NB	63414 AC	63418 LG	63422 AC
63403 NB	63407 NB	63411 AC	63415 AC	63419 AC	63423 PV
63404 SO	63408 BD	63412 NB	63416 AC	63420 NB	

CLASS/SERIE BB 63500 — BoBo

A slightly more powerful version of BB 63000 but with lots of detail variations within the class. The e.t.h. locos at La Villete are used for tripping passenger trains around the Petit Ceinture from Paris Nord to Paris Lyon. Some locos are under conversion to Class BB 64700.

Une version plus puissante des BB 63000. Beaucoup de différences de détails existent. Les 63902/6, équipées du chauffage électrique, remorquent des trains de voyageurs entre Paris Nord et Gare de Lyon sur le «Petite Ceinture». Certaines machines sont en train d'être tranformées en BB 64700.

Built/Construction: 1956–71.
Builder/Constructeur: Brissonneau & Lotz.
Engine/Moteur: MGO V12SH (605 kW).
Transmission: Electric/Electrique (e).
Heating/Chauffage: None/aucun.
Max. T.E./T.E. max.: 167 kN.
Wheel Dia./Dia. des roues: 1050 mm.
Livery/Livrée: V or/ou J.

Weight/Masse: 64–68 tonnes.
Length/Longeur: 14.68 m.
Max. Speed/Vitesse max.: 80 km/h.

m   Multiple working fitted./Couplables en UM.
e   E.t.h. fitted./Équipée de chauffage électrique.
c   Equipped with cab signalling for maintenance work on LGV Atlantique
    Equipées du cab signal pour des trains de travaux sur le LGV Atlantique.

63501 NB	63512 SO	63523 RS	63534 AV	63545 VE	63556 SO
63502 SO	63513 AV	63524 SO	63535 RS	63546 AC	63557 TL
63503 AC	63514 AV	63525 SO	63536 BD	63547 BD	63558 AC
63504 BD	63515 VG	63526 CA	63537 AC	63548 VE	63559 TL
63505 SO	63516 SO	63527 AC	63538 RS	63549 VE	63560 TL
63506 NB	63517 AC	63528 SB	63539 CA	63550 TL	63561 CA
63507 SO	63518 AC	63529 SO	63540 TL	63551 BD	63562 RS
63508 AC	63519 SO	63530 SO	63541 AC	63552 PV	63563 CA
63509 RS	63520 AC	63531 AC	63542 TL	63553 AC	63564 AC
63510 SO	63521 RS	63532 AC	63543 AV	63554 AV	63565 TL
63511 SO	63522 LE	63533 LE	63544 AV	63555 RS	63566 AC

63567	AC	63632	PV	63699	AV	63764	NB	63829 m	SB	63896 e	AV
63568	AC	63633	BD	63700	MN	63765	BD	63830 m	AV	63897	NB
63569	TL	63634	VE	63701	SB	63766	LE	63831 m	AV	63898	SB
63570	LE	63635	AV	63702	AV	63767	NB	63832 m	VG	63899	LN
63571	CA	63636	PV	63703	LN	63768	NB	63833 m	MN	63900	AV
63572	NB	63637	NB	63704	LN	63769	NB	63834 m	MN	63901 e	AV
63573	LE	63638	LN	63705	SB	63770	NB	63835 m	MN	63902 e	PV
63574	LE	63639	SB	63706	LN	63771	MZ	63836 m	LG	63903	SO
63575	MZ	63640	VE	63707	LN	63772	LN	63837 m	AV	63904	PV
63576	LE	63641	NB	63708	MN	63773	LN	63838 m	AV	63905	AC
63577	TL	63642	MN	63709	PV	63774	PV	63839 m	MN	63906 e	PV
63578	BD	63643	LE	63710	AV	63775	BD	63840 m	MN	63907	RS
63579	AV	63645	AC	63711	PV	63776	LN	63841 m	SB	63908	NB
63580	TL	63646	SB	63712	AC	63777	LN	63842 m	LG	63910	SB
63581	SO	63647	RS	63713	SB	63778	LN	63843 m	MN	63911	SB
63582	TL	63648	NB	63714	LN	63779	VG	63844 m	MN	63912	SB
63583	TL	63649	SO	63715	AV	63780	VE	63845 m	MN	63913	MZ
63584	AV	63650	CA	63716	MN	63781	MZ	63846 m	AV	63914	PV
63585	SO	63651	MN	63717	MN	63782	BD	63847 m	MN	63915	SO
63586	BD	63652	LE	63718	SB	63783	PV	63848 m	PV	63916	AV
63587	SB	63653	SO	63719	PV	63784	VE	63849 m	MN	63917	SB
63588	PV	63654	BD	63720	AV	63785	VE	63850 m	MZ	63918	AV
63589	VE	63655	MZ	63721 m	SB	63786	LG	63851 m	MZ	63919	MZ
63590	AC	63656	VE	63722 m	SB	63787	BD	63852 m	MZ	63921	SO
63591	SO	63657	AV	63723 m	SB	63788	PV	63853 m	VG	63922	VE
63592	SB	63658	BD	63724 m	LN	63789	VE	63854 m	VE	63923	LN
63593	BD	63659	AV	63725 m	SB	63790	VE	63855 m	VG	63924	LN
63594	BD	63660	NB	63726 m	MZ	63791	LN	63856 m	LG	63925	MZ
63595	TL	63661	MZ	63727 m	SB	63792	AC	63857 m	SO	63926	VE
63596	SB	63662	MZ	63728 m	SB	63793	SB	63858 m	MZ	63927	RS
63597	LE	63663	RS	63729 m	LN	63794	AC	63859 m	VE	63928	VE
63598	CA	63664	LE	63730 m	SB	63795	VE	63860 m	SB	63929	LN
63599	RS	63665	MN	63731 m	MZ	63796	LN	63861 m	MZ	63930	PV
63600	BD	63666	MZ	63732 m	LN	63797	PV	63862 m	SO	63931	MZ
63601	BD	63667	RS	63733 m	LN	63798	AC	63863 m	MN	63932	VE
63602	AC	63668	LN	63734 m	LN	63799	AC	63864 m	AV	63933	NB
63603	SO	63669	SO	63735 m	LN	63800	AC	63865 m	VE	63934	VE
63604	NB	63670	MN	63736 m	MZ	63801	PV	63866 m	SO	63935	LN
63605	BD	63671	AV	63737 m	LN	63802	AC	63867 m	MZ	63936	LN
63606	AC	63672	BD	63738 m	LN	63803	AC	63868 m	MZ	63937	MZ
63607	SB	63673	LE	63739 m	LN	63804	AC	63869 m	LG	63938	PV
63608	SB	63674	SO	63740 m	LN	63805	VG	63870 m	SB	63939	RS
63609	BD	63675	RS	63741 m	MN	63806	PV	63871 m	MZ	63940	VE
63610	VE	63676	LN	63742 m	MZ	63807	PV	63872 m	MZ	63941	NB
63611	RS	63677	LN	63743 m	MZ	63808	AC	63873 m	SB	63942	MZ
63612	SO	63678	NB	63744 m	LN	63809	AC	63874 m	SB	63943	PV
63613	SO	63679	PV	63745 m	LN	63810	SB	63875 m	SB	63944	BD
63614	SO	63680	MN	63746 m	MN	63811 m	MZ	63876 m	SB	63945	PV
63615	SO	63681	MZ	63747 m	MZ	63812 m	MZ	63877 m	SB	63947	BD
63616	SO	63682	AC	63748 m	MZ	63813 m	AV	63878 m	SB	63948	BD
63617	SB	63683	BD	63749 m	MZ	63814 m	AV	63879 m	SB	63949	MN
63618	SB	63684	BD	63750 m	MZ	63815 m	PV	63880 m	SO	63950	PV
63619	SB	63685	LN	63751	LG	63816 m	MN	63881 m	SB	63951	VE
63620	NB	63686	PV	63752	SB	63817 m	AV	63882 m	MZ	63952	MZ
63621	SO	63687	AC	63753	RS	63818 m	VE	63883 m	SB	63953	PV
63622	SB	63688	VE	63754	RS	63819 m	MZ	63884 m	SB	63954	PV
63623	LE	63689	VE	63755	RS	63820 m	MZ	63885 m	LN	63955	LG
63624	AV	63691	MN	63756	MZ	63821 m	VE	63886	PV	63956	LN
63625	LN	63692	VE	63757	RS	63822 m	SO	63888	MZ	63957	LG
63626	LE	63693	VE	63758	RS	63823 m	MZ	63890	VE	63958	TL
63627	VE	63694	VE	63759	RS	63824 m	MZ	63891	PV	63960	LN
63628	NB	63695	MN	63760	RS	63825 m	AV	63892	MZ	63961	NB
63629	VE	63696	MZ	63761	LE	63826 m	PV	63893	MZ	63962	LG
63630	SO	63697	VE	63762	LE	63827 m	MN	63894	PV	63963	NB
63631	RS	63698	RS	63763	NB	63828 m	MZ	63895	AV	63964	TL

63965 c	AC	63986 m	LG	64005 m	BD	64024	VE	64043	BD	64062	MZ
63966	MN	63987 m	LG	64006 m	BD	64025	SO	64044	AV	64063	PV
63967	NB	63988 m	LN	64007 m	MZ	64026	LG	64045	MZ	64064	MZ
63968	NB	63989 m	BD	64008 m	MZ	64027	LG	64046	PV	64065	LN
63969	AV	63990 m	LG	64009 m	SO	64028	LN	64047	RS	64066	LN
63970	MZ	63991 m	LN	64010 m	SO	64029	AV	64048	RS	64067	LN
63971	VE	63992 m	VE	64011 m	LG	64030	PV	64049	AV	64068	LN
63972	AV	63993 m	LG	64012 m	LG	64031	SO	64050	AV	64069	LN
63973	MN	63994 m	SO	64013 m	LG	64032	LG	64051	MZ	64070	AV
63974	PV	63995 m	LN	64014 m	SO	64033	MZ	64052	RS	64071	AV
63975	VE	63996 m	SO	64015 m	SO	64034	SO	64053	AV	64072	AV
63977	MN	63997 m	PV	64016 m	BD	64035	AV	64054	BD	64073	SB
63978	AV	63998 m	PV	64017 m	BD	64036	MZ	64055	PV	64074	SB
63979 c	AC	63999 m	VE	64018 m	BD	64037	AC	64056	AC	64075	AV
63981 m	BD	64000 m	PV	64019 m	SO	64038	AV	64057	VE	64076	PV
63982 m	BD	64001 m	BD	64020 m	SO	64039	MZ	64058	AC	64077	PV
63983 m	LG	64002 m	BD	64021	LN	64040	LN	64059	SO	64078	SB
63984 m	LN	64003 m	SO	64022	SO	64041	SO	64060	MZ	64079	PV
63985 m	BD	64004 m	BD	64023	AV	64042	SO	64061	MZ	64080	PV

CLASS/SERIE BB 64700/TBB 64800   BoBo+BoBo

Freight train weights continue to increase and SNCF was finding itself short of heavy shunters as the 62000s were being withdrawn. As a first step several 66000s were rebuilt into new shunting locos of class 66700. However it was realised that shunters of greater tractive effort were required. SNCF decided to go back to a system previously tried with Class C 61000, where a number of motored trucks (TC 61100) were coupled to them. BB 63500 was decided on as the master unit and Nevers Works was given the job of rebuilding these locos which are finished off similar to BB 66700. Sotteville Quatre Mares Works was given the job of converting 63000s into the new mates (motors assisting tractive effort). Here the work has been more drastic. The cab has obviously been removed as it is unnecessary but the main frame has been shortened and the two motor bogies are much closer. The overall length of the 64700 remains the same as its predessor but the 64800 measures only 11.40 m. As there are no fuel tanks and no diesel engine in the mate a large deadweight has been added to give good adhesion. The first pair have been allocated to Avignon for work at Miramas and others are likely to go there as well as to Lens (for Dunkerque), Metz (for Woippy) and Vénissieux (for Sibelin). Please note that although the mates are semi-permanently coupled to the locos, there are more locos than mates as the diesel loco will require more maintenance than the mate.

Avec la radiation des 62000, la SNCF s'est trouvée en manque de machines pour manoeuvrer des rames de marchandises qui deviennent de plus en plus lourdes. D'abord quelques BB 66000 ont été transformées en BB 66700 mais dans certains cas encore d'avantage de traction a été necessaire. SNCF a décidé de revenir au système de «locomotive + veau» pratique auparavant avec les C 61000 et «truck moteurs» TC 61100. Les ateliers de Nevers transforment les BB 63500 en BB 64700 qui sont équipées d'une nouvelle cabine dans le style des 66700. Soteville Quatre Mares transforment les BB 63000 en «trucks» TBB 64800. la cabine est otée et le chassis raccourci à seulement 11,40 m. Comme il n'y a plus de moteur dans le truck, celui-ci est lesté pour maintenir une bonne adhésion. Le premier couplage fut affecté à Avignon pour le triage de Miramas. D'autres seront basés a Lens (pour Dunkerque), Metz (pour Woippy) et Vénissieux (pour Sibelin). Les couplages peuvent changer puisqu'il y a plus de locomotives, qui demandent d'avantage d'entretien, que de trucks.

Max. T.E./T.E. max.: 300 kN.
Length/Longeur: 14.68 m. + 11.40 m.
Total Weight/Masse totale: 136.6 tonnes (2 x 68.3).
Livery/Livrée: J.

Class/Série 64700 Locomotives.

64701 (63920)	AV	64709 (63946)		64717 (63)	
64702 (63976)	LE	64710 (63)		64718 (63)	
64703 (63889)	LE	64711 (63)		64719 (63)	
64704 (63959)	AV	64712 (63)		64720 (63)	
64705 (63909)	AV	64713 (63)		64721 (63)	
64706 (63644)	MZ	64714 (63)		64722 (63)	
64707 (63690)	MZ	64715 (63)		64723 (63)	
64708 (63887)		64716 (63)			

Class/Série 64800 Mates/Trucks.

64801 (63024)	AV	64808 (63070)	64814 (63)
64802 (63057)	LE	64809 (63051)	64815 (63)
64803 (63043)	LE	64810 (63)	64816 (63)
64804 (63080)	AV	64811 (63)	64817 (63)
64805 (63001)	AV	64812 (63)	64818 (63)
64806 (63014)	MZ	64813 (63)	64819 (63)
64807 (63059)	MZ		

CLASS/SERIE CC 65500   CoCo

The first heavy duty diesel introduced for freight work around the Grande Ceinture route in Paris. They were made redundant by electrification and the introduction of dual-voltage electric locomotives on transfer freights. Saved from the scrapyard by the need to have powerful locomotives for use on construction trains on LGV Sud Est, they have had a second reprieve as there was a similar need for locomotives for the construction of LGV-Atlantique. Although no longer being overhauled by main works, the workshop at La Plaine depot did a fantastic job refurbishing these locomotives. Many have been given a complete repaint and look as good as new. Some have been sold out of service to track repair contractors or loaned to coal mines. With the completion of LGV Atlantique it was thought that these locos would be scrapped. However then came the Lyon–Valence high speed line and yet again the class has been given a reprieve. All are now based in Lyon which is likely to be their last home as they are now scheduled for withdrawal in 1993.

Les première diesels de ligne en France qui furent utilisées pour des marchandises sur la Grande Ceinture de Paris. L'électrification de cette ligne à rendu la série superflue mais le besoin de machines diesels puissantes pour la construction de la LGV Sud–Est les a épargnées du chalumeau. Elles ont été utilisées pour le constructiron de la LGV Atlantique et puis mutées en bloc à Vénissieux pour les travaux du contournement de Lyon. Quelques machines ont été vendues aux sociétés privées de travaux de voie ou louées aux Houillières de la Lorraine. Leur amortissement est prévu à l'achèvement de ce chantier, mais qui sais?

Built/Construction: 1955–59.
Engine/Moteur: Sulzer 12LDA (1470 kW).
Transmission: Electric/Electrique.
Heating/Chauffage: None/aucun.
Max. T.E./T.E. max.: 359 kN.
Wheel Dia./Dia. des roues: 1200 mm.
Livery/Livrée: V.

Builders/Constructeurs: CAFL/CEM.

Weight/Masse: 123 tonnes.
Length/Longeur: 19.42 m.
Max. Speed/Vitesse max.: 75 km/h.

65501	VE	65508	VE	65518	VE	65521	VE	65529	VE	65533	VE
65502	VE	65515	VE	65519	VE	65524	VE	65530	VE	65534	VE
65503	VE	65516	VE	65520	VE	65527	VE	65531	VE	65535	VE
65506	VE	65517	VE								

CLASS/SERIE BB 66000   BoBo

A mixed traffic locomotive once found on passenger trains but with the introduction of electric heating they are rarely found now on this type of work. At one time they worked in multiple either side of a boiler van. BB 66400 have taken over local passenger train work while BB 67300, 67400 work the heavier trains. Some have been rebuilt into BB 66600 and a further rebuilding programme is now underway converting two a year into BB 66700. During the last few years the class has seen many moves and now Lens has a large allocation with many locos having been drafted in to work on construction trains in connection with the Channel Tunnel and TGV Nord. 66001–40 have different suspension and are relegated to LGV Nord and Lyon by-pass works trains.

Une série pour services mixtes. Avec l'introduction des 66400 avec chauffage électrique et des plus puissantes 67300 et 67400, les 66000 sont maintenant rarement utilisées sur des trains de voyageurs. Quelques unités ont été transformées en BB 66600 et d'autres en BB 66700. Les 66001–40 ont une suspension moins évoluée et sont réservées aux seuls trains de travaux pour le LGV Nord et contournement de Lyon. Récemment, le dépôt de Lens en a reçu un nombre important pour la LGV–Nord.

Built/Construction: 1960–68.
Builders/Constructeurs: CAFL/CEM/Alsthom/Fives-Lille/SACM.
Engine/Moteur: MGO V16BSHR (1030 kW).

BB 66463 + BB 66244. Nevers depot./Dépôt de Nevers. 17/09/89. *Eric Dunkling*

A1AA1A 68036. Chalindrey depot./Dépôt de Chalindrey. 15/07/90. *Eric Dunkling*

Transmission: Electric/Electrique.
Heating/Chauffage: None/aucun.
Max. T.E./T.E. max.: 167 kN.
Wheel Dia./Dia. des roues: 1100 mm.
Livery/Livrée: D.

Weight/Masse: 66/67 tonnes.
Length/Longeur: 14.90 m.
Max. Speed/Vitesse max.: 120 km/h.

Multiple working fitted. Some have snowploughs.
Couplables en UM. Certaines sont équipées d'éperons chasse neige.

66001	LE	66051	TL	66107	LG	66168	NB	66222	AV	66271	LN
66002	LE	66052	TL	66108	NV	66169	NB	66223	LE	66272	TL
66003	LE	66053	NV	66109	TL	66170	NB	66224	SO	66273	VE
66004	LE	66054	LN	66110	LN	66171	NB	66225	SO	66274	LN
66005	LE	66055	TL	66111	NV	66175	LN	66226	SO	66275	LN
66006	LE	66056	TL	66112	NV	66179	SO	66227	CY	66276	LN
66007	AV	66057	NV	66113	LN	66180	SO	66228	NV	66277	LN
66008	LE	66058	TL	66114	LN	66181	SO	66229	SO	66278	CY
66009	VE	66059	NV	66115	TL	66182	SO	66230	VE	66279	LG
66011	LE	66060	TL	66116	LN	66183	SO	66231	CY	66280	LN
66012	AV	66061	AV	66117	NV	66184	NV	66232	SO	66281	LG
66013	VE	66062	TL	66118	LN	66185	NV	66233	VE	66282	VE
66014	LE	66063	LN	66119	LG	66186	SO	66234	VE	66283	LG
66015	LE	66064	TL	66120	NV	66187	VE	66235	VE	66284	LN
66016	VE	66065	AV	66121	LG	66188	TL	66236	VE	66285	SO
66017	VE	66066	LN	66122	LG	66189	VE	66237	VE	66286	LG
66018	LE	66067	LN	66123	AV	66190	LG	66238	SO	66287	LA
66019	VE	66068	AV	66124	AV	66191	CY	66239	LA	66288	LN
66020	LE	66069	NV	66125	SO	66192	LN	66240	LA	66289	LG
66021	LE	66070	TL	66126	LN	66193	LA	66241	LA	66290	AV
66022	LE	66071	TL	66127	AV	66194	LG	66242	NV	66291	AV
66023	LE	66072	TL	66128	VE	66195	LE	66243	NV	66292	CY
66024	LE	66073	NV	66129	LG	66196	LN	66244	NV	66293	NV
66025	AV	66075	NB	66130	LG	66197	VE	66245	NV	66294	SO
66026	TL	66077	NV	66131	TL	66198	AV	66246	NV	66295	LA
66027	LE	66078	LN	66133	TL	66199	VE	66248	NV	66296	LN
66028	TL	66079	NV	66135	NV	66200	LN	66249	LN	66297	AV
66029	AV	66082	TL	66137	VE	66201	NV	66250	NV	66298	AV
66030	LE	66083	TL	66140	SO	66202	LG	66251	CY	66299	AV
66031	LE	66084	TL	66141	TL	66203	NV	66252	SO	66300	LN
66032	AV	66085	TL	66142	LN	66204	NV	66253	LA	66301	SO
66033	LE	66086	TL	66145	AV	66205	LG	66254	LG	66302	LG
66034	LE	66087	TL	66147	NV	66206	AV	66255	VE	66303	AV
66035	TL	66088	LG	66150	VE	66207	VE	66256	SO	66304	LN
66036	TL	66089	NV	66151	SO	66208	SO	66257	LG	66305	LN
66037	AV	66090	LN	66153	SO	66209	LA	66258	SO	66306	LG
66038	AV	66091	LN	66154	NV	66210	AV	66259	NV	66307	LG
66039	LE	66092	LG	66155	NV	66211	LE	66260	LG	66308	LN
66040	AV	66093	LG	66156	NB	66212	LN	66261	LG	66309	LN
66041	TL	66094	LN	66157	NB	66213	SO	66262	LA	66310	LA
66042	LN	66095	LN	66159	NB	66214	VE	66263	SO	66311	TL
66043	TL	66096	LN	66160	LN	66215	LE	66264	SO	66312	SO
66044	NV	66097	LG	66161	NB	66216	LN	66265	VE	66313	LG
66045	LN	66099	LN	66162	NB	66217	LE	66266	VE	66314	LG
66046	TL	66100	LN	66163	NB	66218	SO	66267	LN	66315	LG
66047	TL	66101	LG	66164	NB	66219	NV	66268	VE	66316	VE
66048	TL	66103	LG	66165	NB	66220	LE	66269	LG	66317	TL
66049	NV	66104	LG	66166	NB	66221	LG	66270	LN	66318	SO
66050	TL	66105	LG	66167	NB						

CLASS/SERIE BB 66400   BoBo

This class is a development of BB 66000 and incorporates three-phase transmission. All are fitted with electric train heating and, except those based at Nevers, for push-pull working. They are used out of Lille, Nancy and Paris Est on push-pull stock but are gradually losing this work to the faster and more powerful BB 67400s. 66480 has recently been fitted with asynchronous motors and transferred on loan to Nevers.

Une version plus moderne des 66000 avec transmission triphasée. Toutes sont équipées pour le chauffage électrique des trains et, sauf celles basées à réversabilité. Elles sont utilisées avec des rames réversibles autour de Lille, Nancy et à partir de Paris Est mais cèdent ces trains peu à peu aux plus puissantes et rapides BB 67400. La 66480 à été équipée de moteurs asynchrones à titre experimental et transférée à Nevers.

Built/Construction: 1968–71.
Builders/Constructeurs: CAFL/CEM/Alsthom/Fives-Lille/SACM.
Engine/Moteur: MGO V16BSHR (1030 kW).
Transmission: Electric. Three phase/Electrique triphasé.
Heating/Chauffage: Electric/Electrique   **Weight/Masse:** 64 tonnes.
Max. T.E./T.E. max.: 167 kN.   **Length/Longeur:** 14.97 m.
Wheel Dia./Dia. des roues: 1100 mm.   **Max. Speed/Vitesse max.:** 120 km/h.
Livery/Livrée: D.

Multiple working and e.t.h. fitted./Couplables en UM et équipées du chauffage électrique.

p Push-pull fitted./Dotées de la reversabilité.

66401 p LE	66419 p LE	66437 p CY	66455 p SO	66473 NV	66490 p LE
66402 p LE	66420 p CY	66438 p CY	66456 p SO	66474 NV	66491 p CY
66403 p LE	66421 p CY	66439 p NB	66457 p SO	66475 NV	66492 p CY
66404 p LE	66422 p CY	66440 p CY	66458 p SO	66476 p LE	66493 p CY
66405 p LE	66423 p CY	66441 p CY	66459 p SO	66477 p CY	66494 p CY
66406 p LE	66424 p CY	66442 p CY	66460 p SO	66478 p CY	66495 p CY
66407 p LE	66425 p CY	66443 p CY	66461 p SO	66479 p CY	66496 p LE
66408 p LE	66426 p CY	66444 p CY	66462 p SO	66480 p NV	66497 p NB
66409 p LE	66427 p CY	66445 p LE	66463 NV	66481 p CY	66498 p NB
66410 p LE	66428 p TL	66446 p CY	66464 NV	66482 p NB	66499 p CY
66411 p LE	66429 p LE	66447 p CY	66465 NV	66483 p LE	66500 p NB
66412 p CY	66430 p NB	66448 p CY	66466 NV	66484 p LE	66501 p NB
66413 p CY	66431 p CY	66449 p CY	66467 NV	66485 p LE	66502 p NB
66414 p CY	66432 p TL	66450 p LE	66468 NV	66486 p LE	66503 p CY
66415 p CY	66433 p LE	66451 p SO	66469 NV	66487 p LE	66504 p CY
66416 p CY	66434 p CY	66452 p SO	66470 NV	66488 p LE	66505 p LE
66417 p LE	66435 p NB	66453 p SO	66471 NV	66489 p LE	66506 p LE
66418 p TL	66436 p CY	66454 p SO	66472 NV		

CLASS/SERIE BB 66600   BoBo

Several BB 66000 were rebuilt with a slightly more powerful engine to form this sub-class. The experiment does not appear to have been a success as no more conversion followed. With the closure of Nîmes shed all were transferred to Avignon but their sphere of operation remains unaltered being mostly on the Nîmes–Clermont Ferrand line. Two members of the class are being used on Lyon by-pass works trains.

Cette série est constituée de BB 66000 transformées avec un moteur plus puissant. L'expérience ne semble pas concluante puisque il n'y a pas eu d'autres transformations. A la fermeture du dépôt de Nîmes, elles furent mutées à Avignon mais elles continuent de sillonner la ligne Nîmes–Clermont Ferrand. En 1991, 2 membres de la série sont utilisés sur des trains de travaux pour le contournement de Lyon.

Built/Construction: 1960–62.
Builders/Constructeurs: CAFL/CEM/Alsthom/Fives-Lille.
Engine/Moteur: SEMT 12PA4 (1100 kW).
Transmission: Electric/Electrique.
Heating/Chauffage: None/aucun   **Weight/Masse:** 71 tonnes.
Max. T.E./T.E. max.: 167 kN.   **Length/Longeur:** 14.90 m.
Wheel Dia./Dia. des roues: 1100 mm.   **Max. Speed/Vitesse max.:** 120 km/h.
Livery/Livrée: D.

Multiple working fitted. Most fitted with snowploughs.
Couplable en UM. Le plupart sont équipées d'éperons chasse neige.

66604 (66304)	AV	66608 (66308)	AV	66614 (66098)	AV
66605 (66305)	AV	66610 (66310)	AV	66615 (66102)	AV
66606 (66306)	AV	66611 (66311)	AV	66616 (66106)	AV
66607 (66307)	AV	66612 (66312)	AV		

CLASS/SERIE BB 66700   BoBo

These are converted BB 66000. The ever increasing weight of wagons has led to the need for more powerful shunting locomotives. These locomotives have been regeared at Nevers works and the weight increased slightly. Many of the Lens locomotives are based at Dunkerque whilst those at Vénissieux can be found at Miramas and Sibelin. The Bordeaux locomotives work at the local yard at Hourcade. The last two locos are expected to go to Achères and Strasbourg (for Mulhouse Nord) respectively.

La radiation des 62000 et l'augmentation de poids des rames de marchandises créa un besoin pour des locomotives de manoeuvres plus puissantes. Cette série est une conversion des BB 66000 avec une modification de la réduction et une augmentation du poids. Les machines de Vénissieux sont utilisées à Miramas et Sibelin, celles de Lens à Dunkerque et celles de Bordeaux à Hourcade. En principe les 66723 et 66724 sont destinées à Achères et Strasbourg (pour Mulhouse Nord).

Built/Construction: 1985–91.
Builders/Constructeurs: CAFL/CEM/Alsthom/Fives-Lille/SACM.
Engine/Moteur: MGO V16BSHR (1030 kW).
Transmission: Electric/Electrique.
Heating/Chauffage: None/aucun.   **Weight/Masse:** 71 tonnes.
Max. T.E./T.E. max.: 229kN.   **Length/Longeur:** 14.90 m.
Wheel Dia./Dia. des roues: 1100 mm.   **Max. Speed/Vitesse max.:** 90 km/h.
Livery/Livrée: J.

66701	(66146)	VE	66709	(66148)	VE	66717	(66149)	LE
66702	(66080)	VE	66710	(66134)	VE	66718	(66173)	LE
66703	(66166)	VE	66711	(66158)	VE	66719	(66076)	BD
66704	(66174)	VE	66712	(66144)	LE	66720	(66074)	BD
66705	(66152)	VE	66713	(66139)	LE	66721	(66136)	BD
66706	(66172)	SB	66714	(66143)	LE	66722	(66138)	BD
66707	(66176)	SB	66715	(66081)	LE	66723	(66)	
66708	(66178)	LE	66716	(66177)	LE	66724	(66)	

CLASS/SERIE BB 67000   BB

This is the first of the SNCF big diesels that played a part in the elimination of steam workings. These and subsequent series were one of the first to have the exterior styling by Paul Arzens who has since become responsible for most SNCF locomotive body designs. Originally a mixed traffic locomotive with a two gear bogie, they are now regarded as freight only and the bogie geared accordingly. Never fitted with boiler equipment, they used to operate with boiler vans. Many have been rebuilt into BB 67200 or BB 67300 and the missing numbers will be found under those series except 67036 which became e.t.h. prototype 67291.

Les premières grandes locomotives diesels de ligne de la SNCF, cette série a aidé à éliminer la vapeur en France. A l'origine les BB 67000 furent utilisées pour des services mixtes mais depuis plusieurs années leurs bogies sont bloquées sur le couple marchandises. Beaucoup ont été transformées en 67200 ou 67300 et les numéros manquant sont trouvés sous ces deux titres sauf la 67036 qui fut transformée en 67291, le prototype avec chauffage électrique, et puis en 67390.

Built/Construction: 1963–68.
Builders/Constructeurs: Brissonneau and Lotz/MTE/SEMT.
Engine/Moteur: SEMT 16PA4 (1470 kW).
Transmission: Electric/Electrique.
Heating/Chauffage: None/aucun.   **Weight/Masse:** 80 tonnes.
Max. T.E./T.E. max.: 304/202 kN.   **Length/Longeur:** 17.09 m.
Wheel Dia./Dia. des roues: 1150 mm.   **Max. Speed/Vitesse max.:** 90/130 km/h.
Livery/Livrée: D.

Multiple Working fitted (also with 67200, 68000, 68500).
Couplable en UM entre elles et avec les 67200, 68000 et 68500.

67001	CA	67003	CA	67009	NV	67012	CA	67014	CA	67016	CA
67002	CA	67005	CA	67010	CA	67013	NV	67015	AV	67017	NV

67019	AV	67031	AV	67055	CA	67067	AV	67074	NV	67085	NV
67020	AV	67032	AV	67060	CA	67068	NV	67076	NV	67086	NV
67022	CA	67033	AV	67062	CA	67069	NV	67077	NV	67087	NV
67023	AV	67035	AV	67063	CA	67070	NV	67079	NV	67088	NV
67024	AV	67038	AV	67064	AV	67071	NV	67080	NV	67089	NV
67025	AV	67044	CA	67065	AV	67072	NV	67083	AV	67090	NV
67026	AV	67049	CA	67066	AV	67073	NV	67084	NV	67097	NV
67027	AV	67053	CA								

CLASS/SERIE BB 67200 — BB

With the introduction of the LGV Sud Est route it was realised that some locomotives would be required that could operate over the line on ballast trains and in emergencies. The line does not have conventional signalling and thus 30 BB 67000 were modified and fitted with cab signalling and train-signal box radio. With the construction of the LGV Atlantique, a further 16 were converted. Like Class 67000 their bogies are blocked on the freight gearing. Although based at Nevers and Tours, they have freight duties which take them close to the TGV route. A number of Nevers locos are outstationed at Vénissieux, Montchanin and Laroche-Migennes for night time work. Tours locos can be found outstationed at Chartres.

Transformées des 67000 avec la signalisation en cabine et la radio sol-train pour des trains de travaux sur les lignes à grande vitesse. Comme les 67000 leurs bogies sont bloquées sur la réduction marchandises. Bien que basées à Nevers et Tours, elles sont utilisées sur ces trains de marchandises sur un large champ d'action. Un nombre important des machines de Nevers sont stationnées à Vénissieux, Montchanin et Laroche-Migennes pour se lancer sur la LGV pendant la nuit, tandis que celles de Tours sont souvent à Chartres.

Built/Construction: 1980–89.
Builders/Constructeurs: Brissonneau and Lotz/MTE.
Engine/Moteur: SEMT 16PA4 (1470 kW).
Transmission: Electric/Electrique.
Heating/Chauffage: None/aucun.
Weight/Masse: 80 tonnes.
Max. T.E./T.E. max.: 304/202 kN.
Length/Longeur: 17.09 m.
Wheel Dia./Dia. des roues: 1150 mm.
Max. Speed/Vitesse max.: 90/130 km/h.
Livery/Livrée: D.

Multiple Working fitted (also with 67000, 68000, 68500). Snowplough fitted.
Couplables en UM entre elles et avec les 67000, 68000 et 68500. Equipées d'éperons chasse neige.

67201 (67006)	NV	67217 (67117)	NV	67232 (67043)	TP
67202 (67011)	NV	67218 (67112)	NV	67233 (67046)	TP
67203 (67040)	NV	67219 (67091)	NV	67234 (67051)	TP
67204 (67034)	NV	67220 (67114)	NV	67235 (67041)	TP
67205 (67037)	NV	67221 (67081)	NV	67236 (67042)	TP
67206 (67030)	NV	67222 (67078)	NV	67237 (67054)	TP
67207 (67021)	NV	67223 (67082)	NV	67238 (67057)	TP
67208 (67008)	NV	67224 (67103)	NV	67239 (67052)	TP
67209 (67118)	NV	67225 (67029)	NV	67240 (67056)	TP
67210 (67120)	NV	67226 (67028)	NV	67241 (67059)	TP
67211 (67108)	NV	67227 (67007)	NV	67242 (67045)	TP
67212 (67122)	NV	67228 (67039)	NV	67243 (67047)	TP
67213 (67115)	NV	67229 (67004)	NV	67244 (67061)	TP
67214 (67123)	NV	67230 (67018)	NV	67245 (67058)	TP
67215 (67102)	NV	67231 (67048)	TP	67246 (67050)	TP
67216 (67121)	NV				

CLASS/SERIE BB 67300 — BB

As mentioned under BB 67000 one of that class was modified to provide e.t.h. and became the prototype for this class. The production series featured other improvements such as three-phase transmission. Later, rather than build more new locomotives, some of Class 67000 were converted and the old numbers of these are shown below. A mixed traffic locomotive with some fitted out for working push-pull trains. 67325/40/66 were withdrawn in late 1990 after accidents. Those fitted for push-pull work around Rennes and out of Paris Montparnasse and St. Lazare.

La 67036 fut dotée de chauffage électrique et devient le prototype (numérotée 67291) pour cette série. Il fut décidé aussi d'équiper la série avec des moteurs triphasés. 20 67000 furent transformées en 67300 plus tard. Les BB 67300 sont des machines pour services mixtes. Celles équipées pour la réversabilité sont utilisées sur Paris Montparnasse–Argentan et St Lazare–Serquigny. Les 67325/40/66 ont été radiées en 1990, à la suite d'accidents.

Built/Construction: 1967–79.
Builders/Constructeurs: Brissonneau and Lotz/MTE.
Engine/Moteur: SEMT 16PA4 (1764 kW).
Transmission: Electric. Three phase/Electrique triphasé.
Heating/Chauffage: Electric/Electrique. **Weight/Masse:** 80 tonnes.
Max. T.E./T.E. max.: 304/202 kN. **Length/Longeur:** 17.09 m.
Wheel Dia./Dia. des roues: 1150 mm. **Max. Speed/Vitesse max.:** 90/140 km/h.
Livery/Livrée: D.

Multiple working fitted within class and with BB 67400. Odd examples have snowploughs. 67330–4 are fitted for working the "Catalan Talgo".

Couplable en UM entre elles et avec les 67400. Certaines sont équipées d'éperons chasse neige. Les 67330–34 sont aptes à remorquer des rames «Catalan Talgo».

p push-pull fitted./Équipées pour la reversabilité.

67301	CB	67316	TP	67332	CB	67348 p	NB	67362	CB	67377 p	CA
67302	CB	67317	TP	67333	CB	67349 p	NB	67363	CB	67378 p	CA
67303 p	TP	67318	TP	67334	CB	67350	CB	67364	CB	67379 p	CA
67304 p	CA	67319	TP	67335	CB	67351 p	NB	67365	CB	67380 p	CA
67305 p	NB	67320	TP	67336	CB	67352 p	NB	67367	CB	67381 p	CA
67306 p	NB	67321	TP	67337	CB	67353	CB	67368	CB	67382 p	CA
67307	CB	67322	TP	67338	CB	67354 p	NB	67369	CB	67383 p	CA
67308	CB	67323	TP	67339	CB	67355	CB	67370	CB	67384 p	CA
67309	TP	67324	TP	67341 p	NB	67356 p	NB	67371 p	CA	67385 p	CA
67310	TP	67326	CB	67342	CB	67357	CB	67372 p	CA	67386 p	CA
67311	TP	67327	CB	67343	CB	67358	CB	67373 p	CA	67387 p	NB
67312	TP	67328	CB	67344 p	NB	67359	CB	67374 p	CA	67388 p	NB
67313	TP	67329	CB	67345 p	NB	67360	CB	67375 p	CA	67389 p	NB
67314	TP	67330	CB	67346	CB	67361	CB	67376 p	CA	67390 p	NB
67315	TP	67331	CB	67347	CB						

Old Numbers/Anciens numéros:

67371 (67092)	67375 (67116)	67379 (67113)	67383 (67119)	67387 (67124)
67372 (67107)	67376 (67095)	67380 (67100)	67384 (67099)	67388 (67096)
67373 (67110)	67377 (67104)	67381 (67111)	67385 (67105)	67389 (67093)
67374 (67109)	67378 (67098)	67382 (67101)	67386 (67094)	67390 (67291)

Name/nom:67348 LA BERNERIE EN RETZ

CLASS/SERIE BB 67400   BB

This class is the one a British visitor usually encounters first as they usually haul the boat trains from Calais and Boulogne. The class represents another development of the BB 67000 series. Three-phase transmission and e.t.h. fitted they can be found virtually all over the system on freight and passenger duties. One gear ratio. The bogies are the same as on BB 7200/15000/22200/26000 but with a shorter wheelbase. The bogies on 67419 and 67537 have been modified for 160 km/h running as the bogie rides quite well. However it was also necessary to change the gear ratio and to supplement the air brake with a rheostatic brake. The conversions were thus quite expensive and no more have been carried out.

Développement final des 67000, on trouve cette série presque partout sur le réseau SNCF sur les trains de voyageurs et marchandises. Les 67400 ont des bogies semblables aux BB 7200,15000 22200 et 26000 avec la transmission triphasée et le chauffage électrique. Les bogies des 67419 et 67537 ont été modifiés pour 160 km/h qui nécessitait leur équipement du frein rhéostatique. Cette conversion s'est avérée assez chère et ne sera pas appliquée aux autres locomotives.

Built/Construction: 1969–75.
Builders/Constructeurs: Brissonneau and Lotz/MTE.
Engine/Moteur: SEMT 16PA4 (1765 kW).
Transmission: Electric. Three phase/Electrique triphasé.
Heating/Chauffage: Electric/Electrique. **Weight/Masse:** 83 tonnes.

Max. T.E./T.E. max.: 285 kN.
Wheel Dia./Dia. des roues: 1260 mm.
Livery/Livrée: D.
Length/Longeur: 17.09 m.
Max. Speed/Vitesse max.: 140 km/h.

Multiple working fitted within class and with BB 67300. Some have snowploughs.
Couplables en UM entre elles et avec les 67300. Certaines sont équipées d'éperons chasse neige.
p push-pull fitted./Équipées pour la reversabilité.

67401 p	NV	67440	CA	67479 p	LN	67518 p	SB	67556	NV	67594 p	LN
67402	BD	67441	CA	67480	BD	67519 p	SB	67557 p	NV	67595 p	LN
67403	RS	67442	RS	67481 p	CA	67520 p	SB	67558 p	MB	67596 p	LN
67404	RS	67443	BD	67482 p	MB	67521 p	SB	67559 p	MB	67597 p	LN
67405 p	MB	67444 p	NV	67483 p	LN	67522 p	SB	67560 p	MB	67598 p	LN
67406	RS	67445	RS	67484 p	MB	67523 p	SB	67561 p	MB	67599 p	LN
67407	RS	67446	CA	67485 p	LN	67524 p	SB	67562 p	NV	67600 p	LN
67408	BD	67447 p	CA	67486 p	LN	67525 p	NV	67563	CA	67601 p	LN
67409 p	CY	67448 p	CA	67487 p	MB	67526 p	CY	67564 p	NV	67602 p	LN
67410	RS	67449 p	NV	67488 p	MB	67527	CA	67565 p	MB	67603 p	SB
67411 p	CY	67450 p	NV	67489 p	MB	67528 p	NV	67566 p	NV	67604 p	LN
67412	BD	67451	CA	67490 p	CA	67529	CA	67567 p	NV	67605 p	LN
67413 p	CY	67452 p	NV	67491 p	CA	67530 p	CY	67568 p	MB	67606 p	LN
67414 p	NV	67453 p	NV	67492 p	CA	67531 p	NV	67569 p	SB	67607 p	LN
67415 p	SB	67454	CA	67493 p	MB	67532	CA	67570 p	SB	67608 p	LN
67416 p	LN	67455 p	NV	67494 p	MB	67533	LG	67571 p	SB	67609 p	LN
67417	RS	67456 p	CY	67495 p	MB	67534	CA	67572 p	SB	67610 p	LN
67418	NB	67457 p	CY	67496 p	MB	67535 p	NV	67573 p	NV	67611 p	LG
67419 p	RS	67458 p	NV	67497 p	NV	67536	CA	67574 p	NV	67612 p	LG
67420	RS	67459 p	NV	67498 p	SB	67537 p	RS	67575 p	MB	67613 p	LG
67421	RS	67460 p	NV	67499 p	SB	67538	RS	67576 p	NV	67614 p	LG
67422 p	RS	67461	CA	67500	RS	67539	RS	67577 p	NV	67615 p	LG
67423 p	CY	67462 p	NV	67501 p	NV	67540 p	NV	67578 p	NV	67616 p	LN
67424	RS	67463 p	NV	67502 p	NV	67541 p	MB	67579 p	NV	67617 p	LN
67425 p	RS	67464 p	CY	67503 p	NV	67542 p	NV	67580 p	MB	67618 p	LN
67426	RS	67465	CA	67504 p	NV	67543 p	MB	67581 p	NV	67619 p	LN
67427	RS	67466	CA	67505 p	NV	67544	CA	67582 p	CY	67620 p	LN
67428	RS	67467	CA	67506 p	NV	67545 p	MB	67583 p	CY	67621 p	LG
67429	BD	67468	BD	67507 p	NV	67546 p	NV	67584 p	CY	67622 p	LG
67430 p	RS	67469 p	NV	67508	CA	67547 p	NV	67585 p	NV	67623 p	LG
67431	RS	67470	BD	67509	CA	67548 p	NV	67586 p	SB	67624 p	LG
67432	RS	67471	BD	67510 p	SB	67549 p	MB	67587 p	SB	67625 p	LG
67433 p	CY	67472	CA	67511 p	SB	67550	CA	67588 p	SB	67626 p	LG
67434 p	RS	67473	BD	67512 p	SB	67551	CA	67589 p	LN	67627 p	LG
67435	BD	67474	CA	67513 p	SB	67552	CA	67590 p	LN	67628 p	LG
67436	BD	67475	RS	67514 p	SB	67553 p	CA	67591 p	LN	67629 p	LG
67437	BD	67476	RS	67515 p	SB	67554 p	NV	67592 p	LN	67631 p	LG
67438 p	LN	67477	RS	67516 p	SB	67555 p	NV	67593 p	LN	67632 p	LG
67439 p	LN	67478 p	NV	67517 p	SB						

Names:

67428 DREUX
67530 ROMILLY-SUR-SEINE
67575 DRAGUIGNAN

67580 MONTPELLIER
67581 NEVERS
67620 ABBEVILLE

CLASS/SERIE A1AA1A 68000   A1AA1A

Introduced at the same time as BB 67000 but fitted with steam boilers for passenger train work. These have since been removed or isolated and the class now only works freight. Some BB 68500 have been re-engined and added to this series probably using the redundant engines ex BR Class 48 (re-engined class 47) Nos. D 1702–6, since the engines from these locos were sold to the SNCF. Many of the Chalindrey locos are now being used on LGV Nord construction trains. Those allocated to Chalindrey share a diagram with Class 68500.

Les 68000 furent introduites en même temps que les 67000 mais furent équipées de chaudières furent démontées et maintenant la série ne remorque que des marchandises. Cinq membres de la série sont des 68500 qui ont reçu des moteurs AGO achetés aux chemins de fer britanniques. Les 68000 de Chalindrey partagent un roulement avec les 68500.

Built/Construction: 1963–68.
Builders/Constructeurs: CAFL/CEM/Fives-Lille.
Engine/Moteur: Sulzer 12LVA24 (1950 kW).
Transmission: Electric/Electrique.
Heating/Chauffage: None/aucun.   **Weight/Masse:** 104 tonnes.
Max. T.E./T.E. max.: 298 kN.   **Length/Longeur:** 17.92 m.
Wheel Dia./Dia. des roues: 1250 mm.   **Max Speed/Vitesse max.:** 130 km/h.
Livery/Livrée: D.

Multiple working fitted within class and with 68500. Some fitted with snowploughs.
couplables en UM entre elles et avec les 68500. Certaines sont dotées d'éperons chasse neige.

68001	NB	68015	CY	68030	CY	68044	NB	68058	TP	68073	TP
68002	CY	68016	CY	68031	CY	68045	CY	68059	TP	68074	TP
68003	CY	68017	CY	68032	CY	68046	CY	68060	TP	68075	TP
68004	CY	68018	NB	68033	NB	68047	CY	68061	CY	68076	TP
68005	CY	68019	CY	68034	CY	68048	NB	68063	TP	68077	TP
68006	NB	68020	CY	68035	NB	68049	TP	68064	TP	68078	TP
68007	NB	68021	CY	68036	CY	68050	TP	68065	TP	68079	TP
68008	CY	68022	CY	68037	CY	68051	TP	68066	TP	68080	TP
68009	NB	68023	CY	68038	CY	68052	TP	68067	TP	68081	TP
68010	CY	68024	CY	68039	CY	68053	TP	68068	TP	68082	TP
68011	NB	68025	NB	68040	CY	68054	TP	68069	TP	68083	TP
68012	NB	68026	CY	68041	CY	68055	TP	68070	TP	68084	CY
68013	NB	68027	CA	68042	CY	68056	TP	68071	TP	68085	CY
68014	NB	68029	NB	68043	NB	68057	TP	68072	TP		

Old Numbers/Anciens Numéros:

68005 (68501)   68082 (68529)   68083 (68525)   68084 (68508)   68085 (68510)

CLASS/SERIE A1AA1A 68500   A1AA1A

Similar to Class 68000 but with a different engine. Mainly used on freights on the Paris–Chalindrey–Belfort line. It is expected that some of these locomotives will work LGV Nord construction trains.

Très similaires aux 68000 sauf pour le moteur. Avec les 68000 de Chalindrey, elles sont utilisées principalement pour des marchandises sur Paris–Chalindrey–Belfort. L'utilisation sur des trains de travaux pour la LGV Nord est prévue pour la série.

Built/Construction: 1964–68.
Builders/Constructeurs: CAFL/CEM/SACM/Fives-Lille.
Engine/Moteur: AGO 12DSHR (1985 kW).
Transmission: Electric/Electrique.
Heating/Chauffage: None/aucun.   **Weight/Masse:** 102 tonnes.
Max. T.E./T.E. max.: 298 kN.   **Length/Longeur:** 17.92 m.
Wheel Dia./Dia. des roues: 1250 mm.   **Max. Speed/Vitesse max.:** 130 km/h.
Livery/Livrée: D.

Multiple working fitted within class and with 68000. Some fitted with snowploughs.
Couplables en UM entre elles et avec les 68000. Certaines sont dotées d'éperons chasse neige.

68502	CY	68506	CY	68512	CY	68516	CY	68520	CY	68524	CY
68503	CY	68507	CY	68513	CY	68517	CY	68521	CY	68526	CY
68504	CY	68509	CY	68514	CY	68518	CY	68522	CY	68527	CY
68505	CY	68511	CY	68515	CY	68519	CY	68523	CY	68528	CY

CLASS/SERIE CC 72000   CC

This is SNCF's really big diesel and features monomotor bogies with gear selection. The low gear is intended for freight work but is also used when hauling passenger trains over difficult routes such as Lyon–Roanne–St.Germain des Fosses. After surmounting the gradients out of Lyon the express gear ratio is selected whilst station duties are undertaken at Roanne. Recent electrification projects could see Vénissieux lose its allocation to Nevers and the other depots. Chalindrey has had its fleet augmented allowing 68000s to be redeployed and allows some 72000 to work Paris Nord–Laon releasing 67400 for push-pull work. Although capable of 160 km/h, Rennes locos are limited to 140 km/h.

Les plus grandes locomotives diesel de la SNCF. Equipées de bogies monomoteurs à deux réductions. La réduction «fret» est employée sur des lignes à profil difficile telle que Lyon–St Germain des Fossés. Après avoir surmonte les pentes entre Lyon et Roanne, la réduction «voyageurs» est choisie pendant l'arrêt à Roanne. Après des électrifications successives dans la région, Vénissieux a transféré son affectation à Nevers. Chalindrey a gagné plusieurs unités afin de libérer des 68000 pour le LGV Nord. En plus, les 72000 de Chalindrey ont pris charge des express Paris–Laon afin de libérer des 67400 pour des rames reversibles. Bien que capable de 160 km/h, les machines de Rennes sont limitée à 140 km/h.

Built/Construction: 1967–74.
Builders/Constructeurs: Alsthom/SACM/SEMT.
Engine/Moteur: AGO V16ESHR (2650 kW).   [Pielstick V16PA4-VGA (2350 kW)†].
Transmission: Electric/Electrique.   **Heating/Chauffage:** Electric/Electrique.
Weight/Masse: 114/118 tonnes.   **Wheel Dia./Dia. des roues:** 1140 mm.
Max. T.E./T.E. max.: 362/189 kN.   **Length/Longeur:** 20.19 m.
Max. Speed/Vitesse max.: 85/160 (85/140*)km/h.
Livery/Livrée: D.

Electro-pneumatic braking. Driver-guard communication (not *).
Equipées du frein électropneumatique et liaison train-engin moteur (pas *).

72001	* CY	ANNONAY	72048	CY	HAUTE SAÔNE
72002	* CY		72049	CY	
72003	* CY		72050	NV	LAPALISSE-EN-BOURBONNAIS
72004	* CY		72051	CY	
72005	* CY		72052	RS	LA BAULE
72006	* CY		72053	CY	MONTAUBAN DE BRETAGNE
72007	* CY		72054	NV	
72008	* CY		72055	NV	
72009	* CY		72056	NV	LA BOURBOULE
72010	* CY	BOURG ARGENTAL	72057	RS	
72011	* CY		72058	NV	
72012	* CY		72059	RS	
72013	* CY		72060	CY	GRAY
72014	* RS		72061	NV	AMPLEPUIS
72015	* RS	PARAY-LE-MONIAL	72062	NV	
72016	* RS		72063	RS	LA ROCHE-SUR-YON
72017	* RS		72064	NV	
72018	* RS		72065	RS	
72019	* RS		72066	RS	
72020	* RS		72067	NV	
72021	NV		72068	CY	
72022	CY	VILLEMOMBLE	72069	RS	
72023	NV		72070	NV	
72024	RS	PONT AUDEMER	72071	NV	MARSEILLE
72025	NV	TARARE	72072	RS	SAINT-MALO
72026	CY	LUXEUIL-LES-BAINS	72073	RS	
72027	CY		72074	CY	TOULON
72028	CY		72075 †	CY	
72029	CY		72076	CY	
72030	CY	CHALINDREY	72077	CY	NOISY-LE-SEC
72031	CY	FOUGEROLLES	72078	CY	
72032	RS		72079	CY	
72033	RS		72080	CY	MULHOUSE
72034	CY		72081	RS	
72035	CY		72082	CY	PROVINS
72036	CY	THANN	72083	NV	
72037	RS		72084	NV	
72038	CY	NANGIS	72085	NV	
72039	CY		72086	CY	
72040	NV		72087	RS	
72041	CY	CHAUMONT	72088	RS	
72042	NV		72089	RS	
72043	CY	LANGRES	72090	NV	BELFORT
72044 †	CY		72091	RS	
72045	CY		72092	NV	
72047	CY				

TURBOTRAINS

CLASS/SERIE T 1000   ETG

In 1967 SNCF converted DMU X 4375, XR 8575 into an experimental gas turbine unit. X 4375 had a new cab provided but the diesel motor and transmission retained. The trailer car also had a new cab fitted but this received a gas turbine power unit and was renumbered to X 2061. After detailed testing it was decided to order a production series of 4 car sets. These became the ETGs where the T 1000 are the turbine cars and T 1500 the diesel cars. For many years the class was allocated to Vénissieux but they have moved to Lyon Vaise. Vaise depot. With electrification in the Alps, they have moved mainly to Nevers–Dijon, Clermont Ferrand–Besançon and Lyon–Clermont Ferrand duties.

En 1967, la SNCF transforma l'autorail X 4375 et sa remorque, la XR 8575, en élément à turbine à gaz expérimental. Le X 4375 recevra une nouvelle cabine carénée mais le moteur et transmission conventional a été retenu. La remorque a aussi reçu une nouvelle cabine plus un moteur à turbine à gaz et a été renumérotée X 2061. Après de nombreux essais, il a été décidé de construire une série d'éléments de quatre caisses. Ces «elements à turbine à gaz» (ETG) ont une motrice à turbine à gaz (les T 1000) et une motrice à moteur diesel (les T 1500). Après plusieurs années à Vénissieux, les ETG ont été mutés à Lyon Vaise en 1985. Avec l'electrification des lignes des Alpes, leur travail est principalement sur Nevers–Dijon, Clermont Ferrand–Besançon et Lyon–Clermont Ferrand.

Built/Construction: 1969–72.
Engine/Moteur: Turmo IIIF3 (820 kW) + Saurer SDHR (320 kW).
Transmission: Hydraulic/hydraulique (Voith L 411 r) + mechanical/mécanique.
Formation: TB + TRA + TRB + TBD.
Accomodation: –/44 + 56/– + –/54 + –/48.
Weight/Masse: 42 + 28 + 33 + 44 tonnes.
Length/Longeur: 22.84 + 20.75 + 20.75 + 22.84 m.
Max. Speed/Vitesse max.: 160 km/h.
Livery/Livrée: D.

T 1001	TR 21001	TR 51001	T 1501	LV	T 1009	TR 21009	TR 51009	T 1509	LV
T 1002	TR 21002	TR 51002	T 1502	LV	T 1010	TR 21010	TR 51010	T 1510	LV
T 1003	TR 21003	TR 51003	T 1503	LV	T 1011	TR 21004	TR 51004	T 1504	LV
T 1005	TR 21005	TR 51005	T 1505	LV	T 1012	TR 21012	TR 51012	T 1512	LV
T 1006	TR 21006	TR 51006	T 1506	LV	T 1013	TR 21013	TR 51013	T 1513	LV
T 1007	TR 21007	TR 51007	T 1507	LV	T 1014	TR 21014	TR 51014	T 1514	LV
T 1008	TR 21008	TR 51008	T 1508	LV					

CLASS/SERIE T 2000   RTG

Pleased with the success of the ETGs SNCF went one better and built some 5 car sets with a gas turbine power car at each end. The odd numbered power cars have a slightly more powerful turbine and once on the move the lower powered one is usually shut down. Units are all now fitted for multiple working but until recently two drivers, in contact by intercom, were necessary. Caen based units work most trains on the Paris St Lazare–Cherbourg line and its branches. Those at Vénissieux work mostly on Lyon–Strasbourg. These two routes are being electrified and when finished, all the RTGs will be withdrawn as they are very expensive to operate.

Avec le succes des ETG, le SNCF a décidé de commander des éléments avec deux turbines à gaz. Les motrices à numéros impairs ont un moteur plus puissant que celui de la motrice paire. En général, les deux moteurs sont utilisés au démarrage et puis le «petit» est arrêté. Toutes les rames sont maintenant couplables en UM mais jusqu'en 1987, il a fallu deux conducteurs quand deux rames étaient utilisées ensemble. Les rames de Caen sont utilisées surtout sur la ligne St Lazare–Cherbourg et ses antennes. Celles de Vénissieux forment la plupart des Lyon–Strasbourg. Les RTG sont trés chères a exploiter et des que l'électrification de ces deux axes sera complétés vers 1995, la série entière sera radiée.

Note: Cars marked § are buffet cars, whilst the other catering vehicles have a kitchen.
Nota: Les TR 52000 marquées § sont des buffets, tandis que les autres ont une cuisine.

T 1510/1010. 10.23 Dijon–Clermont Ferrand. 23/03/89.

Keith Grafton

Built/Construction: 1972–76. **Builder/Constructeur:** ANF/MTE.
Engine/Moteur: Turmo XII (1200 kW) (odd/impair), Turmo IIIF1 (820 kW) (even/pair).
Transmission: Hydraulic/hydraulique (Voith L 411 r).
Formation: TBD + TRB (TRAB*) + TRA + TRBr + TBD.
Accomodation/Places: –/48 1T + –/80 2T (29/40 2T*) + 60/– + –/64 1T (–/44+24 chairs/chaises 1T§) + –/48 1T.
Weight/Masse: 54 + 38 + 42 + 37 + 54 tonnes.
Length/Longeur: 26.23 + 25.51 + 25.51 + 25.51 + 26.23 m.
Max. Speed/Vitesse max.: 160 km/h.
Livery/Livrée: D.

Most are fitted with train-signal box radio and cowcatchers.
La plupart sont équipées de la radio soi-train et d'éperons chasse obstacles.

T 2001	TR 32001*	TR 22001	TR 52001§	T 2002 VE	AIX-LES-BAINS
T 2003	TR 32002*	TR 22002	TR 52002§	T 2004 VE	LYON
T 2005	TR 32003*	TR 22003	TR 52003§	T 2006 VE	SAUMUR
T 2007	TR 32004*	TR 22004	TR 52004§	T 2008 VE	VÉNISSIEUX
T 2009	TR 32005*	TR 22005	TR 52005§	T 2010 VE	BOURGES
T 2011	TR 32006*	TR 22006	TR 52006§	T 2012 VE	CLERMONT FERRAND
T 2013	TR 32007*	TR 22007	TR 52007§	T 2014 VE	RIORGES
T 2015	TR 32008*	TR 22008	TR 52008§	T 2016 VE	LE VERDON-SUR-MER
T 2021	TR 32011*	TR 22011	TR 52011§	T 2022 VE	BESANÇON
T 2053	TR 32012*	TR 22012	TR 52012§	T 2024 CA	GUÉRET
T 2025	TR 32013*	TR 22013	TR 52013§	T 2026 VE	EYGURANDE-MERLINES
T 2027	TR 32014*	TR 22014	TR 52014§	T 2028 VE	
T 2029	TR 32015*	TR 22015	TR 52015§	T 2030 VE	MONTBÉLIARD
T 2031	TR 32016*	TR 22016	TR 52016§	T 2032 VE	MONTLUÇON
T 2033	TR 32017*	TR 22017	TR 52017§	T 2034 VE	NANTES
T 2036	TR 32018*	TR 22018	TR 52018	T 2035 CA	PÉRIGUEUX
T 2038	TR 32019*	TR 22019	TR 52019	T 2037 CA	ROYAN
T 2040	TR 32020	TR 22020	TR 52020	T 2039 CA	DINARD
T 2042	TR 42021	TR 22021	TR 52021	T 2041 CA	CAEN
T 2044	TR 42022	TR 22022	TR 52022	T 2043 CA	DINAN
T 2046	TR 42023	TR 22023	TR 52023	T 2045 CA	
T 2048	TR 42024	TR 22024	TR 52024	T 2047 CA	LAON
T 2050	TR 42025	TR 22025	TR 52025	T 2049 CA	ANGERS
T 2052	TR 42026	TR 22026	TR 52026	T 2051 CA	
T 2056	TR 42028	TR 22028	TR 52028	T 2055 CA	
T 2058	TR 42029	TR 22029	TR 52029	T 2057 CA	SANCY LES-CHEMINOTS
T 2060	TR 42030	TR 22030	TR 52030	T 2059 CA	SOISSONS
T 2062	TR 42031	TR 22031	TR 52031	T 2061 CA	CALAIS
T 2064	TR 42032	TR 22032	TR 52032	T 2063 CA	BOULOGNE-SUR-MER
T 2066	TR 42033	TR 22033	TR 52033	T 2065 CA	
T 2068	TR 42034	TR 22034	TR 52034	T 2067 CA	
T 2070	TR 42035	TR 22035	TR 52035	T 2069 CA	
T 2072	TR 42036	TR 22036	TR 52036	T 2071 CA	BERNAY
T 2074	TR 42037	TR 22037	TR 52037	T 2073 CA	TOURS
T 2076	TR 42038	TR 22038	TR 52038	T 2075 CA	
T 2078	TR 42039	TR 22039	TR 52039	T 2077 CA	
T 2080	TR 32040	TR 22040	TR 52040	T 2079 CA	BRIOUZE
T 2082	TR 32041	TR 22041	TR 52041	T 2081 CA	

X 2124. Rennes. Livery/livrée 'M'. 31/07/88. *Eric Dunkling*

X 2250 with stainless steel body at Tours St. Pierre depot. X 2250 fabriqué en acier inox au dépôt de Tours St. Pierre. 13/09/89. *Eric Dunkling*

SNCF DIESEL RAILCARS
AUTORAILS

In this book, a distinction is made between railcars and multiple units. In France there are many services are operated by single unit diesel railcars which tow trailers. At the end of the journey it is necessary to run round the trailer. However, as the trailers are through wired for multiple working, trains often run with a railcar at each end with a trailer or trailers sandwiched between them. Those railcars with a '9' prefix were built specially for regional councils. Increasing numbers of the others are being repainted in regional colours.

Dans ce livre nous séparons les autorails simples et les éléments automoteurs. En France, beaucoup de services sont assurées par des autorails simples avec ou sans remorque. Les remorques peuvent être remorquées ou prises «en sandwich» entre deux motrices. Les autorails dont les numéros portent le préfixe '9' furent construits pour l'une des 22 régions de la France. De plus en plus les autres sont repeints dans la livrée de la région.

CLASS/SERIE X 2100   B2

This class helped to replace the ageing X 2400 and X 3800 series. Toulouse units are mainly used on Toulouse–Auch, Rennes units all over Brittanny and Limoges units in common with X 2200.

Cette série remplaça beaucoup des vieux X 2400 et X 3800. Ceux de Toulouse sont utilisés principalement sur Toulouse–Auch, ceux de Rennes partout en Bretagne et ceux de Limoges en roulement avex les X 2200.

Type: XABD.
Built/Construction: 1980–83.
Engine/Moteur: Saurer S1DHR (440 kW).
Weight/Masse: 44 tonnes.
Max. Speed/Vitesse max.: 140 km/h.

Accommodation/Places: 8/48 1T.
Builders/Constructeurs: ANF/Schneider.
Transmission: Hydraulic/hydraulique. Voith.
Length/Longeur: 22.40 m.

Hydrodynamic braking. Multiple working with X 2200, X 2800, XR 6000 and XR 6200 up to a maximum of 3 railcars and 3 trailers.
Équipés du frein hydrodynamique. Couplables en UM avec les X 2200, X 2800, XR 6000 et XR 6200 jusqu'un maximum de 3 motrices plus 3 remorques.

Note: 92104 was renumbered from 2133./Nota: Le 92104 était rénumeroté de 2133.

2101	M TL	2110	G RS	2119	M LG	2128	M RS	2138	G RS	2147	G RS
2102	M TL	2111	G RS	2120	M LG	2129	M RS	2139	G RS	2148	G RS
2103	M TL	2112	G RS	2121	M LG	2130	M RS	2140	G RS	2149	M RS
2104	M TL	2113	G RS	2122	M LG	2131	M RS	2141	G RS	2150	M RS
2105	M TL	2114	G RS	2123	G RS	2132	M LG	2142	G RS	92101	B NB
2106	M TL	2115	G RS	2124	G RS	2134	G RS	2143	G RS	92102	B NB
2107	M TL	2116	G RS	2125	M TL	2135	G RS	2144	G RS	92103	B NB
2108	G RS	2117	G RS	2126	M RS	2136	G RS	2145	G RS	92104	M TL
2109	G RS	2118	G RS	2127	M RS	2137	G RS	2146	G RS		

Names/Noms:

2132 DUNIÈRES.
92101–3 LES PAYS DE LA LOIRE
92104 CONSEIL RÉGIONAL MIDI PYRÉNÉES

CLASS/SERIE X 2200   B2

An improved version of X 2100 with a modified interior. Limoges units cover a very wide area from the Massif Central to La Rochelle and Mont-de-Marsan. Tours units are mainly used on Tours–Paris Austerlitz via Châteaudun.

Une version ameliorée des X 2100 avec l'interieur modernisé. Ceux de Limoges assurent des omnibus sur une vaste région du Massif Central à La Rochelle et Mont-de-Marsan. De Tours, ils vont surtout à Paris Austerlitz via Châteaudun.

Type: XABD.
Built/Construction: 1985–90.

Accommodation/Places: 8/48 1T.
Builders/Constructeurs: ANF/Schneider.

Engine/Moteur: Saurer S1DHR (440 kW).
Weight/Masse: 44 tonnes.
Max. Speed/Vitesse max.: 140 km/h.

Transmission: Hydraulic/hydraulique. Voith.
Length/Longeur: 22.40 m.

Hydrodynamic braking. Multiple working with X 2100, X 2800, XR 6000 and XR 6200.
Équipés du frein hydrodynamique. Couplables en UM avec les X 2100, X 2800, XR 6000 et XR 6200.

Livery N: Stainless steel body with blue upper bodyside.
Livrée N: Caisse en acier inox avec bande en bleu.

2201	**R** LG	2211	**B** TP	2221	**R** LG	2231	**R** LG	2241	**R** LG	2251	**R** LG
2202	**B** LV	2212	**B** TP	2222	**R** LG	2232	**R** LG	2242	**R** LG	2252	**R** LG
2203	**R** LG	2213	**R** LG	2223	**R** LG	2233	**R** LG	2243	**R** LG	2253	**R** LG
2204	**R** LG	2214	**R** LG	2224	**R** LG	2234	**R** LG	2244	**R** LG	2254	**R** LG
2205	**B** TP	2215	**R** LG	2225	**R** LG	2235	**R** LG	2245	**R** LG	2255	**R** LG
2206	**B** TP	2216	**R** LG	2226	**R** LG	2236	**R** LG	2246	**R** LG	2256	**R** LG
2207	**B** TP	2217	**R** LG	2227	**R** LG	2237	**R** LG	2247	**R** LG	2257	**R** LG
2208	**B** TP	2218	**R** LG	2228	**R** LG	2238	**R** LG	2248	**R** LG	92201	**G** SO
2209	**B** TP	2219	**R** LG	2229	**R** LG	2239	**R** LG	2249	**R** LG	92202	**M** TL
2210	**B** TP	2220	**R** LG	2230	**R** LG	2240	**R** LG	2250	**N** TP	92203	**M** TL

Names/Noms:

2205 CLOYES-SUR-LA-LOIR
92201 NORMANDIE
92202 CONSEIL RÉGIONAL MIDI-PYRÉNÉES
92203 LANGUEDOC ROUSSILLON

CLASS/SERIE XR 6000   22

Trailers constructed to work with X 2100.
Des remorques pour utiliser avec les X 2100.

Type: XRAB.
Built/Construction: 1980–83.
Weight/Masse: 24 tonnes. .
Max. Speed/Vitesse max.: 140 km/h.

Accommodation/Places: 16/60 1T.
Builders/Constructeurs: ANF.
Length/Longeur: 24.04 m.

6001	**M** TL	6030	**M** TL	6060	**M** TL	6090	**M** LV	6119	**R** LG	6148	**R** SA
6002	**M** LG	6031	**M** CF	6061	**M** TL	6091	**M** LV	6120	**R** LG	6149	**R** SA
6003	**M** LG	6032	**M** CF	6062	**M** TL	6092	**M** LV	6121	**R** LG	6150	**R** LG
6004	**M** LG	6033	**M** CF	6063	**M** TL	6093	**M** LV	6122	**R** LG	6151	**R** SA
6005	**M** LG	6034	**M** CF	6064	**M** TL	6094	**M** LV	6123	**R** LG	6152	**R** SA
6006	**M** LG	6035	**M** CF	6065	**M** TL	6095	**M** LV	6124	**R** LG	6153	**R** SA
6007	**M** LG	6036	**M** CF	6066	**M** TL	6096	**M** LV	6125	**R** LG	6154	**R** SA
6008	**M** TL	6037	**M** CF	6067	**M** TL	6097	**M** LV	6126	**R** LG	6155	**R** LG
6009	**M** CF	6038	**M** CF	6068	**B** TL	6098	**M** LV	6127	**R** LG	6156	**R** LG
6010	**M** CF	6039	**M** CF	6070	**M** LG	6099	**M** LV	6128	**R** LG	6157	**R** LG
6011	**M** CF	6040	**M** CF	6071	**M** LG	6100	**M** LV	6129	**R** LG	6158	**R** BD
6012	**M** CF	6041	**M** CF	6072	**M** LG	6101	**G** RS	6130	**R** LG	6159	**R** BD
6013	**M** CF	6042	**M** CF	6073	**M** LG	6102	**G** RS	6131	**R** LG	6160	**R** BD
6014	**M** CF	6043	**M** CF	6074	**M** LG	6103	**G** RS	6132	**R** BD	6161	**R** BD
6015	**M** CF	6044	**M** CF	6075	**M** LG	6104	**G** RS	6133	**R** BD	6162	**R** BD
6016	**M** CF	6045	**M** CF	6076	**M** LG	6105	**G** RS	6134	**R** BD	6163	**G** RS
6017	**M** CF	6046	**M** CF	6077	**M** LG	6106	**G** RS	6135	**R** BD	6164	**G** RS
6018	**M** CF	6047	**M** CF	6078	**M** LG	6107	**G** RS	6136	**R** BD	6165	**G** RS
6019	**M** CF	6048	**M** CF	6079	**M** LG	6108	**G** RS	6137	**R** BD	6166	**G** RS
6020	**M** CF	6049	**M** LV	6080	**M** LG	6109	**G** RS	6138	**R** LG	6167	**G** RS
6021	**M** CF	6050	**M** LV	6081	**M** LG	6110	**G** RS	6139	**R** LG	6168	**G** RS
6022	**M** CF	6051	**M** LV	6082	**M** LG	6111	**R** LV	6140	**R** LV	6169	**G** RS
6023	**M** CF	6052	**M** LV	6083	**M** LG	6112	**R** LG	6141	**R** LG	6170	**G** RS
6024	**M** CF	6053	**M** LV	6084	**M** LG	6113	**R** LV	6142	**R** LG	96001	**B** NB
6025	**M** CF	6054	**M** TL	6085	**M** LG	6114	**R** LV	6143	**R** LG	96002	**B** NB
6026	**M** CF	6055	**M** TL	6086	**M** LG	6115	**R** LV	6144	**R** SA	96003	**B** NB
6027	**M** TL	6056	**M** TL	6087	**M** LG	6116	**R** LV	6145	**R** SA	96004	**M** TL
6028	**M** TL	6058	**M** TL	6088	**M** LV	6117	**R** LG	6146	**R** SA	96005	**G** SO
6029	**M** TL	6059	**M** TL	6089	**M** LV	6118	**R** LG	6147	**R** SA	96006	**M** TL

CLASS/SERIE XR 6200   22

These trailers are similar to Class 6000, but have 2200-style interiors.
Comme les XR 6000 mais avec intérieurs style X 2200.

Type: XRAB.
Built/Construction: 1988–90.
Weight/Masse: 24 tonnes. .
Max. Speed/Vitesse max.: 140 km/h.

Accommodation/Places: 16/60 1T.
Builders/Constructeurs: ANF.
Length/Longeur: 24.04 m.

6201	**G** RS	6215	**R** DP	6229	**R** BD	6242	**R** LV	6255	**R** BD	96213**B** TL
6202	**G** RS	6216	**B** TP	6230	**R** BD	6243	**R** LV	96201**B** TL		96214**B** TL
6203	**R** LV	6217	**B** TP	6231	**R** BD	6244	**R** LV	96202**B** TL		96215**B** TL
6204	**R** LV	6218	**B** TP	6232	**R** BD	6245	**R** LV	96203**B** TL		96216**B** TL
6205	**R** BD	6219	**B** TP	6233	**R** BD	6246	**R** LV	96204**B** TL		96217**B** TL
6206	**R** BD	6220	**B** TP	6234	**R** BD	6247	**R** LV	96205**B** TL		96218**B** TL
6207	**R** TL	6221	**B** TP	6235	**R** BD	6248	**R** LV	96206**B** TL		96219**B** TL
6208	**R** TL	6222	**B** TP	6236	**R** BD	6249	**R** LV	96207**B** TL		96220**B** TL
6209	**R** TL	6223	**B** TP	6237	**R** BD	6250	**R** BD	96208**B** TL		96221**B** TL
6210	**R** DP	6224	**B** TP	6238	**R** BD	6251	**R** BD	96209**B** TL		96222**B** TL
6211	**R** DP	6225	**R** BD	6239	**R** LG	6252	**R** BD	96210**B** TL		96223**B** TL
6212	**R** DP	6226	**R** BD	6240	**R** LG	6253	**R** BD	96211**B** TL		96224**B** TL
6213	**R** DP	6227	**R** BD	6241	**R** LV	6254	**R** BD	96212**B** TL		96225**B** TL
6214	**R** DP	6228	**R** BD							

CLASS/SERIE X 2400   BB

These powerful railcars have now all been withdrawn except 2464 which is in departmental service as a signal department test car.

Ces autorails puissants sont tous radiés mais le 2464 reste en service, hors inventaire, pour des essais sur les relais de voie.

Type: XABDP.
Built/Construction: 1951–56.
Engines/Moteurs: 2 Renault 517G (255 kW).
Weight/Masse: 43 tonnes.
Max. Speed/Vitesse max.: 120 km/h.
Livery: Corail livery of two-tone grey lined in orange.
Livrée: Gris clair et foncé avec bandes oranges.

Accommodation/Places: 12/56 1T.
Builders/Constructeurs: Decauville Aîné.
Transmission: Mechanical/mécanique.
Length/Longeur: 27.73 m.

2464 **M** NV(D)

CLASS/SERIE X 2800   B2

These sets have all been refurbished and are known as "Massif Central sets", although they do also work elsewhere. On refurbishment the sets were painted blue and white. They can work in multiple with other railcars.

Ces autorails sont connus sous le nom «Massif Central» mais sont présents dans les autres massifs montagneux. A l'origine en rouge et blanc cassé, ils ont reçu la livrée bleue en même temps que leur modernisation.

Type: XABD.
Built/Construction: 1957–62.
Engine/Moteur: MGO V12SH (605 kW).
Transmission: Hydraulic/hydraulique. Maybach.
Weight/Masse: 54 tonnes.
Max. Speed/Vitesse max.: 120 km/h.

Accommodation/Places: 12/50 1T.
Builders/Constructeurs: Decauville/Renault.

Length/Longeur: 27.73 m.

Multiple working with X 2100, X 2200, XR 6000 and XR 6200.
Couplables en UM avec les X 2100, X 2200, XR 6000 et XR 6200.

2801 **M** LG	2807 **M** LV	2813 **M** LG	2819 **M** LV	2826 **M** LV	2832 **M** LG
2802 **M** LV	2808 **M** LG	2814 **M** LG	2820 **M** TL	2827 **M** LV	2833 **M** TL
2803 **M** LV	2809 **M** LG	2815 **M** LG	2821 **M** LG	2828 **M** LV	2834 **M** LV
2804 **M** LG	2810 **M** LV	2816 **M** LV	2822 **M** LG	2829 **M** LV	2835 **M** LV
2805 **M** LG	2811 **M** LV	2817 **M** TL	2823 **M** LV	2830 **M** LV	2836 **M** LV
2806 **M** LV	2812 **M** LG	2818 **M** LV	2824 **M** LV	2831 **M** TL	2837 **M** LV
			2825 **M** LV		

2838	M LV	2852	M LV	2866	M LV	2880	M LG	2894	M LG	2907	M LG
2839	M LG	2853	M TL	2867	M LG	2881	M TL	2895	M LV	2908	M LG
2840	M LV	2854	M TL	2868	M LV	2882	M LG	2896	M LV	2909	M TL
2841	M TL	2855	M LV	2869	M LV	2883	M LG	2897	M LV	2910	M TL
2842	M LV	2856	M LV	2870	M LV	2884	M LG	2898	M LV	2911	M LV
2843	M LV	2857	M LG	2871	M LG	2885	M LV	2899	M LV	2912	M LV
2844	M LV	2858	M LV	2872	M LG	2886	M LG	2900	M LG	2913	M LV
2845	M LV	2859	M LV	2873	M LV	2887	M TL	2901	M LG	2914	M LV
2846	M LV	2860	M LV	2874	M LV	2888	M LG	2902	M LG	2915	M LG
2847	M LG	2861	M LG	2875	M LG	2889	M LG	2903	M TL	2916	M LV
2848	M LV	2862	M LV	2876	M LG	2890	M LG	2904	M LG	2917	M TL
2849	M LG	2863	M LV	2877	M LV	2891	M TL	2905	M LG	2918	M LG
2850	M LV	2864	M LV	2878	M LV	2892	M LG	2906	M LG	2919	M LG
2851	M LG	2865	M LG	2879	M LG	2893	M LV				

CLASS/SERIE X 3800 (PICASSO) B2

An SNCF classic diesel railcar known as "Picassos" because of the strange location of the driving cab (on the roof!) and the fact that the driver has to sit side on instead of facing the direction of travel! They were built with one cab as a means of providing a cheap unit that would help to keep branch lines open, the roof cab meaning that the driver did not have to change ends during reversals en route. The remaining units are in departmental use. Many have also been preserved.

Des autorails classiques connus sous le nom de "Picassos" a cause de la position bizarre de la cabine de conduite (sur le toit!). Ils furent construits avec une seule cabine par mesure d'économie. le conducteur n'a donc pas besoin de changer de cabine à un terminus! Les quatre Picassos qui restent ne sont plus sur les inventaires de la SNCF. Beaucoup de la série ont été preservées.

Type: XBD or XABD.
Built/Construction: 1951–62.
Accommodation/Places: –/62 1T or 12/32 1T.
Builders/Constructeurs: ANF/De Dietrich/Renault/Saurer.
Engine/Moteur: Renault 517G (250 kW).
Transmission: Mechanical/mécanique.
Weight/Masse: 53 tonnes.
Length/Longeur: 27.73 m.
Max. Speed/Vitesse max.: 120 km/h.
Livery: X 3896/3900 are in pale green lined in white and have modified front windows for better observation. X 3997 is similar but in Corail livery of two-tone grey lined in orange.
Livrée: X 3896/3900 sont en vert clair avec bandes en blanches avec des fenêtres modifiées pour une meilleure observation. X 3997 est gris clair et foncé avec bandes oranges.

3886	R BD(D)	3896	N MN(D)	3900	N MN(D)	3997	N MN(D)

CLASS/SERIE XR 7800 22

These refurbished 'standard' trailers work Dijon to Dole and Besançon with X 2800 whose internal furnishings they have.

Ces remorques unifiées modernisées sont utilisées de Dijon à Dole et Besançon avec les X 2800, qui ont le même intérieur.

8274	M DV	8281	M DV	8285	M DV	8291	M DV

"Picasso" X 3900. Departmental stock/matériel de service. Paris La Villette. 13/09/89.
Eric Dunkling

EAT X 4920 'SOTTEVILLE-LES-ROUEN'. Caen depot. Dépôt de Caen. 08/89.   *David Haydock*

DIESEL MULTIPLE UNITS
ELEMENTS AUTOMOTEURS DIESEL

Note: All DMUS are assumed to be in livery 'A' unless stated otherwise.
Nota: Tous les éléments sont en livrée 'A' sauf indication contraire.

CLASS/SERIE X 2700   RGP

This departmental unit has been formed from two power cars of former RGP sets (rame à grand parcours). The set was converted from power cars 2707 and 2714 at Bordeaux Works and is used as an ultrasonic rail tester. Numbered as X 2700, it is also known as V4. In each power car the outer engine has been replaced by test equipment leaving the inner engine in each car.

Cette rame a été formée à partir des motrices 2707 et 2714 des anciennes RGP-2 (rame à grand parcours à 2 moteurs). L'élément fut transformée par les ateliers de Bordeaux pour faire des essais d'auscultation des rails pour le division de l'équipment. Dans chaque voiture, un des moteurs a été enlevé et remplacé par du matériel d'essai. Bien que numérotée X 2700, la rame est aussi connu sous le nom de V4.

Built/Construction: 1954–55.   **Builder/Constructeur:** Decauville-Aîné.
Formation: XBD + XBD.
Wheel Arrangement/Disposition des Essieux: 2B + B2.
Engine/Moteur: 1 Renault 517G (250 kW).
Transmission: Mechanical/Mécanique.
Length/Longeur: 26.63 + 26.63 m.   **Max. Speed/Vitesse max.:** 120 km/h.
Livery: Corail livery of two-tone grey lined in orange.
Livrée: Gris clair et foncé avec bandes oranges.

X 2700 X 2700 **N**   NV(D) |

CLASS/SERIE X 2720   RGP

This class was formerly two separate classes. The units are also known as RGPs. Unlike the X 2700 class, they have one large engine instead of two smaller ones. The X 2770 series were former TEE units and are being renumbered in the series X 2739–49 when refurbished. The refurbishment consists of fitting new cabs similar to those on the X 2200 railcars, new seats and automatic doors. Driving trailers X 7721–32 were renumbered X 7757–68 prior to refurbishing and are being renumbered in the same series when refurbished. However they have not necessarily regained their original number. In September 1991, all Metz units (in yellow livery) will be transferred to Lyon Vaise for use on the Nîmes–Clermont Ferrand line.

Cette série sont les RGP-1, rames à grand parcours à un moteur. Les X 2720 étaient auparavant deux séries differents – les X 2770 sont les anciennes rames TEE qui seront renumerotées X 2739–49 quand elles sont modernisées. La modernisation de la série, qui est presque terminée, consiste essentielement à mettre de nouvelles cabines, de nouveaux sièges et des portes automatiques. Les remorques XR 7721–32 étaient rénumerotées XR 7757–68 avant la modernisation. Après modernisation elles reprennent un numéro entre 7721 et 7732 mais pas forcément le numéro original. En septembre 1991, toutes les rames de Metz seront transferées a Lyon Vaise pour le service Nimes–Clermont Ferrand.

Wheel Arrangement/Disposition des Essieux: B2 + 2B.
Built/Construction: 1955–56.   **Builder/Constructeur:** De Dietrich/SACM.
Engine/Moteur: MGO V12SH of 605 kW.   **Transmission:** Hydraulic/hydraulique.
Formation: XBD + XRABx.   **Accommodation/Places:** –/60 + 24/52.
Weight/Masse: 53 + 32 tonnes.   **Max. Speed/Vitesse max.:** 140 km/h.
Length/Longeur: 27.63 + 26.05 (*26.63 + 25.53 unrefurbished/non-modernisé*) m.

X 2721	XR 7721 **R**	r LV	X 2727	XR 7727 **Y**	r MZ	X 2733	XR 7733 **R**	r LV
X 2722	XR 7722 **Y**	r MZ	X 2728	XR 7728 **R**	r LV	X 2734	XR 7734 **R**	r LV
X 2723	XR 7723 **Y**	r MZ	X 2729	XR 7729 **Y**	r MZ	X 2735	XR 7735 **Y**	r MZ
X 2724	XR 7778 **O**	LV	X 2730	XR 7730 **R**	r LV	X 2736	XR 7736 **R**	r LV
X 2725	XR 7763 **O**	LV	X 2731	XR 7731 **Y**	r MZ	X 2737	XR 7759 **O**	LV
X 2726	XR 7726 **R**	r LV	X 2732	XR 7732 **R**	r LV	X 2738	XR 7738 **R**	r LV

X 2739	XR 7739	**R**	r	LV	X 2743	XR 7743	**Y**	r	LV		
X 2740	XR 7740	**R**	r	LV	X 2744	XR 7744	**R**	r	LV		
X 2741	XR 7741	**R**	r	LV	X 2745	XR 7745	**R**	r	LV		
X 2742	XR 7742	**R**	r	LV	X 2778	XR 7751	**O**		LV		

X 2747	XR 7747	**R**	r	LV
X 2780	XR 7757	**O**		LV
X 2749	XR 7749	**R**	r	LV

CLASSES/**SERIES** X 4300+X 4500

These two-car DMUs represent the 1960s generation of DMUs. Introduced in 1963, similar units continued to be built until 1981s. Their introduction led to mass withdrawals of old units many of which dated from pre-war days. The only difference between the two classes is the engine. The trailer cars have different proportions of first and second class and power cars of either class operate with either an XR 8300 or an XR 8500 driving trailer to match seating demand. Formations now tend to be permanent after several years of changes. Both classes are being modernised. The ends have been altered and are now similar to the recently-delivered RRR push-pull sets with large and one small window. Although formations have been permanent for some time, a recent visit to Le Mans workshops discovered that trailers are being exchanged and renumbered as they are modernised!

Ces «éléments automoteurs doubles» (EAD) représentent la génération d'autorails des années 60. Les premiers furent introduits en 1963 mais des éléments similaires sortaient de l'usine jusqu'en 1981. Leur introduction a entamé la radiation de vieux autorails qui datent, dans certains cas, d'avant-guerre. La seule différence entre les X 4300 et les X 4500 est la motorisation. Les remorques XR 8300 et XR 8500, qui ont des répartitions différents de places en première et deuxième classe, peuvent être couplées avec chacune des séries. Les jumelages motrice + remorque sont quasi-permanents. Les deux séries sont en train d' être modernisées. Les éléments sont équipés de nouvelles cabines, proches de celles des rames RRR, et de nouveaux sièges. Les remorques sont renumerotées lors de la modernisation aux ateliers du Mans.

Wheel Arrangement/Disposition des Essieux: B2 + 22.
Built/Construction: 1963–70.　**Builder/Constructeur:** ANF.
Engine/Moteur: Poyaud (X 4300), Saurer SDHR (X 4500) (320 kW).
Transmission: Mechanical/Mécanique.　**Formation:** XBD + XRABx.
Accommodation/Places: –/60 1T + 12/69 1T (XR 8300), 24/49 1T (XR 8500).
Weight/Masse: 34 tonnes (X 4300), 35 tonnes (X 4500) + 23 tonnes.
Length/Longeur: 21.24 + 21.24 m.　**Max. Speed/Vitesse max.:** 120 km/h.

Note: X 4365 became a turbotrain prototype. X 4624/5/6 were rebuilt from X 4351/71/85 respectively.
Nota: La X 4365 est devenu le prototype des turbotrains. Les X 4624/5/6 furent transformés des X 4351/71/85.

r Refurbished units./rames modernisées.

X 4301	XR 8301	TP	X 4324	XR 8533	MZ	X 4348	XR 8328			MZ
X 4302	XR 8302	MZ	X 4325	XR 8315	MZ	X 4349	XR 8598	**B**	r	MZ
X 4303	XR 8557	NV	X 4326	XR 8316	MZ	X 4350	XR 8329			MZ
X 4304	XR 8559	NV	X 4327	XR 8317	MZ	X 4352	XR 8339			MZ
X 4305	XR 8505	NV	X 4328	XR 8318	MZ	X 4353	XR 8343			MZ
X 4306	XR 8504	MZ	X 4329	XR 8540	NV	X 4354	XR 8524			MZ
X 4307	XR 8507	NV	X 4330	XR 8543	MZ	X 4355	XR 8345			MZ
X 4308	XR 8303	TP	X 4331	XR 8319	MZ	X 4356	XR 8344			TP
X 4309	XR 8330	TP	X 4332	XR 8320	MZ	X 4357	XR 8347			MZ
X 4310	XR 8331	TP	X 4333	XR 8544	NV	X 4358	XR 8581	**B**	r	MZ
X 4311	XR 8621	TP	X 4334	XR 8545	NV	X 4359	XR 8568			MZ
X 4312	XR 8306	TP	X 4335	XR 8321	TP	X 4360	XR 8527			TP
X 4313	XR 8309	TP	X 4336	XR 8322	TP	X 4361	XR 8570			MZ
X 4314	XR 8310	TP	X 4337	XR 8554	NV	X 4362	XR 8576			TP
X 4315	XR 8311	TP	X 4338	XR 8536	MZ	X 4363	XR 8577			MZ
X 4316	XR 8312	TP	X 4339	XR 8324	MZ	X 4364	XR 8354	**B**	r	MZ
X 4317	XR 8517	NV	X 4340	XR 8325	TP	X 4366	XR 8356	**B**		MZ
X 4318	XR 8349	MZ	X 4341	XR 8326	MZ	X 4367	XR 8362			TP
X 4319	XR 8519	MZ	X 4342	XR 8340	MZ	X 4368	XR 8357	**B**		MZ
X 4320	XR 8520	MZ	X 4343	XR 8337	MZ	X 4369	XR 8361	**B**		MZ
X 4321	XR 8521	MZ	X 4344	XR 8342	MZ	X 4370	XR 8355	**B**	r	TP
X 4322	XR 8313	MZ	X 4345	XR 8327	MZ	X 4372	XR 8348	**B**	r	TP
X 4323	XR 8314	MZ	X 4346	XR 8555	NV	X 4373	XR 8518	**B**	r	MZ

X 4374	XR 8350			MZ	X 4442	XR 8422			MZ

No.	XR	B/G	r	Code
X 4374	XR 8350			MZ
X 4375	XR 8351			MZ
X 4376	XR 8352	B	r	MZ
X 4377	XR 8359			MZ
X 4378	XR 8578	B	r	MZ
X 4379	XR 8588			NV
X 4380	XR 8580			MZ
X 4381	XR 8582	B	r	MZ
X 4383	XR 8602			MZ
X 4384	XR 8603			MZ
X 4386	XR 8539			NV
X 4387	XR 8606			TP
X 4388	XR 8607			NV
X 4389	XR 8608	B	r	MZ
X 4390	XR 8609			MZ
X 4391	XR 8610	B	r	TP
X 4392	XR 8611			NV
X 4393	XR 8612			TP
X 4394	XR 8501			MZ
X 4395	XR 8549			MZ
X 4396	XR 8363			MZ
X 4397	XR 8560			MZ
X 4398	XR 8605			NV
X 4399	XR 8613			NV
X 4400	XR 8542			NV
X 4401	XR 8367			TP
X 4402	XR 8502	B	r	TP
X 4403	XR 8369	B	r	TP
X 4404	XR 8366			MZ
X 4405	XR 8513			MZ
X 4406	XR 8506			MZ
X 4407	XR 8626	B	r	TP
X 4408	XR 8573			MZ
X 4409	XR 8628			MZ
X 4410	XR 8569			MZ
X 4411	XR 8532			MZ
X 4412	XR 8631			NV
X 4413	XR 8591			NV
X 4414	XR 8558			MZ
X 4415	XR 8586			MZ
X 4416	XR 8381			TP
X 4417	XR 8382			MZ
X 4418	XR 8383			TP
X 4420	XR 8552			MZ
X 4421	XR 8526			MZ
X 4422	XR 8387			MZ
X 4423	XR 8388			MZ
X 4424	XR 8386			MZ
X 4425	XR 8390			MZ
X 4426	XR 8391			TP
X 4427	XR 8392			MZ
X 4428	XR 8393			MZ
X 4429	XR 8394			MZ
X 4430	XR 8395			TP
X 4431	XR 8396			TP
X 4432	XR 8593	B	r	MZ
X 4433	XR 8584	B	r	MZ
X 4434	XR 8523	B	r	MZ
X 4435	XR 8632	B	r	TP
X 4436	XR 8541	B	r	MZ
X 4437	XR 8597	B	r	TP
X 4438	XR 8418			MZ
X 4439	XR 8531	B	r	MZ
X 4440	XR 8420	B	r	TP
X 4441	XR 8421	B	r	TP
X 4442	XR 8422			MZ
X 4443	XR 8423			MZ
X 4444	XR 8424			MZ
X 4445	XR 8425			MZ
X 4446	XR 8426			MZ
X 4447	XR 8427			MZ
X 4448	XR 8428			MZ
X 4449	XR 8429			MZ
X 4450	XR 8430			MZ
X 4451	XR 8431			MZ
X 4501	XR 8503			SO
X 4502	XR 8365			MB
X 4503	XR 8509			RS
X 4504	XR 8304			LN
X 4505	XR 8511			LN
X 4506	XR 8615			LN
X 4507	XR 8370			MB
X 4509	XR 8512			SO
X 4510	XR 8514			SO
X 4511	XR 8515			LN
X 4512	XR 8432			LN
X 4513	XR 8522			LN
X 4514	XR 8414			LN
X 4515	XR 8332			MB
X 4516	XR 8525			SO
X 4517	XR 8389			LN
X 4518	XR 8629			LN
X 4519	XR 8528			SO
X 4520	XR 8604			LN
X 4521	XR 8614			MB
X 4522	XR 8419			LN
X 4523	XR 8360			RS
X 4524	XR 8534			LN
X 4525	XR 8535			LN
X 4526	XR 8364			LN
X 4527	XR 8537			LN
X 4528	XR 8538			LN
X 4529	XR 8371			LN
X 4530	XR 8416			LN
X 4531	XR 8529			MB
X 4532	XR 8546			SO
X 4533	XR 8547			LN
X 4534	XR 8548			LN
X 4535	XR 8307			LN
X 4536	XR 8530			LN
X 4537	XR 8368			MB
X 4538	XR 8508			SO
X 4539	XR 8510			SO
X 4540	XR 8550			RS
X 4541	XR 8566			MB
X 4542	XR 8333	G	r	RS
X 4543	XR 8562			SO
X 4544	XR 8335			MB
X 4545	XR 8601			LN
X 4546	XR 8385			LN
X 4547	XR 8379			LN
X 4548	XR 8561			LN
X 4549	XR 8353			MB
X 4550	XR 8563			LN
X 4551	XR 8553	B	r	SO
X 4552	XR 8334			MB
X 4553	XR 8565			LN
X 4554	XR 8564			MB
X 4555	XR 8567			LN
X 4556	XR 8551	G	r	RS
X 4557	XR 8571			LN
X 4558	XR 8572			MB
X 4559	XR 8372			LN
X 4560	XR 8622			MB
X 4561	XR 8575	B	r	SO
X 4563	XR 8341			LN
X 4564	XR 8630			LN
X 4565	XR 8583			LN
X 4566	XR 8585			LN
X 4567	XR 8380			LN
X 4568	XR 8384			LN
X 4569	XR 8413			LN
X 4570	XR 8589			RS
X 4571	XR 8590			LN
X 4572	XR 8378			LN
X 4573	XR 8592			LN
X 4574	XR 8412			LN
X 4575	XR 8594			LN
X 4576	XR 8308			LN
X 4577	XR 8596			LN
X 4578	XR 8417			LN
X 4579	XR 8338			LN
X 4580	XR 8599			LN
X 4581	XR 8600			LN
X 4582	XR 8373			LN
X 4583	XR 8374			LN
X 4584	XR 8375			LN
X 4585	XR 8376			LN
X 4586	XR 8377			LN
X 4587	XR 8616			LN
X 4588	XR 8617			RS
X 4589	XR 8618			LN
X 4590	XR 8619	B	r	SO
X 4591	XR 8620			RS
X 4592	XR 8305			LN
X 4593	XR 8641	B	r	SO
X 4594	XR 8627	B	r	SO
X 4595	XR 8624			LN
X 4596	XR 8404			LN
X 4597	XR 8397	B	r	SO
X 4598	XR 8398			LN
X 4599	XR 8399			LN
X 4600	XR 8667	G	r	RS
X 4601	XR 8401			LN
X 4602	XR 8402			LN
X 4603	XR 8323			LN
X 4604	XR 8625			LN
X 4605	XR 8405			LN
X 4606	XR 8406			LN
X 4607	XR 8415			LN
X 4608	XR 8633			MB
X 4609	XR 8634			LN
X 4610	XR 8635			RS
X 4611	XR 8636			MB
X 4612	XR 8637			MB
X 4613	XR 8638			MB
X 4614	XR 8639			MB
X 4615	XR 8640			MB
X 4616	XR 8516			MB
X 4617	XR 8407			LN
X 4618	XR 8358			LN
X 4619	XR 8409			LN
X 4620	XR 8410			LN
X 4621	XR 8411			LN
X 4622	XR 8574			LN

X 4623	XR 8433	MB		X 4625	XR 8623	RS		X 4626	XR 8408	LN
X 4624	XR 8336	MB								

CLASS/SERIE X 4630

A development of the preceding classes but featuring hydraulic transmission. The trailers are interchangeable with those of X 4300 and X 4500 units. The Nantes units in 'W' livery have been refurbished internally. They carry "Pays de la Loire" markings.

Une version des X 4300 avec transmission hydraulique. Les remorques sont utilisables avec les X 4300 et X 4500 mais les jumelages sont quasi-permanent. Les éléments de Nantes en livrées W ont des intérieurs modernisés mais pas de cabines nouvelles. Ils portent des sigles «Pays de la Loire».

Wheel Arrangement/Disposition des Essieux: B2 + 22.
Built/Construction: 1974–77. **Builder/Constructeur:** ANF.
Engine/Moteur: Saurer SDHR (320 kW). **Transmission:** Hydraulic/hydraulique. Voith.
Formation: XBD + XRABx. **Weight/Masse:** 39 + 24 tonnes.
Length/Longeur: 21.24 + 21.24 m. **Max. Speed/Vitesse max.:** 120 km/h.
Accommodation/Places: –/60 1T + 24/49 1T (–/89 1T†).

† X 94630 is owned by the local transport authority in Cannes for working the Cannes–Ranguin service on which SNCF tickets are not valid. Livery is blue and yellow.
† X 94630 qui exploite la ligne Cannes–Ranguin n'appartient pas à la SNCF et les billets SNCF ne sont pas valables. La livrée est bleu et jaune.

X 4630	XR 8642			LV		X 4668	XR 8665	W	NB		X 4706	XR 8703		LV
X 4631	XR 8643	B	r	NB		X 4669	XR 8666		LV		X 4707	XR 8704		LV
X 4632	XR 8644			NV		X 4670	XR 8556	W	NB		X 4708	XR 8705		LV
X 4633	XR 8645			NV		X 4671	XR 8648	W	NB		X 4709	XR 8706		LN
X 4634	XR 8646			NV		X 4672	XR 8595	W	NB		X 4710	XR 8707		LV
X 4635	XR 8647			LN		X 4673	XR 8670	W	NB		X 4711	XR 8708		LN
X 4636	XR 8669	W		NB		X 4674	XR 8671	W	NB		X 4712	XR 8709		LN
X 4637	XR 8649	W		NB		X 4675	XR 8672	W	NB		X 4713	XR 8710		NV
X 4638	XR 8650			NV		X 4676	XR 8673	W	NB		X 4714	XR 8711		LN
X 4639	XR 8651			NV		X 4677	XR 8674		LV		X 4715	XR 8712		NV
X 4640	XR 8652			NV		X 4678	XR 8675	W	NB		X 4716	XR 8713		LN
X 4641	XR 8653			NV		X 4679	XR 8676	W	NB		X 4717	XR 8714		LN
X 4642	XR 8654			LV		X 4680	XR 8677	W	NB		X 4718	XR 8715		LN
X 4643	XR 8655			LN		X 4681	XR 8678	W	NB		X 4719	XR 8716		LN
X 4644	XR 8656			NV		X 4682	XR 8679	W	NB		X 4720	XR 8717		LN
X 4645	XR 8434			LV		X 4683	XR 8680		LV		X 4721	XR 8718		LN
X 4646	XR 8435			LN		X 4684	XR 8681	W	NB		X 4722	XR 8719		LN
X 4647	XR 8436			NV		X 4685	XR 8682		LV		X 4723	XR 8720		LV
X 4648	XR 8437			LV		X 4686	XR 8683	W	NB		X 4724	XR 8721		LN
X 4649	XR 8444			LV		X 4687	XR 8684		LV		X 4725	XR 8722		LV
X 4650	XR 8439			NV		X 4688	XR 8685	W	NB		X 4726	XR 8723		LN
X 4651	XR 8440			NV		X 4689	XR 8686		LV		X 4727	XR 8724		LN
X 4652	XR 8441			LV		X 4690	XR 8687		LV		X 4728	XR 8725		LN
X 4653	XR 8442			NV		X 4691	XR 8688		LV		X 4729	XR 8726		NV
X 4654	XR 8443			NV		X 4692	XR 8689		LV		X 4730	XR 8727		NB
X 4655	XR 8445			NV		X 4693	XR 8690	W	NB		X 4731	XR 8728		NV
X 4656	XR 8661	W		NB		X 4694	XR 8691		LV		X 4732	XR 8729		LN
X 4657	XR 8446			NV		X 4695	XR 8692		LV		X 4733	XR 8730		NV
X 4658	XR 8447			NV		X 4696	XR 8693		LN		X 4734	XR 8731		NV
X 4659	XR 8448			LV		X 4697	XR 8694	W	NB		X 4735	XR 8732		NV
X 4660	XR 8657			NV		X 4698	XR 8695		LV		X 4736	XR 8733		NB
X 4661	XR 8658			NV		X 4699	XR 8696	R	r	LV		X 4737	XR 8734		NB
X 4662	XR 8659			LV		X 4700	XR 8697		LV		X 4738	XR 8735		NV
X 4663	XR 8660			NV		X 4701	XR 8698		LV		X 4739	XR 8736		NV
X 4664	XR 8438			NV		X 4702	XR 8699		LV		X 4740	XR 8737		NB
X 4665	XR 8662			LV		X 4703	XR 8700		LV		X 4741	XR 8738		NB
X 4666	XR 8663			NV		X 4704	XR 8701		LV		X 4742	XR 8739		NV
X 4667	XR 8664			LV		X 4705	XR 8702	R	r	LV		X 94630	XR 98630	N	† MB

CLASS/SERIE X 4750

The last of the two car sets to appear were this series having a more powerful engine and a higher maximum speed.
La version finale des EAD qui a un moteur plus puissant et une vitesse maximale plus élévee.

Wheel Arrangement/Disposition des Essieux: B2 + 22.
Built/Construction: 1977–81.
Engine/Moteur: Saurer (440 kW).
Formation: XBD + XRABx.
Length/Longeur: 21.24 + 21.24 m.
Accommodation/Places: –/60 1T + 24/49 1T.

Builder/Constructeur: ANF.
Transmission: Hydraulic/hydraulique. Voith.
Weight/Masse: 39 + 24 tonnes.
Max. Speed/Vitesse max.: 140 km/h.

X 4750	XR 8750	MZ	X 4764	XR 8764	SO	X 4777	XR 8777	MZ
X 4751	XR 8751	MZ	X 4765	XR 8765	SO	X 4778	XR 8778	MZ
X 4752	XR 8752	MZ	X 4766	XR 8766	SO	X 4779	XR 8779	MZ
X 4753	XR 8753	MZ	X 4767	XR 8767	SO	X 4780	XR 8780	SO
X 4754	XR 8754	MZ	X 4768	XR 8768	MZ	X 4781	XR 8781	MZ
X 4755	XR 8755	SO	X 4769	XR 8769	SO	X 4782	XR 8782	MZ
X 4756	XR 8756	SO	X 4770	XR 8770	SO	X 4783	XR 8783	MZ
X 4757	XR 8757	SO	X 4771	XR 8771	SO	X 4784	XR 8784	MZ
X 4758	XR 8758	SO	X 4772	XR 8772	SO	X 4785	XR 8785	MZ
X 4759	XR 8759	SO	X 4773	XR 8773	SO	X 4786	XR 8786	MZ
X 4760	XR 8760	SO	X 4774	XR 8774	SO	X 4787	XR 8787	MZ
X 4761	XR 8761	SO	X 4775	XR 8775	MZ	X 4788	XR 8788	MZ
X 4762	XR 8762	SO	X 4776	XR 8776	MZ	X 4789	XR 8789	SO
X 4763	XR 8763	SO						

CLASS/SERIE X 4790

These units are similar to X 4750 but have lower density seating. They used to carry orange/grey livery and work the Paris–Granville service. However this service is now loco-hauled and the units are used on other services in the Basse-Normandie region. All have now been refurbished with the new front ends.

Ces éléments sont similaires aux X 4750 mais ont des sièges individuels au lieu de banquettes. A l'origine ils arboraient une livrée orange et exploitaient le service Paris–Granville. Ce service est maintenant exploité par des rames tractées et les X 4790 sont utilisés sur d'autres services en Basse-Normandie. Tous ont reçu des cabines de conduite renforcées du style RRR.

Wheel Arrangement/Disposition des Essieux: B2 + 22.
Built/Construction: 1980–81.
Engine/Moteur: Saurer (440 kW).
Formation: XBD + XRABx.
Length/Longeur: 21.24 + 21.24 m.
Accommodation/Places: –/47 1T + 24/36 1T (–/89 1T*).

Builder/Constructeur: ANF.
Transmission: Hydraulic/hydraulique. Voith.
Weight/Masse: 39 + 24 tonnes.
Max. Speed/Vitesse max.: 140 km/h.

X 4790	XR 8790 **B**	SO	BAGNOLES-DE-L'ORNE
X 4791	XR 8791 **B**	SO	GRANVILLE
X 4792	XR 8792 **B**	SO	VILLEDIEU-LES-POELES
X 4793	XR 8793 **B**	SO	VIRE
X 4794	XR 8794 **B**	SO	L'AIGLE
X 4795	XR 8795 **B**	SO	FLERS
X 4796	XR 8796 **B**	SO	ARGENTAN

CLASS/SERIE X 4900

These are 3-car versions low density units and, like X 4790, are intended for long distance work as a higher standard of comfort is provided. They are known as EATs ("Éléments au-tomoteurs triples") and are used mainly on Rouen–Caen–Rennes and Caen–Tours. X 4901–12 have snowploughs.

Ces «Éléments automoteurs triples» (EAT) sont une version à 3 voitures des EAD avec des sièges plus confortables pour de plus longues distances. Ils sont utilisés principalement sur Rouen–Caen–Rennes et Caen–Tours. Les X 4901–12 ont des éperons chasse neige.

Wheel Arrangement/Disposition des Essieux: B2 + 22 + 2B.
Built/Construction: 1975–77.
Engine/Moteur: Saurer SHDR (320 kW).
Formation: XBD + XRAB + XBD.
Length/Longeur: 21.24 + 20.75 + 21.24 m.
Accommodation/Places: –47 1T + 32/28 1T + –/47 1T.
Builder/Constructeur: ANF.
Transmission: Hydraulic/hydraulique. Voith.
Weight/Masse: 39 + 28 + 39 tonnes.
Max. Speed/Vitesse max.: 140 km/h.

X 4901	XR 8901	X 4902 **M**	SO	VEYNES
X 4903	XR 8902	X 4904 **M**	SO	MONOSQUE
X 4905	XR 8903	X 4906 **M**	SO	
X 4907	XR 8904	X 4908 **M**	SO	
X 4909	XR 8905	X 4910 **M**	SO	
X 4911	XR 8906	X 4912 **M**	SO	
X 4913	XR 8907	X 4914 **M**	SO	
X 4915	XR 8908	X 4916 **M**	SO	
X 4917	XR 8909	X 4918 **M**	SO	
X 4919	XR 8910	X 4920 **M**	SO	SOTTEVILLE-LES-ROUEN
X 4921	XR 8911	X 4922 **M**	SO	
X 4923	XR 8912	X 4924 **M**	SO	
X 4925	XR 8913	X 4926 **M**	SO	

CLASS/SERIE X 94750

These 2-car units belong to the postal authorities and are used exclusively as mail trains. They are only used on the Paris–Sotteville line.

Ces éléménts double appartiennent aux PTT et sont utilisés exclusivement sur des trains postaux Paris–Sotteville.

Wheel Arrangement/Disposition des Essieux: B2 + 22.
Built/Construction: 1978–79.
Engine/Moteur: Saurer (440 kW).
Formation: XP + XRPx.
Weight/Masse: 39 + 23 tonnes.
Livery/Livrée: Maroon and cream./Rouge bordeaux et blanc cassé.
Builder/Constructeur: ANF.
Transmission: Hydraulic/hydraulique. Voith.
Length/Longeur: 21.24 + 21.24 m.
Max. Speed/Vitesse max.: 140 km/h.

X 94750	XR 98750 **N**	SO		X 94755	XR 98755 **N**	SO		X 94757	XR 98757 **N**	SO	
X 94753	XR 98753 **N**	SO		X 94756	XR 98756 **N**	SO					

Y 2206. Chalindrey depot./Dépôt de Chalindrey. 14/07/90. *Eric Dunkling*

Y 2460. Villeneuve St. Georges depot./Dépôt de Villeneuve St. Georges. 14/09/89.

Eric Dunkling

TRACTORS/**LOCOTRACTEURS**

These small diesel shunters are known as tractors (locotracteurs) in France and can be operated by station staff as well as locomen.

Les locotracteurs peuvent être conduits per le personnel des gares aussi bien que par les conducteurs.

CLASS/**SERIE** Y 2200   B

This series of light shunters is mostly in use as depots/works shunters. They rarely get out on main line but some are allowed to and are fitted with scrapers to ensure the operation of track circuits. Some are fitted with a form of automatic coupling for shunting work. Most of the class has now been withdrawn, but some have been retained as shed shunters and as such are counted as departmental stock. For example, 0006 (2237), 0007 (2266) and 0030 (2285).

Bien que hors inventaire SNCF maintenant, ces petits locotracteurs sont toujours utilisés dans les dépôts et ateliers SNCF bien que interdit en ligne. Tous ont perdu leurs sigles et numéros SNCF et certains ont des nouveaux numéros. Par exemple, 0006 (2237), 0007 (2266) et 0030 (2285). Afin d'aider le lecteur, tous les Y 2200 encore en service sont listés ici.

Built/Construction: 1956–60.
Builder/Constructeur: Moyse (2201–49) Decauville (2250–2340).
Engine/Moteur: Poyaud 2BDT (44 kW) [* Agron (40 kW)].
Transmission: Mechanical/Mécanique.   **Weight/Masse:** 16 tonnes.
Max. T.E./E.T. max.:   kN.   **Length/Longeur:** 5.78 m.
Wheel Dia./Dia. des roues: 1050 mm.   **Max. Speed/Vitesse max.:** 50 km/h.
Livery/Livrée: V.

Y 2206	CY	Y 2243	CY	Y 2280	LG	Y 2310	LV	Y 2319	LM
Y 2208	CY	Y 2255	BZ	Y 2282	HE	Y 2311	CB	Y 2321	PV
Y 2215	CY	Y 2257	BZ	Y 2285	TA	Y 2314	AV	Y 2322	MZ
Y 2237	NV	Y 2260	CB	Y 2298	CB	Y 2315	MB	Y 2330	NB
Y 2240	DP	Y 2266	NV	Y 2301	MB	Y 2316	AV	Y 2336	AV
Y 2242	CB	Y 2267	BZ	Y 2306	SO	Y 2317	LV		

CLASS/**SERIE** Y 2400   B

Another small light duty shunter with almost all being used within depot and carriage siding limits.

Une autre série de petits locotracteurs. Comme les Y 2200, ils sortent rarement des dépôts et ateliers.

Built/Construction: 1962–69.
Builder/Constructeur: Decauville.   **Engine/Moteur:** Agron (45 kW).
Transmission: Mechanical/Mécanique.   **Weight/Masse:** 17 tonnes.
Max. T.E./E.T. max.:   kN.   **Length/Longeur:** 7.18 m.
Wheel Dia./Dia. des roues: 1050 mm.   **Max. Speed/Vitesse max.:** 50 km/h.
Livery/Livrée: V.

Y 2401	CA	Y 2426	CB	Y 2455	LV	Y 2482	TL	Y 2505	RS
Y 2403	TA	Y 2427	NV	Y 2456	MB	Y 2483	VG	Y 2506	VG
Y 2404	LG	Y 2428	DP	Y 2460	VG	Y 2485	HE	Y 2507	VG
Y 2405	TA	Y 2431	SO	Y 2465	DP	Y 2486	SO	Y 2508	TL
Y 2409	CY	Y 2435	NV	Y 2466	NV	Y 2487	SO	Y 2509	LV
Y 2410	CY	Y 2438	DP	Y 2467	CB	Y 2488	NV	Y 2510	LG
Y 2413	CB	Y 2439	BZ	Y 2468	BZ	Y 2490	RS	Y 2511	BZ
Y 2414	CB	Y 2440	LV	Y 2471	LV	Y 2492	AC	Y 2512	CB
Y 2415	DP	Y 2441	DP	Y 2473	LV	Y 2493	BD	Y 2513	LV
Y 2416	LG	Y 2444	AV	Y 2474	CB	Y 2496	SO	Y 2514	NV
Y 2417	BZ	Y 2447	MB	Y 2476	CB	Y 2499	LV	Y 2515	LV
Y 2418	LG	Y 2449	DP	Y 2477	NV	Y 2500	MB	Y 2516	CB
Y 2421	TL	Y 2450	LV	Y 2478	DP	Y 2501	MB	Y 2517	CB
Y 2424	BZ	Y 2452	AV	Y 2480	NV	Y 2502	TP	Y 2518	NV
Y 2425	BZ	Y 2453	AV	Y 2481	AC	Y 2504	BZ	Y 2519	CB

Y 6252. Villeneuve St. Georges depot./Dépôt de Villeneuve St. Georges. 14/09/89.

Eric Dunkling

Y 6317. Rennes depot./Dépôt de Rennes. 30/07/88.

Eric Dunkling

CLASS/SERIE Y 5100 B

Another small, light duty shunter virtually all being used as depot/workshops shunters. Being so small they can often fit on a turntable or traverser with a locomotive or carriage.

Encore une série de petits locotracteurs utilisés dans les dépôts et ateliers. Leur petite taile leur permet de se placer sur un pont tournant ou pont transbordeur avec une locomotive ou voiture.

Built/Construction: 1960–63.
Builder/Constructeur: De Dietrich.　　　　**Engine/Moteur:** Poyaud 4PYT (81 kW).
Transmission: Hydraulic/hydraulique.　　　**Weight/Masse:** 20 tonnes.
Max. T.E./E.T. max.:　　kN.　　　　　　　**Length/Longeur:** 7.18 m.
Wheel Dia./Dia. des roues: 1050 mm.　　　**Max. Speed/Vitesse max.:** 18 km/h.
Livery/Livrée: V.

Y 5101	LV	Y 5117	LN	Y 5133	MN	Y 5148	LE	Y 5201	AC
Y 5102	LM	Y 5118	LE	Y 5135	LE	Y 5149	NB	Y 5203	LN
Y 5103	LM	Y 5119	LN	Y 5136	TP	Y 5150	LM	Y 5204	TA
Y 5104	NB	Y 5120	NB	Y 5137	LG	Y 5151	VG	Y 5205	LG
Y 5105	AC	Y 5121	SO	Y 5138	LM	Y 5152	VG	Y 5207	LV
Y 5106	PO	Y 5122	AC	Y 5139	LM	Y 5154	LE	Y 5209	SB
Y 5107	LA	Y 5123	BD	Y 5140	VG	Y 5155	PV	Y 5210	SB
Y 5108	TL	Y 5124	LG	Y 5142	NV	Y 5156	LE	Y 5211	LN
Y 5109	PO	Y 5125	LA	Y 5143	PV	Y 5157	LN	Y 5212	LE
Y 5110	LG	Y 5126	TL	Y 5144	LE	Y 5159	TV	Y 5213	TP
Y 5111	BZ	Y 5127	PO	Y 5145	CY	Y 5160	NB	Y 5214	CY
Y 5113	LE	Y 5129	MZ	Y 5146	DP	Y 5162	PV	Y 5215	LE
Y 5116	NV	Y 5131	SB	Y 5147	LN				

CLASS/SERIE Y 6200 B

This is another class that can be considered to be in departmental use as most of them seem to be used on short ballast trains etc. The series now being withdrawn.

Beaucoup de cette série sont utilisée pour des trains de travaux sur les voies. Une série en cours d'amortissement.

Built/Construction: 1949–58.
Builders/Constructeurs: BDR (6201–26) St. Lilloise (6227–59) Moyse (6260–97).
Engine/Moteur: Poyaud 6PDT (132 kW).　　**Transmission:** Electric./électrique.
Weight/Masse: 30 tonnes.　　　　　　　　**Length/Longeur:** 8.90 m.
Wheel Dia./Dia. des roues: 1050 mm.　　　**Max. Speed/Vitesse max.:** 60 km/h.
Livery/Livrée: V.

Y 6201	MZ	Y 6229	PO	Y 6248	MB	Y 6270	TL	Y 6286	VG
Y 6205	MZ	Y 6230	LE	Y 6252	VG	Y 6271	TL	Y 6288	MZ
Y 6206	TL	Y 6244	VG	Y 6262	TL	Y 6276	TA	Y 6289	PV
Y 6213	DP	Y 6246	CY	Y 6267	MB	Y 6281	TP	Y 6293	LM
Y 6225	PV								

CLASSES/SERIES Y 6300 & Y 6400 B

These low powered shunters are found all over France on light shunting duties and works trains.

Ces locotracteurs de faible puissance sont utilisés partout en France sur des manoeuvres légères et des trains de travaux.

Built/Construction: 1949–58.
Builders/Constructeurs: BDR (6301–30), De Dietrich (6401–30, 6501–6625), Decauville (6431–6500).
Engine/Moteur: Poyaud 6PDT (132 kW).　　**Transmission:** Electric/électrique.
Weight/Masse: 30 tonnes.　　　　　　　　**Length/Longeur:** 8.90 m.
Wheel Dia./Dia. des roues: 1050 mm.　　　**Max. Speed/Vitesse max.:** 60 km/h.
Livery/Livrée: V.

Y 6569. Lens depot./Dépôt de Lens. 25/04/87. *Eric Dunkling*

Y 7114. Reims. Livery/livrée 'J'. 24/02/90. *Eric Dunkling*

CLASS/SERIE Y 6300

Y 6303 CB	Y 6308 NV	Y 6317 RS	Y 6321 MZ	Y 6329 SB
Y 6307 VG	Y 6312 LE	Y 6318 NB	Y 6323 MN	

CLASS/SERIE Y 6400

Y 6401 MZ	Y 6450 TL	Y 6489 AV	Y 6532 NB	Y 6581 PO
Y 6404 PV	Y 6454 SO	Y 6490 DP	Y 6533 CA	Y 6585 SO
Y 6408 PV	Y 6456 AC	Y 6493 DP	Y 6535 CA	Y 6591 LA
Y 6410 LE	Y 6457 RS	Y 6494 VG	Y 6536 TL	Y 6595 CA
Y 6411 CY	Y 6458 CA	Y 6495 CB	Y 6537 TP	Y 6600 LM
Y 6412 MZ	Y 6459 LM	Y 6497 CB	Y 6539 TL	Y 6601 LM
Y 6413 AC	Y 6460 CA	Y 6500 DP	Y 6547 LM	Y 6604 CA
Y 6414 NB	Y 6461 RS	Y 6501 MZ	Y 6553 MZ	Y 6605 RS
Y 6416 AC	Y 6463 AC	Y 6502 MN	Y 6554 BD	Y 6606 PV
Y 6419 BD	Y 6464 NB	Y 6507 LE	Y 6556 LE	Y 6607 PO
Y 6422 LV	Y 6467 CA	Y 6508 LE	Y 6561 PV	Y 6608 TP
Y 6426 VG	Y 6468 VG	Y 6509 LN	Y 6565 VG	Y 6609 LA
Y 6429 LV	Y 6472 MB	Y 6510 TV	Y 6566 MN	Y 6612 BD
Y 6430 LV	Y 6475 BZ	Y 6513 VG	Y 6567 PV	Y 6613 PO
Y 6431 MN	Y 6477 BZ	Y 6514 AV	Y 6569 LE	Y 6615 PO
Y 6432 MN	Y 6478 CY	Y 6517 MB	Y 6571 PV	Y 6616 VG
Y 6436 MZ	Y 6479 AV	Y 6520 MB	Y 6573 PV	Y 6617 LA
Y 6438 PO	Y 6482 LV	Y 6521 RS	Y 6574 CB	Y 6620 SO
Y 6440 TL	Y 6483 VG	Y 6522 SO	Y 6575 PV	Y 6621 RS
Y 6441 BD	Y 6487 LV	Y 6525 CA	Y 6576 PV	Y 6623 LE
Y 6444 TL	Y 6488 LV	Y 6531 SO	Y 6580 DP	Y 6625 NB
Y 6449 LA				

CLASS/SERIE Y 7100   B

The Y 6xxx series were built after World War Two and virtually continued pre-war designs. The Y 7100 series was a completely fresh design and featured hydraulic transmission. However this form of transmission was dropped for future classes after Y 7192 had been converted to mechanical transmission and renumbered Y 7001.

Bien que les Y 6xxx soient d'une conception d'avant-guerre, la série Y 7100 est un modèle complètement nouveau avec transmission hydraulique. Cependant, le Y 7192 (renuméroté Y 7001) a été doté d'une transmission mécanique, ce qui a été aussi adopté pour les Y 7400.

Built/Construction: 1958–62.
Builder/Constructeur: Billard (7101–7230), Decauville (7231–7310).
Engine/Moteur: Poyaud 6PYT (150 kW).   **Transmission:** Hydraulic/hydraulique.
Weight/Masse: 32 tonnes.
Max. T.E./E.T. max.: 73 kN.   **Length/Longeur:** 8.94 m.
Wheel Dia./Dia. des roues: 1050 mm.   **Max. Speed/Vitesse max.:** 54 km/h.
Livery/Livrée: V or/ou J.

Y 7101 MN	Y 7120 BZ	Y 7139 BZ	Y 7158 MZ	Y 7177 MB
Y 7102 MN	Y 7121 BZ	Y 7140 AV	Y 7159 NV	Y 7178 CA
Y 7103 MZ	Y 7122 LE	Y 7141 MB	Y 7160 TP	Y 7179 DP
Y 7104 MZ	Y 7123 LE	Y 7142 MB	Y 7161 LE	Y 7180 PO
Y 7105 BZ	Y 7124 LN	Y 7143 LG	Y 7162 AC	Y 7181 BZ
Y 7106 BZ	Y 7125 MZ	Y 7144 MZ	Y 7163 TP	Y 7182 MB
Y 7107 LE	Y 7126 LE	Y 7145 DP	Y 7164 BD	Y 7183 LG
Y 7108 MZ	Y 7127 LE	Y 7146 LE	Y 7165 AC	Y 7184 LE
Y 7109 SO	Y 7128 SO	Y 7147 LN	Y 7166 DP	Y 7185 AC
Y 7110 AC	Y 7129 AC	Y 7148 DP	Y 7167 LV	Y 7186 BD
Y 7111 MN	Y 7130 SO	Y 7149 SO	Y 7168 TP	Y 7187 LG
Y 7112 MZ	Y 7131 BZ	Y 7150 LN	Y 7169 HE	Y 7188 LE
Y 7113 MN	Y 7132 MZ	Y 7151 NV	Y 7170 CA	Y 7189 AC
Y 7114 MN	Y 7133 MZ	Y 7152 PV	Y 7171 HE	Y 7190 MN
Y 7115 MN	Y 7134 MZ	Y 7153 TP	Y 7172 MZ	Y 7191 LE
Y 7116 MN	Y 7135 MZ	Y 7154 TA	Y 7173 BZ	Y 7193 LN
Y 7117 MN	Y 7136 PV	Y 7155 LN	Y 7174 LE	Y 7194 MN
Y 7118 SO	Y 7137 MB	Y 7156 LV	Y 7175 BZ	Y 7195 MZ
Y 7119 MB	Y 7138 MB	Y 7157 BZ	Y 7176 BZ	Y 7196 MN

Y 7197	LV	Y 7220	LG	Y 7243	AV	Y 7266	TP	Y 7289	LV
Y 7198	LN	Y 7221	NV	Y 7244	AV	Y 7267	LG	Y 7290	MN
Y 7199	PV	Y 7222	NV	Y 7245	MZ	Y 7268	BZ	Y 7291	MN
Y 7200	MZ	Y 7223	NV	Y 7246	AV	Y 7269	AC	Y 7292	SO
Y 7201	MN	Y 7224	MZ	Y 7247	MZ	Y 7270	LV	Y 7293	AC
Y 7202	VG	Y 7225	LN	Y 7248	MN	Y 7271	PV	Y 7294	CA
Y 7203	SO	Y 7226	CA	Y 7249	VG	Y 7272	LE	Y 7295	AC
Y 7204	MN	Y 7227	AC	Y 7250	DP	Y 7273	VG	Y 7296	LE
Y 7205	MN	Y 7228	MB	Y 7251	LN	Y 7274	LN	Y 7297	LE
Y 7206	VG	Y 7229	AV	Y 7252	LE	Y 7275	MB	Y 7298	LN
Y 7207	LE	Y 7230	NV	Y 7253	LN	Y 7276	LV	Y 7299	LN
Y 7208	BZ	Y 7231	MN	Y 7254	NV	Y 7277	AV	Y 7300	VG
Y 7209	BZ	Y 7232	MZ	Y 7255	HE	Y 7278	LV	Y 7301	CB
Y 7210	LN	Y 7233	MZ	Y 7256	NV	Y 7279	CB	Y 7302	VG
Y 7211	PV	Y 7234	DP	Y 7257	TP	Y 7280	VG	Y 7303	AV
Y 7212	BD	Y 7235	LV	Y 7258	BZ	Y 7281	VG	Y 7304	MB
Y 7213	LG	Y 7236	LE	Y 7259	MB	Y 7282	SO	Y 7305	BZ
Y 7214	NV	Y 7237	LE	Y 7260	MB	Y 7283	LN	Y 7306	BZ
Y 7215	LV	Y 7238	LE	Y 7261	MB	Y 7284	PV	Y 7307	MB
Y 7216	LE	Y 7239	TA	Y 7262	MZ	Y 7285	LE	Y 7308	VG
Y 7217	LE	Y 7240	LG	Y 7263	MN	Y 7286	PV	Y 7309	DP
Y 7218	SO	Y 7241	HE	Y 7264	MZ	Y 7287	MB	Y 7310	VG
Y 7219	TP	Y 7242	BZ	Y 7265	BD	Y 7288	MB		

CLASS/SERIE Y 7400   B

After succesful trials the mechanical transmission applied to 7001 became standard and the production run lasted nearly 10 years. They are found all over the network on a variety of shunting and trip duties.The original green livery is now giving way to the yellow livery first applied to the Y 8000 series.

Après le succès de l'essai de transmission mécanique sur le Y 7001, ce type de transmission est devenu standard et la production des Y 7400 a continué pendent 10 ans. Comme les Y 7100, on trouve les Y 7400 partout en France sur des manoeuvres et des trains de service légers.

Built/Construction: 1959/1963–72.
Builder/Constructeur: Billard (7001), Decauville (7401–7520), De Dietrich (7521–7625), Moyse (7626–7888).
Engine/Moteur: Poyaud 6PYT (150 kW).   **Transmission:** Mechanical/Mécanique.
Weight/Masse: 32 tonnes.
Max. T.E./E.T. max.: 73 kN.   **Length/Longeur:** 8.94 m.
Wheel Dia./Dia. des roues: 1050 mm.   **Max. Speed/Vitesse max.:** 60 km/h.
Livery/Livrée: V or/ou J.

Y 7001	AC	Y 7421	NV	Y 7442	TP	Y 7463	LV	Y 7484	LE
Y 7401	PV	Y 7422	VG	Y 7443	BD	Y 7464	PV	Y 7485	BD
Y 7402	LN	Y 7423	LV	Y 7444	LE	Y 7465	CB	Y 7486	BD
Y 7403	PV	Y 7424	AV	Y 7445	LN	Y 7466	AV	Y 7487	NV
Y 7404	PV	Y 7425	MB	Y 7446	CB	Y 7467	PV	Y 7488	VG
Y 7405	PV	Y 7426	BZ	Y 7447	RS	Y 7468	RS	Y 7489	MB
Y 7406	LN	Y 7427	BZ	Y 7448	NB	Y 7469	VG	Y 7490	BZ
Y 7407	RS	Y 7428	AV	Y 7449	NB	Y 7470	AC	Y 7491	SB
Y 7408	LE	Y 7429	BZ	Y 7450	RS	Y 7471	PV	Y 7492	PV
Y 7409	RS	Y 7430	NV	Y 7451	LV	Y 7472	VG	Y 7493	PO
Y 7410	RS	Y 7431	MB	Y 7452	LV	Y 7473	LN	Y 7494	LN
Y 7411	AC	Y 7432	PV	Y 7453	LV	Y 7474	LN	Y 7495	BD
Y 7412	TP	Y 7433	VG	Y 7454	NV	Y 7475	LG	Y 7496	NV
Y 7413	BD	Y 7434	NV	Y 7455	LN	Y 7476	LG	Y 7497	DP
Y 7414	CB	Y 7435	DP	Y 7456	LN	Y 7477	NV	Y 7498	CB
Y 7415	NB	Y 7436	VG	Y 7457	AC	Y 7478	DP	Y 7499	MB
Y 7416	LV	Y 7437	PV	Y 7458	PV	Y 7479	BZ	Y 7500	LE
Y 7417	DP	Y 7438	PV	Y 7459	BZ	Y 7480	AV	Y 7501	LN
Y 7418	DP	Y 7439	LE	Y 7460	MB	Y 7481	RS	Y 7502	DP
Y 7419	VG	Y 7440	TP	Y 7461	LV	Y 7482	DP	Y 7503	CB
Y 7420	NV	Y 7441	TP	Y 7462	MB	Y 7483	LN	Y 7504	BZ

Y 7505	PV	Y 7570	NB	Y 7635	LE	Y 7700	PO	Y 7765	LV
Y 7506	VG	Y 7571	PV	Y 7636	LE	Y 7701	NB	Y 7766	NV
Y 7507	LE	Y 7572	VG	Y 7637	LN	Y 7702	RS	Y 7767	LG
Y 7508	BZ	Y 7573	LG	Y 7638	RS	Y 7703	CY	Y 7768	BD
Y 7509	LN	Y 7574	BD	Y 7639	AC	Y 7704	NV	Y 7769	LN
Y 7510	LN	Y 7575	CB	Y 7640	NV	Y 7705	RS	Y 7770	CY
Y 7511	LN	Y 7576	DP	Y 7641	VG	Y 7706	PO	Y 7771	NB
Y 7512	LV	Y 7577	CY	Y 7642	LV	Y 7707	SB	Y 7772	LE
Y 7513	AC	Y 7578	SB	Y 7643	NV	Y 7708	CY	Y 7773	DP
Y 7514	LN	Y 7579	SB	Y 7644	LV	Y 7709	CY	Y 7774	LE
Y 7515	LG	Y 7580	SB	Y 7645	BZ	Y 7710	BD	Y 7775	NB
Y 7516	AC	Y 7581	PV	Y 7646	NV	Y 7711	TL	Y 7776	NB
Y 7517	AC	Y 7582	CA	Y 7647	LG	Y 7712	LN	Y 7777	NB
Y 7518	SB	Y 7583	AC	Y 7648	TP	Y 7713	AC	Y 7778	LG
Y 7519	SO	Y 7584	CA	Y 7649	PO	Y 7714	BD	Y 7779	LG
Y 7520	SB	Y 7585	LN	Y 7650	PO	Y 7715	NB	Y 7780	TA
Y 7521	CY	Y 7586	LE	Y 7651	TP	Y 7716	LA	Y 7781	NV
Y 7522	CY	Y 7587	LE	Y 7652	CY	Y 7717	TP	Y 7782	DP
Y 7523	CY	Y 7588	LV	Y 7653	NB	Y 7718	TL	Y 7783	CB
Y 7524	CY	Y 7589	AV	Y 7654	LV	Y 7719	CB	Y 7784	AV
Y 7525	PV	Y 7590	BZ	Y 7655	LN	Y 7720	VG	Y 7785	LV
Y 7526	CB	Y 7591	CB	Y 7656	LN	Y 7721	VG	Y 7786	MB
Y 7527	TP	Y 7592	BD	Y 7657	PV	Y 7722	LV	Y 7787	LG
Y 7528	BD	Y 7593	LG	Y 7658	LE	Y 7723	BZ	Y 7788	PO
Y 7529	CB	Y 7594	TP	Y 7659	AC	Y 7724	AV	Y 7789	LG
Y 7530	VG	Y 7595	AC	Y 7660	AC	Y 7725	LG	Y 7790	TP
Y 7531	NV	Y 7596	DP	Y 7661	NB	Y 7726	BD	Y 7791	BD
Y 7532	SB	Y 7597	DP	Y 7662	DP	Y 7727	TL	Y 7792	TL
Y 7533	NV	Y 7598	CB	Y 7663	DP	Y 7728	BD	Y 7793	CY
Y 7534	SB	Y 7599	CY	Y 7664	NV	Y 7729	SB	Y 7794	CY
Y 7535	SB	Y 7600	SB	Y 7665	NV	Y 7730	CY	Y 7795	TP
Y 7536	SB	Y 7601	RS	Y 7666	BZ	Y 7731	LN	Y 7796	SB
Y 7537	SB	Y 7602	NB	Y 7667	MB	Y 7732	DP	Y 7797	SB
Y 7538	LE	Y 7603	RS	Y 7668	BZ	Y 7733	LN	Y 7798	SB
Y 7539	LN	Y 7604	LA	Y 7669	LN	Y 7734	RS	Y 7799	PV
Y 7540	RS	Y 7605	NB	Y 7670	PO	Y 7735	RS	Y 7800	LE
Y 7541	TP	Y 7606	LE	Y 7671	LA	Y 7736	TL	Y 7801	NB
Y 7542	CB	Y 7607	LN	Y 7672	BD	Y 7737	TL	Y 7802	TL
Y 7543	LV	Y 7608	LE	Y 7673	BD	Y 7738	TL	Y 7803	NB
Y 7544	MB	Y 7609	LV	Y 7674	PV	Y 7739	VG	Y 7804	BZ
Y 7545	BZ	Y 7610	LV	Y 7675	CY	Y 7740	CY	Y 7805	CB
Y 7546	CY	Y 7611	LN	Y 7676	AC	Y 7741	NV	Y 7806	NV
Y 7547	CY	Y 7612	BD	Y 7677	LN	Y 7742	BZ	Y 7807	PO
Y 7548	SB	Y 7613	BD	Y 7678	LN	Y 7743	AV	Y 7808	LA
Y 7549	PV	Y 7614	BD	Y 7679	LN	Y 7744	TL	Y 7809	NB
Y 7550	DP	Y 7615	BD	Y 7680	RS	Y 7745	LA	Y 7810	LG
Y 7551	TL	Y 7616	VG	Y 7681	NB	Y 7746	LA	Y 7811	SB
Y 7552	TP	Y 7617	VG	Y 7682	AC	Y 7747	BD	Y 7812	NB
Y 7553	CB	Y 7618	VG	Y 7683	BD	Y 7748	CY	Y 7813	NB
Y 7554	DP	Y 7619	NV	Y 7684	LG	Y 7749	SB	Y 7814	RS
Y 7555	MB	Y 7620	PV	Y 7685	TL	Y 7750	SO	Y 7815	CY
Y 7556	SB	Y 7621	CY	Y 7686	TP	Y 7751	LV	Y 7816	SB
Y 7557	SB	Y 7622	LE	Y 7687	BD	Y 7752	LN	Y 7817	CY
Y 7558	SB	Y 7623	CY	Y 7688	NV	Y 7753	LN	Y 7818	PV
Y 7559	SB	Y 7624	SB	Y 7689	LV	Y 7754	RS	Y 7819	LN
Y 7560	TL	Y 7625	BD	Y 7690	VG	Y 7755	NB	Y 7820	BZ
Y 7561	TL	Y 7626	LG	Y 7691	CB	Y 7756	NB	Y 7821	SB
Y 7562	VG	Y 7627	DP	Y 7692	MB	Y 7757	BD	Y 7822	RS
Y 7563	VG	Y 7628	PO	Y 7693	LV	Y 7758	PO	Y 7823	RS
Y 7564	SB	Y 7629	PO	Y 7694	BZ	Y 7759	PO	Y 7824	SO
Y 7565	SB	Y 7630	PO	Y 7695	LV	Y 7760	LV	Y 7825	HE
Y 7566	CY	Y 7631	BD	Y 7696	DP	Y 7761	VG	Y 7826	TP
Y 7567	CY	Y 7632	BD	Y 7697	TL	Y 7762	LV	Y 7827	BD
Y 7568	RS	Y 7633	CY	Y 7698	LG	Y 7763	MB	Y 7828	LN
Y 7569	NB	Y 7634	SB	Y 7699	LG	Y 7764	BZ	Y 7829	TL

Y 7001 (ex Y 7192). Achères depot./Dépôt d'Achères. 12/09/89. *Eric Dunkling*

Y 7627. Roche-Jean (between/entre Frasne and/et Vallorbe). 02/08/88. *G.B. Wise*

Y 7830	VG	Y 7842	TL	Y 7854	LN	Y 7866	NB	Y 7878	NV
Y 7831	NV	Y 7843	TL	Y 7855	CA	Y 7867	LG	Y 7879	RS
Y 7832	NV	Y 7844	PO	Y 7856	NB	Y 7868	PO	Y 7880	RS
Y 7833	DP	Y 7845	LG	Y 7857	NB	Y 7869	TP	Y 7881	LN
Y 7834	CY	Y 7846	BD	Y 7858	AC	Y 7870	CA	Y 7882	AC
Y 7835	CY	Y 7847	CB	Y 7859	CA	Y 7871	NB	Y 7883	DP
Y 7836	LE	Y 7848	DP	Y 7860	NV	Y 7872	RS	Y 7884	DP
Y 7837	DP	Y 7849	VG	Y 7861	CB	Y 7873	RS	Y 7885	LV
Y 7838	RS	Y 7850	VG	Y 7862	LV	Y 7874	SB	Y 7886	NV
Y 7839	CA	Y 7851	LV	Y 7863	RS	Y 7875	SB	Y 7887	CB
Y 7840	RS	Y 7852	CY	Y 7864	CA	Y 7876	SB	Y 7888	LV
Y 7841	RS	Y 7853	CY	Y 7865	SO	Y 7877	VG		

CLASS/**SERIE** Y 8000   B

This is the new standard hydraulic shunter in the new yellow livery. Being more powerful and with a higher speed than previous designs the class sees more main line use on trip workings and they are allocated to fewer depots. Those at AV are maintained by MB, those at CB by LV and those at VG by NV. Some are radio fitted for use in stations. Y 8300 was tested with remote control as a prototype for the Y 8400 series.

Le nouveau locotracteur standard de la SNCF. Les Y 8000 furent les premières machines à sortir dans la livrée jaune, maintenant adoptée pour toutes les machines de manoeuvres. Avec plus de puissance que les anciennes séries, les Y 8000 sont utilisées plus souvent pour des trains de marchandises locaux. Leur entretien est concentré sur un nombre restraint de dépôts – MB fournit les Y 8000 pour AV. LV pour CB et NV pour VG, par exemple. Beaucoup sont équipés de la radio. Le Y 8300 fut testé avec la télécommande comme prototype des Y 8400.

Built/Construction: 1977–90.
Builder/Constructeur: Moyse/Fauvet Girel.
Engine/Moteur: Poyaud V12-520NS [Renault MIDRO63540*, Unidiesel UDL6R3†] (219 kW).
Transmission: Hydraulic/hydraulique. Voith.   **Weight/Masse:** 36 tonnes.
Max. T.E./E.T. max.: 118/62 kN.   **Length/Longeur:** 10.14 m.
Wheel Dia./Dia. des roues: 1050 mm.   **Max. Speed/Vitesse max.:** 30/60 km/h.
Livery/Livrée: J.

Y 8001	TP	Y 8031	RS	Y 8061	MB	Y 8091	LN	Y 8121	NB
Y 8002	MZ	Y 8032	NB	Y 8062	BZ	Y 8092	CY	Y 8122	AC
Y 8003	CY	Y 8033	RS	Y 8063	MB	Y 8093	SO	Y 8123	MZ
Y 8004	MZ	Y 8034	NV	Y 8064	DP	Y 8094	CB	Y 8124	MZ
Y 8005	CY	Y 8035	NV	Y 8065	MB	Y 8095	NV	Y 8125	CY
Y 8006	SB	Y 8036	CB	Y 8066	LN	Y 8096	DP	Y 8126	PV
Y 8007	MZ	Y 8037	CB	Y 8067	TP	Y 8097	NB	Y 8127	PV
Y 8008	MZ	Y 8038	PV	Y 8068	TP	Y 8098	NB	Y 8128	PV
Y 8009	MZ	Y 8039	SO	Y 8069	TP	Y 8099	NB	Y 8129	PV
Y 8010	MZ	Y 8040	NB	Y 8070	LE	Y 8100	NB	Y 8130	LG
Y 8011	MZ	Y 8041	NB	Y 8071	LN	Y 8101	NB	Y 8131	TP
Y 8012	MZ	Y 8042	MB	Y 8072	BD	Y 8102	AC	Y 8132	TP
Y 8013	MZ	Y 8043	MB	Y 8073	BD	Y 8103	BZ	Y 8133	TP
Y 8014	SB	Y 8044	MB	Y 8074	LE	Y 8104	MB	Y 8134	CY
Y 8015	MZ	Y 8045	BZ	Y 8075	LE	Y 8105	BZ	Y 8135	PV
Y 8016	MB	Y 8046	DP	Y 8076	TP	Y 8106	DP	Y 8136	MZ
Y 8017	MB	Y 8047	DP	Y 8077	TP	Y 8107	RS	Y 8137	MZ
Y 8018	MB	Y 8048	NB	Y 8078	BD	Y 8108	MZ	Y 8138	LE
Y 8019	MB	Y 8049	TL	Y 8079	LN	Y 8109	CY	Y 8139	CB
Y 8020	TP	Y 8050	TL	Y 8080	BD	Y 8110	MZ	Y 8140	NB
Y 8021	DP	Y 8051	SO	Y 8081	TP	Y 8111	TL	Y 8141	NV
Y 8022	DP	Y 8052	DP	Y 8082	LN	Y 8112	SB	Y 8142	LV
Y 8023	RS	Y 8053	DP	Y 8083	LN	Y 8113	LV	Y 8143	RS
Y 8024	SO	Y 8054	LV	Y 8084	TL	Y 8114	CB	Y 8144	SO
Y 8025	NB	Y 8055	LV	Y 8085	TL	Y 8115	PV	Y 8145	SB
Y 8026	BZ	Y 8056	PV	Y 8086	LN	Y 8116	SB	Y 8146	AC
Y 8027	DP	Y 8057	MZ	Y 8087	LE	Y 8117	SB	Y 8147	MB
Y 8028	LV	Y 8058	RS	Y 8088	LE	Y 8118	MZ	Y 8148	BZ
Y 8029	LV	Y 8059	SO	Y 8089	LG	Y 8119	DP	Y 8149	PV
Y 8030	RS	Y 8060	SO	Y 8090	LG	Y 8120	CB	Y 8150	PV

Y 8151	PV	Y 8196	BD	Y 8241	LN	Y 8286	LE	Y 8331	LE
Y 8152	MZ	Y 8197	TL	Y 8242	LN	Y 8287	TL	Y 8332	CY
Y 8153	PV	Y 8198	LG	Y 8243	LE	Y 8288	LG	Y 8333	TP
Y 8154	BD	Y 8199	TP	Y 8244	CY	Y 8289	LG	Y 8334	PV
Y 8155	CY	Y 8200	LE	Y 8245	RS	Y 8290	LE	Y 8335	PV
Y 8156	LG	Y 8201	PV	Y 8246	NB	Y 8291	NV	Y 8336	PV
Y 8157	LG	Y 8202	PV	Y 8247	SO	Y 8292	LG	Y 8337	NV
Y 8158	TP	Y 8203	SO	Y 8248	RS	Y 8293	CB	Y 8338	MB
Y 8159	TP	Y 8204	NB	Y 8249	RS	Y 8294	LV	Y 8339	LV
Y 8160	RS	Y 8205	SO	Y 8250	SO	Y 8295	MB	Y 8340	MZ
Y 8161	NB	Y 8206	NV	Y 8251	RS	Y 8296	TP	Y 8341	CB
Y 8162	SO	Y 8207	NV	Y 8252	AC	Y 8297	SB	Y 8342	BD
Y 8163	AC	Y 8208	NV	Y 8253	SO	Y 8298	LG	Y 8343	TP
Y 8164	SO	Y 8209	CB	Y 8254	AC	Y 8299	NV	Y 8344	NV
Y 8165	SO	Y 8210	MB	Y 8255	SO	Y 8300	LN	Y 8345	LE
Y 8166	TL	Y 8211	CY	Y 8256	CB	Y 8301	CB	Y 8346	MZ
Y 8167	BD	Y 8212	SB	Y 8257	DP	Y 8302	MB	Y 8347	CB
Y 8168	TL	Y 8213	SB	Y 8258	CB	Y 8303	LV	Y 8348	NV
Y 8169	LE	Y 8214	MZ	Y 8259	BD	Y 8304	BD	Y 8349	NV
Y 8170	SB	Y 8215	MZ	Y 8260	NV	Y 8305	LE	Y 8350	NV
Y 8171	RS	Y 8216	SB	Y 8261	LE	Y 8306	AC	Y 8351	NV
Y 8172	MB	Y 8217	TP	Y 8262	LE	Y 8307	AC	Y 8352	NV
Y 8173	MB	Y 8218	TP	Y 8263	TP	Y 8308	AC	Y 8353	NV
Y 8174	BZ	Y 8219	BD	Y 8264	LG	Y 8309	AC	Y 8354	NV
Y 8175	SB	Y 8220	TL	Y 8265	BD	Y 8310	AC	Y 8355	NV
Y 8176	LV	Y 8221	PV	Y 8266	LE	Y 8311	LG	Y 8356	NV
Y 8177	NV	Y 8222	LE	Y 8267	LE	Y 8312	TL	Y 8357	NV
Y 8178	MB	Y 8223	LN	Y 8268	LN	Y 8313	TP	Y 8358	TL
Y 8179	MB	Y 8224	LN	Y 8269	TP	Y 8314	TP	Y 8359	TP
Y 8180	DP	Y 8225	SO	Y 8270	LG	Y 8315	TP	Y 8360	LN
Y 8181	CY	Y 8226	NB	Y 8271	TL	Y 8316	TP	Y 8361	TP
Y 8182	CY	Y 8227	RS	Y 8272	LG	Y 8317	RS	Y 8362	BD
Y 8183	PV	Y 8228	NB	Y 8273	NV	Y 8318	TP	Y 8363	LV
Y 8184	SB	Y 8229	AC	Y 8274	NV	Y 8319	AC	Y 8364	LV
Y 8185	SB	Y 8230	AC	Y 8275	PV	Y 8320	TP	Y 8365	LV
Y 8186	CY	Y 8231	MB	Y 8276	PV	Y 8321	RS	Y 8366	LV
Y 8187	AC	Y 8232	CB	Y 8277	CY	Y 8322	MZ	Y 8367	LV
Y 8188	PV	Y 8233	BZ	Y 8278	LE	Y 8323	LE	Y 8368	BD
Y 8189	BD	Y 8234	MB	Y 8279	LE	Y 8324	CB	Y 8369	LE
Y 8190	TP	Y 8235	NV	Y 8280	LE	Y 8325	LG	Y 8370	AC
Y 8191	TP	Y 8236	NV	Y 8281	LE	Y 8326	PV	Y 8371	CB
Y 8192	TL	Y 8237	BZ	Y 8282	PV	Y 8327	MZ	Y 8372	CB
Y 8193	LG	Y 8238	AC	Y 8283	BZ	Y 8328	LN	Y 8373	BD
Y 8194	BD	Y 8239	MB	Y 8284	BZ	Y 8329	BZ	Y 8374	LE
Y 8195	BD	Y 8240	CB	Y 8285	NB	Y 8330	MZ	Y 8375	BZ

CLASS/SERIE Y 8400 B

After testing remote control on No. Y 8300, the SNCF decided to follow the DB and go for radio control on its new small shunters thus allowing the duties of driver and shunter to be combined. The loco can either be controlled from a portable radio, or from the cab. Externally the locos are similar to Class Y 8000, but there is an illuminated "TELE" sign at cab roof level and there are marker lights at the four corners to indicate to staff that remote control is in operation.

Après des essais sur le Y 8300, la SNCF a décidé d'équiper ses nouveaux locotracteurs de la télécommande comme au Deutsche Bundesbahn. Cette mesure permet le travail du conducteur et de l'agent de manoeuvre d'être intégré. Les Y 8400 peuvent être contrôlés d'un poste de radio portable ou de la cabine. Les Y 8400 sont identiques aux Y 8000 mais sont équipées d'un panneau lumineux sur lequel est marqué «TELE» et des feux aux quatres extrémités de la machine. Tous s'allument pendant la télécommande pour mettre en garde le personnel.

Details as Y 8000 except/details comme pour Y 8000 sauf:

Built/Construction: 1990–. **Builder/Constructeur:** Fauvet Girel.

Y 8401	AC	Y 8419	BZ	Y 8437	DP	Y 8455	DP	Y 8473
Y 8402	PV	Y 8420	LE	Y 8438	SO	Y 8456	AC	Y 8474
Y 8403	AC	Y 8421	LE	Y 8439	SO	Y 8457	DP	Y 8475
Y 8404	PV	Y 8422	LE	Y 8440	MB	Y 8458	DP	Y 8476
Y 8405	AC	Y 8423	PV	Y 8441	MB	Y 8459	AC	Y 8477
Y 8406	AC	Y 8424	PV	Y 8442	MB	Y 8460	MB	Y 8478
Y 8407	PV	Y 8425	PV	Y 8443	MB	Y 8461		Y 8479
Y 8408	PV	Y 8426	LE	Y 8444	BZ	Y 8462		Y 8480
Y 8409	AC	Y 8427	LE	Y 8445	BZ	Y 8463		Y 8481
Y 8410	PV	Y 8428	LE	Y 8446	BZ	Y 8464		Y 8482
Y 8411	AC	Y 8429	MB	Y 8447	PV	Y 8465		Y 8483
Y 8412	PV	Y 8430	MB	Y 8448	MB	Y 8466		Y 8484
Y 8413	AC	Y 8431	MB	Y 8449	CB	Y 8467		Y 8485
Y 8414	LE	Y 8432	SO	Y 8450	SO	Y 8468		Y 8486
Y 8415	LE	Y 8433	BZ	Y 8451	DP	Y 8469		Y 8487
Y 8416	LE	Y 8434	BZ	Y 8452	DP	Y 8470		Y 8488
Y 8417	SO	Y 8435	BZ	Y 8453	BD	Y 8471		Y 8489
Y 8418	MB	Y 8436	AC	Y 8454	DP	Y 8472		Y 8490

CLASS/SERIE Y BL   B

These are two small tractors for which details are not available which work at the bogie changing shed at Hendaye. BL 160 is standard gauge and BL 161 is broad gauge. It is possible that they may be withdrawn and replaced by Y 2282.

Ces deux locotracteurs, qui sont hors inventaire SNCF, sont utilisés sur le chantier de changement de bogies de Hendaye. Ils sont si petits qu'ils peuvent retirer ou placer une bogie sous une voiture surélevée. BL 160 est à voie normale et BL 161 à voie large (RENFE). Il est possible qu'ils soient radiés et remplacés par le Y 2282.

Transmission: Hydrostatic/hydrostatique

Y BL 160	HEN	Y BL 161	HEN

Y 8021. Besançon depot./Dépôt de Besançon. 25/02/90.   *Eric Dunkling*

ELECTRIC MULTIPLE UNITS
AUTOMOTRICES ELECTRIQUE

CLASS/SERIE Z 5100

These 3-car stainless steel units used to work suburban trains out of Paris Montparnasse and Lyon stations, but delivery of new stock to the Paris area has seen the class moving out to the provinces.

Z 5100F (f) are modified Z 5100 for working on the last remenant of the once extensive third rail network in Paris. Reduced to 2-car units and pantographs removed, they operate the service from Puteaux to Issy-Plaine. Despite operating on lower power they are still more powerful than the units they replaced. (Z 1500s from 1931). Puteaux–Issy Plaine will be converted to a tramway in 1995.

Ces éléments de 3 voitures en inox furent introduits sur les services de banlieue de Paris Lyon et Montparnasse, mais avec la livraisons de matériels plus modernes, plusieurs Z 5100 ont migrées vers la province.
Les Z 5100F (indiquées avec un f comme frotteurs) ont été modifiées pour l'utilisation sur le dernier vestige du réseau à troisième rail à l'ouest de Paris. A cause de cela, elles ont perdu leur remorque centrale et reçu des frotteurs au lieu du pantographe. Leur fief, la ligne Puteaux–Issy Plaine, va être transformée en tramway d'ici 1995.

System/Système: 1500 V d.c./continu.
Built/Construction: 1954–57.
Builder-Mech. Parts/Constructeur-Partie mécanique: Carel & Fouché.
Builder-Elec. Parts/Constructeur-Partie électrique: MTE.
Formation: ZBD + ZRB + ZRABx. Non-gangwayed.
Wheel Arrangement/Disposition des Essieux: BoBo + 22 + 22.
Accommodation/Places: –/60 1T + –/86 1T + 24/46 1T.
Traction Motors/Moteurs de traction: 4 x 225 kW.
Weight/Masse: 57 + 34 + 36 tonnes.
Length/Longeur: 22.85 + 22.40 + 22.85 m.
Max. Speed/Vitesse max.: 120 km/h.
Livery/Livrée: Stainless steel/Acier inoxydible.

Z 5101	25101	15101	TP	Z 5135	25135	15135	TP
Z 5102	25102	15102	VG	Z 5136	25136	15136	MR
Z 5104	25104	15104	TP	Z 5137	25137	15137	TP
Z 5105	25105	15105	MR	Z 5138	25138	15138	TP
Z 5106	25183	15106	TP	Z 5140	25140	15140	VG
Z 5108	25108	15108	TP	Z 5141	25141	15141	TP
Z 5109	25109	15109	VG	Z 5143	25143	15143	TP
Z 5110	25110	15110	TP	Z 5145	25145	15145	VG
Z 5111	25111	15111	MR	Z 5146	25146	15146	TP
Z 5112	25112	15112	TP	Z 5147	25147	15147	VG
Z 5113	25113	15113	TP	Z 5148	25148	15148	TP
Z 5114	25114	15114	TP	Z 5149	25149	15149	TP
Z 5115	25115	15115	VG	Z 5150	25184	15144	TP
Z 5116	25116	15116	TP	Z 5151	25151	15151	VG
Z 5117	25117	15117	TP	Z 5152	25152	15152	MR
Z 5119	25119	15119	TP	Z 5153	25153	15153	VG
Z 5120	25120	15120	TP	Z 5154	25154	15154	VG
Z 5121	25121	15121	VG	Z 5155	25155	15155	MR
Z 5125	25125	15125	TP	Z 5156	25156	15156	MR
Z 5126	25126	15126	VG	Z 5157	25157	15157	MR
Z 5127	25127	15127	TP	Z 5158	25158	15158	MR
Z 5128	25128	15128	TP	Z 5159	25159	15159	MR
Z 5129	25177	15129	TP	Z 5160	25160	15160	MR
Z 5130	25130	15130	TP	Z 5161	25161	15161	MR
Z 5131	25131	15131	VG	Z 5162	25162	15162	MR
Z 5132	25132	15132	MR	Z 5163	25163	15163	MR
Z 5133	25133	15133	VG	Z 5164	25164	15164	MR
Z 5134	25134	15134	TP	Z 5165	25165	15165	MR

Z 5166	25166	15166	MR		Z 5175	25175	15175	MR
Z 5167	25167	15167	MR		Z 5176		15176	f PS
Z 5168	25168	15168	MR		Z 5177		15177	f PS
Z 5169	25169	15169	MR		Z 5178		15178	f PS
Z 5170	25170	15170	MR		Z 5180		15180	f PS
Z 5171	25171	15171	MR		Z 5181		15181	f PS
Z 5173	25173	15173	MR		Z 5182		15182	f PS
Z 5174	25174	15174	TP					

Spare trailers/Réserve:

Z 25122	TP	Z 25179	MR	Z 25181	MR	Z 25184	MR	Z 25186	MR
Z 25144	MR	Z 25180	MR	Z 25182	MR	Z 25185	MR	Z 25187	MR
Z 25178	MR							

CLASS/SERIE Z 5300

With suburban traffic increasing these 4-car units were delivered and again features stainless steel bodywork. For years they have worked out of Paris Austerlitz and Lyon stations on suburban trains but the development of the Paris RER services and the introduction of double-deck EMUs has seen more congregating on Paris Lyon services allowing Z 5100s to be released to other areas. There has also been a knock on effect to BB 8500 which have been transferred away from Villeneuve. In connection with RER duties, all PA-allocated units are fitted with headcode panels.

Avec l'augmentation du trafic à Paris, la SNCF commande des rames à quatre caisses, encore en inox. Depuis longtemps les Z 6300 ont exploité des services à partir de Paris Lyon et Austerlitz. L'introduction d'automotrices à deux niveaux aur la ligne C du RER a permis le transfert d'un grand nombre aux lignes de Paris Lyon, qui à son tour a libéré des Z 5100. Les Z 5300 des Ardoines sont toutes équipées de panneaux lumineux RER.

System/Système: 1500 V d.c./continu.
Built/Construction: 1965–75.
Builders/Constructeurs: Carel & Fouché/MTE/TCO.
Formation: ZBD + ZRB + ZRB + ZRABx.
Wheel Arrangement/Disposition des Essieux: BoBo + 22 + 22 + 22.
Accommodation/Places: –/87 1T + –/112 + –/106 1T + 44/40.
Traction Motors/Moteurs de traction: 4 x 245 kW.
Weight/Masse: 62 + 30 + 30 + 42 tonnes.
Length/Longeur: 25.925 (25.80*) + 25.60 (25.85*) + 25.60 (25.85*) + 25.925 (25.80*) m.
Max. Speed/Vitesse max.: 120 km/h.
Livery/Livrée: Stainless steel/Acier inoxydible.

Z 5301–5361 are non-gangwayed. Z 5362–5445 have gangways for staff use only.
5301–61 n'ont pas de portes d'intercirculation. Z 5362–5445 a des portes d'intercirculation seulement pour des cheminots.

Z 5301	25302	25301	15301	*VG	Z 5322	25344	25343	15322	*VG
Z 5302	25304	25303	15302	*VG	Z 5323	25346	25345	15323	*VG
Z 5303	25306	25305	15303	*VG	Z 5324	25348	25347	15324	*VG
Z 5304	25308	25307	15304	*VG	Z 5325	25350	25349	15325	*VG
Z 5305	25310	25309	15305	*VG	Z 5326	25352	25351	15326	*VG
Z 5306	25312	25311	15306	*VG	Z 5327	25354	25353	15327	*VG
Z 5307	25314	25313	15307	*VG	Z 5328	25356	25355	15328	*VG
Z 5308	25316	25315	15308	*VG	Z 5329	25358	25357	15329	*VG
Z 5309	25318	25317	15309	*VG	Z 5330	25360	25359	15330	*VG
Z 5310	25320	25319	15310	*VG	Z 5331	25362	25361	15331	*VG
Z 5311	25322	25321	15311	*VG	Z 5332	25364	25363	15332	*VG
Z 5312	25324	25323	15312	*VG	Z 5333	25366	25415	15333	*VG
Z 5313	25326	25325	15313	*VG	Z 5334	25368	25367	15334	*VG
Z 5314	25328	25327	15314	*VG	Z 5335	25370	25369	15335	*VG
Z 5315	25330	25329	15315	*VG	Z 5336	25372	25371	15336	*VG
Z 5316	25332	25591	15316	VG	Z 5337	25374	25373	15337	*VG
Z 5317	25334	25333	15317	*VG	Z 5338	25376	25375	15338	*VG
Z 5318	25336	25335	15318	*VG	Z 5339	25378	25377	15339	VG
Z 5319	25338	25337	15319	*VG	Z 5340	25380	25379	15340	*VG
Z 5320	25340	25339	15320	*VG	Z 5341	25382	25381	15341	*VG
Z 5321	25342	25341	15321	*VG	Z 5342	25384	25383	15342	*VG

Z 5360. Paris Austerlitz. 23/02/85.   *Eric Dunkling*
Z 5613. Villeneuve St. Georges. 23/02/85.   *Eric Dunkling*

Z 5343	25386	25385	15343	* VG
Z 5344	25388	25387	15344	* VG
Z 5345	25390	25389	15345	* VG
Z 5346	25392	25391	15346	* VG
Z 5347	25394	25393	15347	* VG
Z 5348	25396	25395	15348	* VG
Z 5349	25398	25397	15349	* VG
Z 5350	25400	25399	15350	* VG
Z 5351	25402	25401	15351	* VG
Z 5352	25404	25403	15352	* VG
Z 5353	25406	25405	15353	* VG
Z 5354	25408	25407	15354	* VG
Z 5355	25410	25409	15355	* VG
Z 5356	25412	25411	15356	* VG
Z 5357	25414	25413	15357	* VG
Z 5358	25416	25415	15358	* VG
Z 5359	25592	25593	15359	* VG
Z 5360	25594	25595	15360	* VG
Z 5361	25596	25597	15361	* VG
Z 5362	25424	25423	15362	VG
Z 5363	25426	25425	15363	VG
Z 5364	25428	25427	15364	VG
Z 5365	25430	25429	15365	VG
Z 5366	25432	25331	15366	VG
Z 5367	25434	25433	15367	VG
Z 5368	25436	25435	15368	VG
Z 5369	25438	25437	15369	VG
Z 5370	25440	25439	15370	VG
Z 5371	25442	25441	15371	VG
Z 5372	25444	25443	15372	VG
Z 5373	25446	25445	15373	PA
Z 5374	25448	25447	15374	PA
Z 5375	25450	25449	15375	PA
Z 5376	25452	25451	15376	PA
Z 5377	25454	25453	15377	PA
Z 5378	25456	25455	15378	PA
Z 5379	25458	25457	15379	PA
Z 5380	25460	25459	15380	PA
Z 5381	25462	25461	15381	PA
Z 5382	25464	25463	15382	PA
Z 5383	25466	25465	15383	PA
Z 5384	25468	25467	15384	PA
Z 5385	25470	25469	15385	PA
Z 5386	25472	25471	15386	PA
Z 5387	25474	25473	15387	PA
Z 5388	25476	25475	15388	PA
Z 5389	25478	25477	15389	PA
Z 5390	25480	25479	15390	PA
Z 5391	25482	25481	15391	PA
Z 5392	25484	25483	15392	PA
Z 5393	25486	25485	15393	PA
Z 5394	25488	25487	15394	PA
Z 5395	25490	25489	15395	PA
Z 5396	25492	25491	15396	PA
Z 5397	25494	25493	15397	PA
Z 5398	25496	25495	15398	PA
Z 5399	25498	25497	15399	PA
Z 5400	25500	25499	15400	PA
Z 5401	25502	25501	15401	PA
Z 5402	25504	25503	15402	PA
Z 5403	25506	25505	15403	PA
Z 5404	25508	25507	15404	PA
Z 5405	25510	25509	15405	PA
Z 5406	25512	25511	15406	PA
Z 5407	25514	25513	15407	PA
Z 5408	25516	25515	15408	PA
Z 5409	25518	25517	15409	PA
Z 5410	25520	25519	15410	PA
Z 5411	25522	25521	15411	PA
Z 5412	25416	25523	15412	PA
Z 5413	25526	25525	15413	PA
Z 5414	25528	25527	15414	PA
Z 5415	25530	25529	15415	PA
Z 5416	25532	25531	15416	PA
Z 5417	25534	25533	15417	PA
Z 5418	25536	25535	15418	PA
Z 5419	25538	25537	15419	PA
Z 5420	25540	25539	15420	PA
Z 5421	25542	25541	15421	PA
Z 5422	25544	25543	15422	PA
Z 5423	25546	25545	15423	PA
Z 5424	25548	25547	15424	PA
Z 5425	25550	25549	15425	PA
Z 5426	25552	25551	15426	VG
Z 5427	25554	25553	15427	PA
Z 5428	25556	25555	15428	PA
Z 5429	25558	25557	15429	PA
Z 5430	25560	25559	15430	PA
Z 5431	25562	25561	15431	PA
Z 5432	25564	25563	15432	PA
Z 5433	25566	25565	15433	PA
Z 5434	25568	25567	15434	PA
Z 5435	25570	25569	15435	PA
Z 5436	25572	25571	15436	PA
Z 5437	25574	25573	15437	PA
Z 5438	25576	25575	15438	PA
Z 5439	25578	25577	15439	PA
Z 5440	25580	25579	15440	PA
Z 5441	25582	25581	15441	PA
Z 5442	25584	25583	15442	PA
Z 5443	25586	25585	15443	PA
Z 5444	25588	25587	15444	PA
Z 5445	25590	25589	15445	PA

Name/Nom: 5395 ISSY-LES-MOLINEAUX

CLASS/SERIE Z 5600

These units followed Z 8100 in breaking away from the stainless steel bodywork. This class of double-deck EMUs (Z2N) is operating between Paris Lyon and Melun and on RER line C. VG units are made up into 5 car sets. These sets carry a plate on the side giving the set number (eg Z 01 being 5601/2) and is often also shown in the headcode panel on stabled units. The sets run as pairs of power cars with loose (or at any rate non-sequential) trailers in between. The trailers are common with the trailers of the new dual-voltage Z 8800 class.

Cette série d'automotrices à deux niveaux (Z2N) est utilisée sur Paris Lyon–Melun et sur la ligne C du RER. Les rames de VG ont 5 remorques et portent une plaque avec la numéro de la rame (par example Z O1 = 5601/2) qui est aussi affiché sur le panneau lumineux quand la rame est garée. Bien que le jumelage des motrices soit consécutif, l'affectation des remorques est complètement aléatoire. Ces remorques sont partagées entre les Z 5600 et les Z 8800.

System/Système: 1500 V d.c./continu.
Built/Construction: 1983–85.
Builder-Mech. Parts/Constructeur-Partie mécanique: ANF/CIMT.
Builder-Elec. Parts/Constructeur-Partie électrique: Alsthom/TCO.
Formation: ZB + ZRB + (+ZRB) + ZRAB + ZB.
Traction Motors/Moteurs de traction: 4 x 350 kW per power car/par motrice.
Max. Speed/Vitesse max.: 140 km/h.
Livery/Livrée: P.

Some VG units have VDUs in the cabs which display the view along the platform at certain stations for one-man operation.
Certaines rames de VG ont des moniteurs vidéos en cabine pour l'exploitation à agent seul.

Power Car Sets/Rames motrice. Accommodation/Places –/115. 25.10 m. 66 tonnes. BoBo + BoBo.

Z 5601	VG	Z 5637	PO	Z 5671	PO
Z 5603	VG	Z 5639	PO	Z 5673	PO
Z 5605	VG	Z 5641	PO	Z 5675	PO
Z 5607	VG	Z 5643	PO	Z 5677	PO
Z 5609	VG	Z 5645	PO	Z 5679	PO
Z 5611	VG	Z 5647	PO	Z 5681	PO
Z 5613	VG	Z 5649	PO	Z 5683	PO
Z 5615	VG	Z 5651	PO	Z 5685	PO
Z 5617	VG	Z 5653	PO	Z 5687	PO
Z 5619	VG	Z 5655	PO	Z 5689	PO
Z 5621	VG	Z 5657	PO	Z 5691	PO
Z 5623	VG	Z 5659	PO	Z 5693	PO
Z 5625	VG	Z 5661	PO	Z 5695	PO
Z 5627	VG	Z 5663	PO	Z 5697	PO
Z 5629	VG	Z 5665	PO	Z 5699	PO
Z 5631	VG	Z 5667	PO	Z 5701	PO
Z 5633	PO	Z 5669	PO	Z 5703	PO
Z 5635	PO				

Names/Noms:

Z 5601/5602	SAVIGNY-LE-TEMPLE	Z 5697/5698	BRÉTIGNY-SUR-ORGE
Z 5633/5634	ATHIS-MONS	Z 5699/5700	ÉTAMPES
Z 5635/5636	VIROFLAY		

Trailer Seconds/Remorques B. Accommodation/Places –/168. 24.28 m. 42 tonnes.

ZR 25601	ZR 25624	ZR 25647	ZR 25670	ZR 25693
ZR 25602	ZR 25625	ZR 25648	ZR 25671	ZR 25694
ZR 25603	ZR 25626	ZR 25649	ZR 25672	ZR 25695
ZR 25604	ZR 25627	ZR 25650	ZR 25673	ZR 25696
ZR 25605	ZR 25628	ZR 25651	ZR 25674	ZR 25697
ZR 25606	ZR 25629	ZR 25652	ZR 25675	ZR 25698
ZR 25607	ZR 25630	ZR 25653	ZR 25676	ZR 25699
ZR 25608	ZR 25631	ZR 25654	ZR 25677	ZR 25700
ZR 25609	ZR 25632	ZR 25655	ZR 25678	ZR 25701
ZR 25610	ZR 25633	ZR 25656	ZR 25679	ZR 25702
ZR 25611	ZR 25634	ZR 25657	ZR 25680	ZR 25703
ZR 25612	ZR 25635	ZR 25658	ZR 25681	ZR 25704
ZR 25613	ZR 25636	ZR 25659	ZR 25682	ZR 25705
ZR 25614	ZR 25637	ZR 25660	ZR 25683	ZR 25706
ZR 25615	ZR 25638	ZR 25661	ZR 25684	ZR 25707
ZR 25616	ZR 25639	ZR 25662	ZR 25685	ZR 25708
ZR 25617	ZR 25640	ZR 25663	ZR 25686	ZR 25709
ZR 25618	ZR 25641	ZR 25664	ZR 25687	ZR 25710
ZR 25619	ZR 25642	ZR 25665	ZR 25688	ZR 25711
ZR 25620	ZR 25643	ZR 25666	ZR 25689	ZR 25712
ZR 25621	ZR 25644	ZR 25667	ZR 25690	ZR 25713
ZR 25622	ZR 25645	ZR 25668	ZR 25691	ZR 25714
ZR 25623	ZR 25646	ZR 25669	ZR 25692	ZR 25715

ZR 25716	ZR 25717	

Trailer Composites/Remorques AB. Accommodation/Places 70/82. 24.28 m. 42 tonnes.

ZR 35601	ZR 35621	ZR 35641	ZR 35661	ZR 35681
ZR 35602	ZR 35622	ZR 35642	ZR 35662	ZR 35682
ZR 35603	ZR 35623	ZR 35643	ZR 35663	ZR 35683
ZR 35604	ZR 35624	ZR 35644	ZR 35664	ZR 35684
ZR 35605	ZR 35625	ZR 35645	ZR 35665	ZR 35685
ZR 35606	ZR 35626	ZR 35646	ZR 35666	ZR 35686
ZR 35607	ZR 35627	ZR 35647	ZR 35667	ZR 35687
ZR 35608	ZR 35628	ZR 35648	ZR 35668	ZR 35688
ZR 35609	ZR 35629	ZR 35649	ZR 35669	ZR 35689
ZR 35610	ZR 35630	ZR 35650	ZR 35670	ZR 35690
ZR 35611	ZR 35631	ZR 35651	ZR 35671	ZR 35691
ZR 35612	ZR 35632	ZR 35652	ZR 35672	ZR 35692
ZR 35613	ZR 35633	ZR 35653	ZR 35673	ZR 35693
ZR 35614	ZR 35634	ZR 35654	ZR 35674	ZR 35694
ZR 35615	ZR 35635	ZR 35655	ZR 35675	ZR 35695
ZR 35616	ZR 35636	ZR 35656	ZR 35676	ZR 35696
ZR 35617	ZR 35637	ZR 35657	ZR 35677	ZR 35697
ZR 35618	ZR 35638	ZR 35658	ZR 35678	ZR 35698
ZR 35619	ZR 35639	ZR 35659	ZR 35679	ZR 35699
ZR 35620	ZR 35640	ZR 35660	ZR 35680	ZR 35700

CLASSES/SERIES Z 6000 & Z 6100

The Z 6000 series were prototypes for the Z 6100s. Like the early dc units these are finished off in stainless steel. They operate suburban services out of Paris Nord as far north as Amiens. The last three digits of the running number also appear on cabsides and in cab windows as set numbers. Z 6124 is withdrawn whilst Z 6168/9 have been sold to Luxembourg where they operate as CFL 262/1 respectively. These units have a monomotor bogie, which is the same type as on Class BB 67000/67300 up to Z 6120. From Z 6121, the bogie is similar to those on Class BB 67400.

Les Z 6000 furent les prototypes pour les Z 6100 et comme les Z 6100, elles furent construites en acier inox. Les Z 6100 exploitent des services de banlieue de Paris Nord jusqu'à Amiens. Les trois derniers chiffres du numéro sont marqués dans et sur la côté de la cabine. La 6124 fut radiée tandis que les Z 6168/9 ont été vendues au chemins de fer luxembourgeois où elles portent les numéros 262/1. Ces automotrices ont une bogie monomoteur. Celle-ci est proche à la bogie du type BB 67000 pour les 6006 à 6120 et à celle des BB 67400 pour les 6121–84.

System/Système: 25 kV a.c./monophasé.
Built/Construction: 1960–61*/1965–71.
Builder-Mech. Parts/Constructeur-Partie mécanique: Carel & Fouché/Schneider/De Dietrich.
Builder-Elec. Parts/Constructeur-Partie électrique: CEM/Siemens/Alsthom.
Formation: ZBD + ZRB + ZRABx.
Wheel Arrangement/Disposition des Essieux: 2B + 22 + 22.
Accommodation/Places: –/86 1T + –/107 1T + 36/51 1T.
Traction Motor/Moteur de traction: 690 kW.
Weight/Masse: 51 + 28 + 28 tonnes.
Length/Longeur: 25.50 + 23.80 + 25.15 m.
Max. Speed/Vitesse max.: 120 km/h.
Livery/Livrée: Stainless steel/Acier inoxydible.

Z 6006	26006	16006	* PJ		Z 6108	26108	16108	PJ
Z 6007	26007	16007	* PJ		Z 6109	26109	16109	PJ
Z 6008	26008	16008	* PJ		Z 6110	26110	16110	PJ
Z 6009	26009	16009	* PJ		Z 6111	26111	16111	PJ
Z 6101	26101	16101	PJ		Z 6112	26112	16112	PJ
Z 6102	26102	16102	PJ		Z 6113	26113	16113	PJ
Z 6103	26103	16103	PJ		Z 6114	26114	16114	PJ
Z 6104	26104	16104	PJ		Z 6115	26115	16115	PJ
Z 6105	26105	16105	PJ		Z 6116	26116	16116	PJ
Z 6106	26106	16106	PJ		Z 6117	26117	16117	PJ
Z 6107	26107	16107	PJ		Z 6118	26118	16118	PJ

Z 6119	26119	16119	PJ	Z 6152	26152	16152	PJ
Z 6120	26120	16120	PJ	Z 6153	26153	16153	PJ
Z 6121	26121	16121	PJ	Z 6154	26154	16154	PJ
Z 6122	26122	16122	PJ	Z 6155	26155	16155	PJ
Z 6123	26123	16123	PJ	Z 6156	26156	16156	PJ
Z 6125	26125	16125	PJ	Z 6157	26157	16157	PJ
Z 6126	26126	16126	PJ	Z 6158	26158	16158	PJ
Z 6127	26127	16127	PJ	Z 6159	26159	16159	PJ
Z 6128	26128	16128	PJ	Z 6160	26160	16160	PJ
Z 6129	26129	16129	PJ	Z 6161	26161	16161	PJ
Z 6130	26130	16130	PJ	Z 6162	26162	16162	PJ
Z 6131	26131	16131	PJ	Z 6163	26163	16163	PJ
Z 6132	26132	16132	PJ	Z 6164	26164	16164	PJ
Z 6133	26133	16133	PJ	Z 6165	26165	16165	PJ
Z 6134	26134	16134	PJ	Z 6166	26166	16166	PJ
Z 6135	26135	16135	PJ	Z 6167	26167	16167	PJ
Z 6136	26136	16136	PJ	Z 6170	26170	16170	PJ
Z 6137	26137	16137	PJ	Z 6171	26171	16171	PJ
Z 6138	26138	16138	PJ	Z 6172	26172	16172	PJ
Z 6139	26139	16139	PJ	Z 6173	26173	16173	PJ
Z 6140	26140	16140	PJ	Z 6174	26174	16174	PJ
Z 6141	26141	16141	PJ	Z 6175	26175	16175	PJ
Z 6142	26142	16142	PJ	Z 6176	26176	16176	PJ
Z 6143	26143	16143	PJ	Z 6177	26177	16177	PJ
Z 6144	26144	16144	PJ	Z 6178	26178	16178	PJ
Z 6145	26145	16145	PJ	Z 6179	26179	16179	PJ
Z 6146	26146	16146	PJ	Z 6180	26180	16180	PJ
Z 6147	26147	16147	PJ	Z 6181	26181	16181	PJ
Z 6148	26148	16148	PJ	Z 6182	26182	16182	PJ
Z 6149	26149	16149	PJ	Z 6183	26183	16183	PJ
Z 6150	26150	16150	PJ	Z 6184	26184	16184	PJ
Z 6151	26151	16151	PJ				

CLASS/SERIE Z 6300

These units operate services out of Paris St. Lazare. Based on Z 6100 they are in fact shorter as several St. Lazare routes have tight curves. These routes also have low platforms and the steps on the EMUs are adjustable according to the type of platform. Those units allocated to Thionville and Longueau are recent transfers and have taken over workings previously covered by DMUs under the catenary. These units also have a monomotor bogie, which is the same type as on Class BB 67000/67300.

Cette série est basée sur les Z 6100 mais les caisses sont plus courtes pour tenir compte des courbes plus prononcées sur les lignes à partir de St. Lazare pour lesquelles elles furent commandées. Les lignes exploitées ont des gares à quais bas alors les X 6300 ont des marchepieds qui changent de hauteur. Récemment, quelques rames ont été mutées à Thionville et Longueau où elles ont replacé des autorails utilisés sous caténaires, surtout autour de Metz et entre Amiens et Rouen. Les X 6300 ont une bogie monomoteur proche à celle des BB 67000.

System/Système: 25 kV a.c./monophasé.
Built/Construction: 1967–70.
Builder-Mech. Parts/Constructeur-Partie mécanique: Carel & Fouché/Fives-Lille/De Dietrich.
Builder-Elec. Parts/Constructeur-Partie électrique: CEM/Siemens/Alsthom.
Formation: ZBD + ZRAB + ZRBx. Non-gangwayed/Pas de portes d'intercirculation.
Wheel Arrangement/Disposition des Essieux: 2B + 22 + 22.
Accommodation/Places: –/39 1T + 40/21 1T + –/67 1T.
Traction Motor/Moteur de traction: 615 kW.
Weight/Masse: 52 + 26 + 28 tonnes.
Length/Longeur: 20.75 + 18.825 + 20.525 m.
Max. Speed/Vitesse max.: 120 km/h.
Livery/Livrée: Stainless steel/Acier inoxydible.

Z 6301	26301	16301	TV	Z 6304	26304	16304	TV
Z 6302	26302	16302	PS	Z 6305	26305	16305	TV
Z 6303	26303	16303	TV	Z 6306	26306	16306	TV

Z 6307	26307	16307	PS		Z 6322	26322	16322	PS
Z 6308	26308	16308	LN		Z 6323	26323	16323	PS
Z 6309	26309	16309	TV		Z 6324	26324	16324	PS
Z 6310	26310	16310	LN		Z 6325	26325	16325	PS
Z 6311	26311	16311	PS		Z 6326	26326	16326	PS
Z 6312	26312	16312	LN		Z 6327	26327	16327	PS
Z 6313	26313	16313	TV		Z 6328	26328	16328	LN
Z 6314	26314	16314	PS		Z 6329	26329	16329	PS
Z 6315	26315	16315	TV		Z 6330	26330	16330	LN
Z 6316	26316	16316	LN		Z 6331	26331	16331	TV
Z 6317	26317	16317	PS		Z 6332	26332	16332	LN
Z 6318	26318	16318	PS		Z 6333	26333	16333	LN
Z 6319	26319	16319	PS		Z 6334	26334	16334	LN
Z 6320	26320	16320	TV		Z 6335	26335	16335	LN
Z 6321	26321	16321	PS					

CLASS/SERIE Z 6400

This was the last type of EMU to feature stainless steel bodywork. Introduced for services out of Paris St. Lazare some operated out of Paris Nord for a while. Part of the fleet has high platform steps for use on the "Group II" lines out if Paris St. Lazare (i.e. the lines to Versailles and Marly), whereas the rest has steps fitted for low platforms to serve the "Group III" line to Poissy. The last three digits of the power car number appear in the cab window.

Ces automotrices ont été les dernières à être construites en acier inox. A l'origine elles furent utilisées sur Paris Nord–Roissy mais elles sont maintenant concentrées sur St. Lazare. Les premières rames ont des marchepieds bas pour les quais bas du «Groupe III» – la ligne de Poissy, tandis que les autres ont des marchepieds hauts pour la «Groupe II» – St. Lazare–Versailles et Marly. Les trois derniers chiffres du numéro sont marqués dans la cabine de conduite.

System/Système: 25 kV a.c./monophasé.
Built/Construction: 1976–79.
Builder-Mech. Parts/Constructeur-Partie mécanique: Carel & Fouché.
Builder-Elec. Parts/Constructeur-Partie électrique: Alsthom/Oerlikon.
Formation: ZAD + ZRB + ZRB + ZBD.
Wheel Arrangement/Disposition des Essieux: BoBo + 22 + 22 + BoBo.
Accommodation/Places: 72/– + –/102 + –/102 + –/84.
Traction Motors/Moteurs de traction: 4 x 295 kW per power car.
. Weight/Masse: 64 + 32 + 32 + 63 tonnes.
Length/Longeur: 22.70 + 22.39 + 22.39 + 22.70 m.
Max. Speed/Vitesse max.: 120 km/h.
Livery/Livrée: Stainless steel with blue around the windows/Livrée: Acier inoxydable avec une bande bleue.

h Fixed steps for high platform use only./Marchepieds fixes pour quais hauts.

Z 6401	26401	26402	6402	PS		Z 6435	26435	26436	6436	PS
Z 6403	26403	26404	6404	PS		Z 6437	26437	26438	6438	PS
Z 6405	26405	26406	6406	PS		Z 6439	26439	26440	6440	PS
Z 6407	26407	26408	6408	PS		Z 6441	26441	26442	6442	h PS
Z 6409	26409	26410	6410	PS		Z 6443	26443	26444	6444	h PS
Z 6411	26411	26412	6412	PS		Z 6445	26445	26446	6446	h PS
Z 6413	26413	26414	6414	PS		Z 6447	26447	26448	6448	h PS
Z 6415	26415	26416	6416	PS		Z 6449	26449	26450	6450	h PS
Z 6417	26417	26418	6418	PS		Z 6451	26451	26452	6452	h PS
Z 6419	26419	26420	6420	PS		Z 6453	26453	26454	6454	h PS
Z 6421	26421	26422	6422	PS		Z 6455	26455	26456	6456	h PS
Z 6423	26423	26424	6424	PS		Z 6457	26457	26458	6458	h PS
Z 6425	26425	26426	6426	PS		Z 6459	26459	26460	6460	h PS
Z 6427	26427	26428	6428	PS		Z 6461	26461	26462	6462	h PS
Z 6429	26429	26430	6430	PS		Z 6463	26463	26464	6464	h PS
Z 6431	26431	26432	6432	PS		Z 6465	26465	26466	6466	h PS
Z 6433	26433	26434	6434	PS		Z 6467	26467	26468	6468	h PS

Z 6469	26469	26470	6470	h PS		Z 6511	26511	26512	6512	h PS
Z 6471	26471	26472	6472	h PS		Z 6513	26513	26514	6514	h PS
Z 6473	26473	26474	6474	h PS		Z 6515	26515	26516	6516	h PS
Z 6475	26475	26476	6476	h PS		Z 6517	26517	26518	6518	h PS
Z 6477	26477	26478	6478	h PS		Z 6519	26519	26520	6520	h PS
Z 6479	26479	26480	6480	h PS		Z 6521	26521	26522	6522	h PS
Z 6481	26481	26482	6482	h PS		Z 6523	26523	26524	6524	h PS
Z 6483	26483	26484	6484	h PS		Z 6525	26525	26526	6526	PS
Z 6485	26485	26486	6486	h PS		Z 6527	26527	26528	6528	PS
Z 6487	26487	26488	6488	h PS		Z 6529	26529	26530	6530	PS
Z 6489	26489	26490	6490	h PS		Z 6531	26531	26532	6532	PS
Z 6491	26491	26492	6492	h PS		Z 6533	26533	26534	6534	PS
Z 6493	26493	26494	6494	h PS		Z 6535	26535	26536	6536	PS
Z 6495	26495	26496	6496	h PS		Z 6537	26537	26538	6538	PS
Z 6497	26497	26498	6498	h PS		Z 6539	26539	26540	6540	PS
Z 6499	26499	26500	6500	h PS		Z 6541	26541	26542	6542	PS
Z 6501	26501	26502	6502	h PS		Z 6543	26543	26544	6544	PS
Z 6503	26503	26504	6504	h PS		Z 6545	26545	26546	6546	PS
Z 6505	26505	26506	6506	h PS		Z 6547	26547	26548	6548	PS
Z 6507	26507	26508	6508	h PS		Z 6549	26549	26550	6550	PS
Z 6509	26509	26510	6510	h PS						

Names/Noms:

Z 6447/6448	CHAVILLE		Z 6505/6506	VAUCRESSON
Z 6449/6450	COURBEVOIE		Z 6519/6520	LA CELLE-SAINT CLOUD
Z 6457/6458	LOUVECIENNES		Z 6523/6524	MARLY-LE-ROI
Z 6485/6486	GARCHES		Z 6549/6550	LA GARENNE-COLOMBES

CLASS/SERIE Z 7100

This class carried on the diesel tradition of single power cars hauling loose trailers. They have now all been refurbished and formed into fixed two or four car formations. The trailer cars gained the number appropriate to the power car of the set which they happened to be in at the time of refurbishing. This was not necessarily their original number in the same series!

A l'origine, les Z 7100 étaient des motrices attachées à un nombre variable de remorques. Elles ont toutes été modernisées récemment avec des formations fixes de deux ou quatre voitures. Dès leur modernisation, les remorques ont été renumérotées et ont pris les derniers deux chiffres de la motrice.

System/Système: 1500 V d.c./continu.
Built/Construction: 1960–62.
Builder-Mech. Parts/Constructeur-Partie mécanique: Decauville/De Dietrich.
Builder-Elec. Parts/Constructeur-Partie électrique: Oerlikon.
Formation: ZABD (+ ZRAB + ZRB) + ZRBDx. Non-gangwayed/Pas de portes d'intercirculation.
Wheel Arrangement/Disposition des Essieux: 2Bo (+ 22 + 22) + 22.
Accommodation/Places: 12/46 1T (+ 12/62 1T + –/78 1T) + –/65 1T.
Traction Motors/Moteurs de traction: 2 x 470 kW.
Weight/Masse: 56 + 26 + 26 + 27 tonnes.
Length/Longueur: 26.13 (+ 22.68 + 22.68) + 22.68 mm.
Max. Speed/Vitesse max.: 130 km/h.
Livery/Livrée: M.

* Rheostatic braking.
* Equipées du freinage rhéostatique.

Z 7101	27201	27101	17101	VE		Z 7111	27211	27111	17111	VE
Z 7102	27202	27102	17102	VE		Z 7112	27212	27112	17112	VE
Z 7103	27203	27103	17103	VE		Z 7113	27213	27113	17113	VE
Z 7104	27204	27104	17104	VE		Z 7114	27214	27114	17114	VE
Z 7105	27205	27105	17105	VE		Z 7116	27216	27116	17116	VE
Z 7106	27206	27106	17106	VE		Z 7117	27217	27117	17117	VE
Z 7107	27207	27107	17107	VE		Z 7118	27218	27118	17118	VE
Z 7108	27208	27108	17108	VE		Z 7119	27219	27119	17119	VE
Z 7109	27209	27109	17109	VE		Z 7120	27220	27120	17120	VE
Z 7110	27210	27110	17110	VE		Z 7121			17121	* AV

Z 7122	17122	* AV		Z 7128	17128	* AV
Z 7123	17123	* AV		Z 7129	17129	* AV
Z 7124	17124	* AV		Z 7130	17130	* AV
Z 7125	17125	* AV		Z 7131	17131	* AV
Z 7126	17126	* AV		Z 7132	17132	* AV
Z 7127	17127	* AV		Z 7133	17133	* AV

CLASS/SERIE Z 7300

The first of a new generation of EMUs not intended for Paris suburban work and known as Z2 type. (Z1 being Z 7100). Those at Bordeaux have replaced old PO/Midi units on stopping services along the Paris–Bordeaux–Hendaye main line. Facing seats.

La première série d'une nouvelle génération d'automotrices doubles, connues sous le nom Z2, pour les services régionaux. Beaucoup remplacement les très anciennes automotrices du PO/Midi. Sièges en vis-à-vis.

System/Système: 1500 V d.c./continu.   **Built/Construction:** 1980–85.
Builder/Constructeur: Alsthom/Francorail-MTE.
Wheel Arrangement/Disposition des Essieux: BoBo + 22.
Traction Motors/Moteurs de traction: 4 x 305 kW.
Formation: ZABP + ZRBx.   **Accommodation/Places:** 24/43 1T + –/84 1T.
Weight/Masse: 64 + 40 tonnes.   **Length/Longeur:** 25.10 + 25.10 m.
Max. Speed/Vitesse max.: 160 km/h.

Z 7301	17301	Z	BD		Z 7327	17327	R	BD	Z 7353	17353	Z	TP
Z 7302	17302	Z	BD		Z 7328	17328	R	BD	Z 7354	17354	Z	TP
Z 7303	17303	Z	BD		Z 7329	17329	R	BD	Z 7355	17355	B	TP
Z 7304	17304	Z	BD		Z 7330	17330	R	BD	Z 7356	17356	Z	TP
Z 7305	17305	Z	BD		Z 7331	17331	R	BD	Z 7357	17357	Y	MB
Z 7306	17306	Z	BD		Z 7332	17332	R	BD	Z 7358	17358	Z	TP
Z 7307	17307	Z	BD		Z 7333	17333	R	BD	Z 7359	17359	Z	TP
Z 7308	17308	Z	BD		Z 7334	17334	R	BD	Z 7360	17360	Z	TP
Z 7309	17309	Z	BD		Z 7335	17335	R	BD	Z 7361	17361	Z	TP
Z 7310	17310	Z	BD		Z 7336	17336	R	BD	Z 7362	17362	Z	TP
Z 7311	17311	Z	BD		Z 7337	17337	R	BD	Z 7363	17363	B	TP
Z 7312	17312	Z	BD		Z 7338	17338	R	BD	Z 7364	17364	Y	MB
Z 7313	17313	Z	BD		Z 7339	17339	R	BD	Z 7365	17365	Y	MB
Z 7314	17314	Z	BD		Z 7340	17340	R	BD	Z 7366	17366	Y	MB
Z 7315	17315	R	BD		Z 7341	17341	R	BD	Z 7367	17367	Y	MB
Z 7316	17316	R	BD		Z 7342	17342	R	BD	Z 7368	17368	B	MB
Z 7317	17317	R	BD		Z 7343	17343	R	BD	Z 7369	17369	Y	MB
Z 7318	17318	R	BD		Z 7344	17344	R	BD	Z 7370	17370	Y	MB
Z 7319	17319	R	BD		Z 7345	17345	R	BD	Z 7371	17371	Y	MB
Z 7320	17320	R	BD		Z 7346	17346	R	BD	Z 7372	17372	Y	MB
Z 7321	17321	R	BD		Z 7347	17347	R	BD	Z 7373	17373	Z	TP
Z 7322	17322	R	BD		Z 7348	17348	Z	TP	Z 97381	917381	B	BD
Z 7323	17323	R	BD		Z 7349	17349	Z	TP	Z 97382	917382	B	BD
Z 7324	17324	R	BD		Z 7350	17350	Z	TP	Z 97383	917383	Y	MB
Z 7325	17325	R	BD		Z 7351	17351	Z	TP	Z 97384	917384	Y	MB
Z 7326	17326	R	BD		Z 7352	17352	Z	TP				

Names/Noms:

Z 7314	SOULAC-SUR-MER		Z 97381	MIDI-PYRENÉES
Z 7321	LESPARRE-MEDOC		Z 97382	MIDI-PYRENÉES
Z 7339	PESSAC		Z 97383	LANGUEDOC-ROUSILLON
Z 7346	MARMANDE		Z 97384	LANGUEDOC-ROUSILLON
Z 7370	MONTEUX			

CLASS/SERIE Z 7500

This class is similar to Z 7300 but has more first class and unidirectional seating.

Cette série est similaire aux Z 7300 mais a plus de places en première et des places unidirectionelles en deuxième.

System/Système: 1500 V d.c./continu.

Built/Construction: 1982–83. **Builder/Constructeur:** Alsthom/Francorail-MTE.
Wheel Arrangement/Disposition des Essieux: BoBo + 22.
Traction Motors/Moteurs de traction: 4 x 305 kW.
Formation: ZABD + ZRBx. **Accommodation/Places:** 32/35 1T + –/84 1T.
Weight/Masse: 64 + 40 tonnes. **Length/Longeur:** 25.10 + 25.10 m.
Max. Speed/Vitesse max.: 160 km/h.

Z 7501	17501	**Z**	MB		Z 7506	17506	**Z**	MB		Z 7511	17511	**Z**	MB
Z 7502	17502	**Z**	MB		Z 7507	17507	**Z**	MB		Z 7512	17512	**Z**	MB
Z 7503	17503	**Z**	MB		Z 7508	17508	**Z**	MB		Z 7513	17513	**Z**	MB
Z 7504	17504	**Z**	MB		Z 7509	17509	**Z**	MB		Z 7514	17514	**Z**	MB
Z 7505	17505	**Z**	MB		Z 7510	17510	**Z**	MB		Z 7515	17515	**Z**	MB

Names/Noms:

Z 7502	CHATEAUNEUF DU PAPE	Z 7515	ORANGE
Z 7513	BARBENTANE		

CLASS/SERIE Z 8100

This Paris area suburban stock is known as MI 79 *(Matériel Interconnection 79)* stock and broke away from tradition by not using stainless steel bodywork. They are dual-voltage units for working over RER line B which incorporates SNCF lines to Roissy and Mitry Claye. The units are owned by SNCF or RATP and are shown as allocated to La Chapelle or RER respectively. All maintenance is carried out by RATP. The units carry cabside markings to show whether they are RATP or SNCF. The "first class seating" is identical to the second class! The units are made from aluminium alloy extrusions and have adjustable steps as the platforms on RER line B are at different levels on the RER and SNCF parts of the line.

Les Z 8100 sont connues sous le nom MI79 – Matériel Interconnexion 1979 – car elles sont des rames bi-courant pour la ligne B du RER qui fut créer par l'interconnexion des lignes Paris Nord–Aulnay de la SNCF (25 kV) et Luxembourg–St Rémy–Les Chevreuse de la RATP (1500 V). Les rames ont des sigles SNCF ou RATP près de la cabine pour montrer leurs propriètaires. Celles de la SNCF sont nominalement affectées à La Chapelle mais toute la série est entretenue à Massy par la RATP. Les places «première classe» sont identiques à celles de deuxième. Les rames sont construites en aluminium et ont des marchepieds qui changent de hauteur pour les quais SNCF et RATP.

Systems/Systèmes: 1500 V d.c./continu/25 kV a.c./monophasé.
Built/Construction: 1980–84.
Builder-Mech. Parts/Constructeur-Partie mécanique: Alsthom/Soc. Franco-Belge, ANF.
Builder-Elec. Parts/Constructeur-Partie électrique: Alsthom/TCO.
Formation: ZBD + ZRB + ZRAB + ZBD.
Wheel Arrangement/Disposition des Essieux: BoBo + 22 + 22 + BoBo.
Accommodation/Places: –/72 + –/84 + 32/52 + –/72.
Traction Motors/Moteurs de traction: 4 x 350 kW per power car/par motrice.
Weight/Masse: 56 + 48 + 48 + 56 tonnes.
Length/Longeur: 26.08 + 26.00 + 26.00 + 26.08 m.
Max. Speed/Vitesse max.: 140 km/h.
Livery/Livrée: P.

Z 8101	28101	28102	8102	MY		Z 8135	28135	28136	8136	PL
Z 8103	28103	28104	8104	PL		Z 8137	28137	28138	8138	MY
Z 8105	28105	28106	8106	MY		Z 8139	28139	28140	8140	PL
Z 8107	28107	28108	8108	MY		Z 8141	28141	28142	8142	PL
Z 8109	28109	28110	8110	MY		Z 8143	28143	28144	8144	PL
Z 8111	28111	28112	8112	MY		Z 8145	28145	28146	8146	MY
Z 8113	28113	28114	8114	MY		Z 8147	28147	28148	8148	PL
Z 8115	28115	28116	8116	MY		Z 8149	28149	28150	8150	PL
Z 8117	28117	28118	8118	MY		Z 8151	28151	28152	8152	PL
Z 8119	28119	28120	8120	MY		Z 8153	28153	28154	8154	MY
Z 8121	28121	28122	8122	PL		Z 8155	28155	28156	8156	PL
Z 8123	28123	28124	8124	MY		Z 8157	28157	28158	8158	PL
Z 8125	28125	28126	8126	PL		Z 8159	28159	28160	8160	PL
Z 8127	28127	28128	8128	PL		Z 8161	28161	28162	8162	MY
Z 8129	28129	28130	8130	MY		Z 8163	28163	28164	8164	PL
Z 8131	28131	28132	8132	PL		Z 8165	28165	28166	8166	PL
Z 8133	28133	28134	8134	PL		Z 8167	28167	28168	8168	PL

Z 8169	28169	28170	8170	MY	Z 8299	28299	28300	8300	MY
Z 8171	28171	28172	8172	PL	Z 8301	28301	28302	8302	MY
Z 8173	28173	28174	8174	PL	Z 8303	28303	28304	8304	MY
Z 8175	28175	28176	8176	PL	Z 8305	28305	28306	8306	MY
Z 8177	28177	28178	8178	MY	Z 8307	28307	28308	8308	MY
Z 8179	28179	28180	8180	PL	Z 8309	28309	28310	8310	MY
Z 8181	28181	28182	8182	PL	Z 8311	28311	28312	8312	MY
Z 8183	28183	28184	8184	PL	Z 8313	28313	28314	8314	MY
Z 8185	28185	28186	8186	PL	Z 8315	28315	28316	8316	MY
Z 8187	28187	28188	8188	MY	Z 8317	28317	28318	8318	MY
Z 8189	28189	28190	8190	PL	Z 8319	28319	28320	8320	MY
Z 8191	28191	28192	8192	PL	Z 8321	28321	28322	8322	MY
Z 8193	28193	28194	8194	MY	Z 8323	28323	28324	8324	MY
Z 8195	28195	28196	8196	MY	Z 8325	28325	28326	8326	MY
Z 8197	28197	28198	8198	PL	Z 8327	28327	28328	8328	MY
Z 8199	28199	28200	8200	PL	Z 8329	28329	28330	8330	MY
Z 8201	28201	28202	8202	MY	Z 8331	28331	28332	8332	MY
Z 8203	28203	28204	8204	MY	Z 8333	28333	28334	8334	MY
Z 8205	28205	28206	8206	PL	Z 8335	28335	28336	8336	MY
Z 8207	28207	28208	8208	PL	Z 8337	28337	28338	8338	MY
Z 8209	28209	28210	8210	MY	Z 8339	28339	28340	8340	MY
Z 8211	28211	28212	8212	MY	Z 8341	28341	28342	8342	MY
Z 8213	28213	28214	8214	PL	Z 8343	28343	28344	8344	MY
Z 8215	28215	28216	8216	PL	Z 8345	28345	28346	8346	MY
Z 8217	28217	28218	8218	MY	Z 8347	28347	28348	8348	MY
Z 8219	28219	28220	8220	MY	Z 8349	28349	28350	8350	MY
Z 8221	28221	28222	8222	PL	Z 8351	28351	28352	8352	MY
Z 8223	28223	28224	8224	PL	Z 8353	28353	28354	8354	MY
Z 8225	28225	28226	8226	MY	Z 8355	28355	28356	8356	MY
Z 8227	28227	28228	8228	MY	Z 8357	28357	28358	8358	MY
Z 8229	28229	28230	8230	PL	Z 8359	28359	28360	8360	MY
Z 8231	28231	28232	8232	PL	Z 8361	28361	28362	8362	MY
Z 8233	28233	28234	8234	MY	Z 8363	28363	28364	8364	MY
Z 8235	28235	28236	8236	MY	Z 8365	28365	28366	8366	MY
Z 8237	28237	28238	8238	PL	Z 8367	28367	28368	8368	MY
Z 8239	28239	28240	8240	PL	Z 8369	28369	28370	8370	MY
Z 8241	28241	28242	8242	MY	Z 8371	28371	28372	8372	MY
Z 8243	28243	28244	8244	PL	Z 8373	28373	28374	8374	MY
Z 8245	28245	28246	8246	PL	Z 8375	28375	28376	8376	MY
Z 8247	28247	28248	8248	PL	Z 8377	28377	28378	8378	MY
Z 8249	28249	28250	8250	PL	Z 8379	28379	28380	8380	MY
Z 8251	28251	28252	8252	PL	Z 8381	28381	28382	8382	MY
Z 8253	28253	28254	8254	PL	Z 8383	28383	28384	8384	MY
Z 8255	28255	28256	8256	PL	Z 8385	28385	28386	8386	MY
Z 8257	28257	28258	8258	PL	Z 8387	28387	28388	8388	MY
Z 8259	28259	28260	8260	PL	Z 8389	28389	28390	8390	MY
Z 8261	28261	28262	8262	PL	Z 8391	28391	28392	8392	MY
Z 8263	28263	28264	8264	PL	Z 8393	28393	28394	8394	MY
Z 8265	28265	28266	8266	MY	Z 8395	28395	28396	8396	MY
Z 8267	28267	28268	8268	MY	Z 8397	28397	28398	8398	MY
Z 8269	28269	28270	8270	MY	Z 8399	28399	28400	8400	MY
Z 8271	28271	28272	8272	MY	Z 8401	28401	28402	8402	MY
Z 8273	28273	28274	8274	MY	Z 8403	28403	28404	8404	MY
Z 8275	28275	28276	8276	MY	Z 8405	28405	28406	8406	MY
Z 8277	28277	28278	8278	MY	Z 8407	28407	28408	8408	MY
Z 8279	28279	28280	8280	MY	Z 8409	28409	28410	8410	MY
Z 8281	28281	28282	8282	MY	Z 8411	28411	28412	8412	MY
Z 8283	28283	28284	8284	MY	Z 8413	28413	28414	8414	MY
Z 8285	28285	28286	8286	MY	Z 8415	28415	28416	8416	MY
Z 8287	28287	28288	8288	MY	Z 8417	28417	28418	8418	MY
Z 8289	28289	28290	8290	MY	Z 8419	28419	28420	8420	MY
Z 8291	28291	28292	8292	MY	Z 8421	28421	28422	8422	MY
Z 8293	28293	28294	8294	MY	Z 8423	28423	28424	8424	MY
Z 8295	28295	28296	8296	MY	Z 8425	28425	28426	8426	MY
Z 8297	28297	28298	8298	MY	Z 8427	28427	28428	8428	MY

Z 8107. RER line/ligne 'B'. Aulnay-sous-Bois. 05/08/89.   *Adrian Norton*
Z 8877. Paris Austerlitz. 28/05/90.   *Adrian Norton*

Z 8429	28429	28430	8430	MY
Z 8431	28431	28432	8432	MY
Z 8433	28433	28434	8434	MY
Z 8435	28435	28436	8436	MY
Z 8437	28437	28438	8438	MY
Z 8439	28439	28440	8440	MY
Z 8441	28441	28442	8442	MY
Z 8443	28443	28444	8444	MY
Z 8445	28445	28446	8446	MY
Z 8447	28447	28448	8448	MY
Z 8449	28449	28450	8450	MY
Z 8451	28451	28452	8452	MY
Z 8453	28453	28454	8454	MY
Z 8455	28455	28456	8456	MY
Z 8457	28457	28458	8458	MY
Z 8459	28459	28460	8460	MY
Z 8461	28461	28462	8462	MY
Z 8463	28463	28464	8464	MY
Z 8465	28465	28466	8466	MY
Z 8467	28467	28468	8468	MY
Z 8469	28469	28470	8470	MY
Z 8471	28471	28472	8472	MY
Z 8473	28473	28474	8474	MY
Z 8475	28475	28476	8476	MY
Z 8477	28477	28478	8478	MY
Z 8479	28479	28480	8480	MY
Z 8481	28481	28482	8482	MY
Z 8483	28483	28484	8484	MY
Z 8485	28485	28486	8486	MY

Names/Noms:

Z 8121/8122	EPINAY-SUR-SEINE
Z 8257/8258	RAISMES
Z 8261/8262	MITRY-MORY
Z 8263/8264	PERSAN
Z 8313/8314	POISSY
Z 8441/8442	INTERLAKEN

CLASS/SERIE 8800   4-CAR UNITS

These are a dual voltage version of Z 5600 and are used on RER line C. The trailer cars are common with the Z 5600 class.

La série est une version bi-courant des Z 5600 et partagent les remorques de ces dernières. Les Z 8800 sont utilisée sur la ligne C du RER, surtout sur la branche vers Ermont sur le réseau Nord.

Systems/Systèmes: 1500 V d.c./continu/25 kV a.c./monophasé.
Built/Construction: 1986–88.
Builder-Mech. Parts/Constructeur-Partie mécanique: ANF/CIMT.
Builder-Elec. Parts/Constructeur-Partie électrique: Alsthom/TCO.
Formation: ZB + ZRB + ZRAB + ZB.
Traction Motors/Moteurs de traction: 4 x 350 kW per power car/par motrice.
Max. Speed/Vitesse max.: 140 km/h.
Livery/Livrée: P.

Power Car Sets/Rames motrices. Accommodation/Places –/107. 25.10 m. 69 tonnes. BoBo + BoBo.

Z 8801	8802	PA	Z 8841	8842	PA	Z 8879	8880	PA
Z 8803	8804	PA	Z 8843	8844	PA	Z 8881	8882	PA
Z 8805	8806	PA	Z 8845	8846	PA	Z 8883	8884	PA
Z 8807	8808	PA	Z 8847	8848	PA	Z 8885	8886	PA
Z 8809	8810	PA	Z 8849	8850	PA	Z 8887	8888	PA
Z 8811	8812	PA	Z 8851	8852	PA	Z 8889	8890	PA
Z 8813	8814	PA	Z 8853	8854	PA	Z 8891	8892	PA
Z 8815	8816	PA	Z 8855	8856	PA	Z 8893	8894	PA
Z 8817	8818	PA	Z 8857	8858	PA	Z 8895	8896	PA
Z 8819	8820	PA	Z 8859	8860	PA	Z 8897	8898	PA
Z 8821	8822	PA	Z 8861	8862	PA	Z 8899	8900	PA
Z 8823	8824	PA	Z 8863	8864	PA	Z 8901	8902	PA
Z 8825	8826	PA	Z 8865	8866	PA	Z 8903	8904	PA
Z 8827	8828	PA	Z 8867	8868	PA	Z 8905	8906	PA
Z 8829	8830	PA	Z 8869	8870	PA	Z 8907	8908	PA
Z 8831	8832	PA	Z 8871	8872	PA	Z 8909	8910	PA
Z 8833	8834	PA	Z 8873	8874	PA	Z 8911	8912	PA
Z 8835	8836	PA	Z 8875	8876	PA	Z 8913	8914	PA
Z 8837	8838	PA	Z 8877	8878	PA	Z 8915	8916	PA
Z 8839	8840	PA						

Names/Noms:

Z 8801/8802	SAINT GRATIEN
Z 8803/8804	FRANCONVILLE
Z 8805/8806	GROSLAY
Z 8807/8808	SANNOIS
Z 8809/8810	ERMONT-EAUBONNE
Z 8811/8812	GENNEVILLIERS

CLASS/SERIE Z 9500

This is a dual-voltage version of Z 7500 and has unidirectional seating. Used in the Jura and in the Alps.

Une version bi-courant des Z 7500. Elles sont utilisées dans le Jura et les Alpes.

Systems/Systèmes: 1500 V d.c./continu/25 kV a.c./monophasé.

Built/Construction: 1982–83.   **Builders/Constructeurs:** Alsthom/Francorail-MTE.
Wheel Arrangement/Disposition des Essieux: BoBo + 22.
Traction Motors/Moteurs de traction: 4 x 305 kW.
Formation: ZABD + ZRBx.
Weight/Masse: 66 + 50 tonnes.
Max. Speed/Vitesse max.: 160 km/h.
Accommodation/Places: 32/35 1T + –/84 1T.
Length/Longeur: 25.10 + 25.10 m.

Z 9501	19501	Z	VE		Z 9508	19508	Z	VE		Z 9515	19515	Z	VE
Z 9502	19502	Z	VE		Z 9509	19509	Z	VE		Z 9516	19516	Z	VE
Z 9503	19503	Z	VE		Z 9510	19510	Z	VE		Z 9517	19517	Z	VE
Z 9504	19504	Z	VE		Z 9511	19511	Z	VE		Z 9518	19518	Z	VE
Z 9505	19505	Z	VE		Z 9512	19512	Z	VE		Z 99581	919581	Z	VE
Z 9506	19506	Z	VE		Z 9513	19513	Z	VE		Z 99582	919582	Z	VE
Z 9507	19507	Z	VE		Z 9514	19514	Z	VE					

Names/Noms:

Z 9502 ARLES
Z 9517 SAINT-PRIEST
Z 99581 EPR BOURGOGNE FRANCHE-COMPE
Z 99582 EPR BOURGOGNE FRANCHE-COMTE

CLASS/SERIE Z 9600

This is the dual-voltage version of Z 7300 and is used to the west of Le mans and in the Alps.

Une version bi-courant des Z 7300. Elles sont utilisées à l'ouest du Mans et dans les Alpes.

Systems/Systèmes: 1500 V d.c./continu/25 kV a.c./monophasé.

Built/Construction: 1984–87.   **Builders/Constructeurs:** Alsthom/Francorail-MTE.
Wheel Arrangement/Disposition des Essieux: BoBo + 22.
Traction Motors/Moteurs de traction: 4 x 305 kW.
Formation: ZABD + ZRBx.
Weight/Masse: 66 + 50 tonnes.
Max. Speed/Vitesse max.: 160 km/h.
Accommodation/Places: 24/43 1T + –/84 1T.
Length/Longeur: 25.10 + 25.10 m.

Many Rennes units are named 'LES PAYS DE LA LOIRE'.
Plusieurs éléments a Rennes portent le nom «LES PAYS DE LA LOIRE».

Z 9601	19601	Z	RS		Z 9613	19613	B	RS		Z 9625	19625	B	RS
Z 9602	19602	Z	RS		Z 9614	19614	Z	VE		Z 9626	19626	B	RS
Z 9603	19603	Z	RS		Z 9615	19615	Z	VE		Z 9627	19627	B	RS
Z 9604	19604	G	RS		Z 9616	19616	Z	VE		Z 9628	19628	Z	RS
Z 9605	19605	Z	RS		Z 9617	19617	Z	VE		Z 9629	19629	B	RS
Z 9606	19606	Z	RS		Z 9618	19618	Z	VE		Z 9630	19630	B	RS
Z 9607	19607	Z	RS		Z 9619	19619	Z	VE		Z 9631	19631	Z	VE
Z 9608	19608	B	RS		Z 9620	19620	Z	VE		Z 9632	19632	Z	VE
Z 9609	19609	B	RS		Z 9621	19621	B	RS		Z 9633	19633	Z	VE
Z 9610	19610	B	RS		Z 9622	19622	B	RS		Z 9634	19634	Z	VE
Z 9611	19611	B	RS		Z 9623	19623	B	RS		Z 9635	19635	Z	VE
Z 9612	19612	B	RS		Z 9624	19624	B	RS		Z 9636	19636	Z	VE

Names/Noms:

Z 9617 FIRMINY
Z 9633 RIVES
Z 9635 CHENE BOURG, CHENE BOURGERIES, THÔNEX

CLASS/SERIE 11500

An a.c. only version of Z 7300 for use around Metz.
Une version monophasédes Z 7300. Utilisées autour de Metz.

Systems/Systèmes: 25 kV a.c./monophasé.

Built/Construction: 1986–67.　　**Builders/Constructeurs:** Alsthom/Francorail-MTE.
Wheel Arrangement/Disposition des Essieux: BoBo + 22.
Traction Motors/Moteurs de traction: 4 x 305 kW.
Formation: ZABD + ZRBx.　　**Accommodation/Places:** 24/43 1T + –/84 1T.
Weight/Masse: 66 + 50 tonnes.　　**Length/Longeur:** 25.10 + 25.10 m.
Max. Speed/Vitesse max.: 160 km/h.

11501	111501 Z	TV		11509	111509 Z	TV		11516	111516 Y	TV
11502	111502 Y	TV		11510	111510 Y	TV		11517	111517 Z	TV
11503	111503 Y	TV		11511	111511 Y	TV		11518	111518 Z	TV
11504	111504 Z	TV		11512	111512 Y	TV		11519	111519 Z	TV
11505	111505 Z	TV		11513	111513 Y	TV		11520	111520 Y	TV
11506	111506 Z	TV		11514	111514 Y	TV		11521	111521 Y	TV
11507	111507 Y	TV		11515	111515 Y	TV		11522	111522 Y	TV
11508	111508 Z	TV								

Names/Noms:

11501　SCHILTIGHEIM　　　　　　　11521　WOIPPY

CLASS/SERIE 20500

These units are a further development of Z 8800 with an improved appearance and longer trailers. They have asynchronous motors and are used on RER line D. They are used on RER line D from Orry-la-Ville to Châtelet. This line will be extended to Gare de Lyon in 1995 and Orry–Paris services extended through to Melun on the Sud-Est.

Une version plus moderne de Z 8800 avec des moteurs asynchrones. L'extérieur est plus carré des Z 8800 et les remorques sont plus longues. Elles sont utilisées sur la ligne D du RER entre Orry-la-Ville et Châtelet. En 1995, cette ligne sera prolongée jusqu'à Paris Lyon et les services Orry–Paris et Paris–Melun seront interconnectés.

Systems/Systèmes: 1500 V d.c./continu/25 kV a.c./monophasé.
Built/Construction: 1988– .
Builder-Mech. Parts/Constructeur-Partie mécanique: CIMT/ANF.
Builder-Elec. Parts/Constructeur-Partie électrique: Alsthom.
Formation: ZB + ZRB + ZRAB + ZB.
Traction Motors/Moteurs de traction: 4 x 350 kW per power car/par motrice.
Max. Speed/Vitesse max.: 140 km/h.
Livery/Livrée: P.

Power Car Sets/Rames motrices. Accommodation/Places –/115 per car/par motrice. 25.10 m. 69 tonnes. BoBo + BoBo.

20501	20502	PJ		20537	20538	PJ		20573	20574	PJ
20503	20504	PJ		20539	20540	PJ		20575	20576	PJ
20505	20506	PJ		20541	20542	PJ		20577	20578	PJ
20507	20508	PJ		20543	20544	PJ		20579	20580	PJ
20509	20510	PJ		20545	20546	PJ		20581	20582	PJ
20511	20512	PJ		20547	20548	PA		20583	20584	
20513	20514	PJ		20549	20550	PA		20585	20586	
20515	20516	PJ		20551	20552	PJ		20587	20588	
20517	20518	PJ		20553	20554	PJ		20589	20590	
20519	20520	PJ		20555	20556	PA		20591	20592	
20521	20522	PJ		20557	20558	PJ		20593	20594	
20523	20524	PJ		20559	20560	PJ		20595	20596	
20525	20526	PJ		20561	20562	PJ		20597	20598	
20527	20528	PA		20563	20564	PJ		20599	20600	
20529	20530	PA		20565	20566	PJ		20601	20602	
20531	20532	PA		20567	20568	PJ		20603	20604	
20533	20534	PA		20569	20570	PJ		20605	20606	
20535	20536	PJ		20571	20572	PA		20607	20608	

20609	20610	20653	20654	20697	20698
20611	20612	20655	20656	20699	20700
20613	20614	20657	20658	20701	20702
20615	20616	20659	20660	20703	20704
20617	20618	20661	20662	20705	20706
20619	20620	20663	20664	20707	20708
20621	20622	20665	20666	20709	20710
20623	20624	20667	20668	20711	20712
20625	20626	20669	20670	20713	20714
20627	20628	20671	20672	20715	20716
20629	20630	20673	20674	20717	20718
20631	20632	20675	20676	20719	20720
20633	20634	20677	20678	20721	20722
20635	20636	20679	20680	20723	20724
20637	20638	20681	20682	20725	20726
20639	20640	20683	20684	20727	20728
20641	20642	20685	20686	20729	20730
20643	20644	20687	20688	20731	20732
20645	20646	20689	20690	20733	20734
20647	20648	20691	20692	20735	20736
20649	20650	20693	20694	20737	20738
20651	20652	20695	20696		

Names/Noms:

20501	LE PLESSIS-BOUCHARD	20531	BEAUCHAMP
20513	VILLIERS-LE-BEL		

Trailer Seconds/Remorques B. Accommodation/Places –/204. 26.40 m.   tonnes.

Trailer Composites/Remorques AB. Accommodation/Places 80/108. 26.40 m.   tonnes.

11506. Thionville depot/Dépôt de Thionville. 19/04/87.   *E. Dunkling*

SNCF NARROW GAUGE LINES
LIGNES À VOIE ÉTROITE DE LA SNCF

There are three metre gauge lines in France operated by the SNCF, plus the Chemins de Fer de la Corse (Corsica) which is now owned by the SNCF. These lines are described separately.

Il y a trois lignes à voie métrique exploitées par la SNCF, plus les Chemins de Fer Corses qui appartiennent maintenant à la SNCF.

SNCF LIGNE DE CERDAGNE ("LE PETIT TRAIN JAUNE")

This line opened 1910–29 was electrified from opening at 850 V dc third rail. Running from Villefranche-le-Conflent to La Tour-de-Carol it traverses mountain scenery with extremely sharp curves and steep gradients and several spectacular bridges. The line was under threat of closure for several years and freight traffic ceased in 1974. However efforts to promote the tourist potential of the line seem to have been successful. All the stock was refurbished in 1962–8 and painted in the then current red and yellow railcar livery. Commencing in 1983 the stock has been undergoing further refurbishment and painting in a mainly yellow livery. The depot is at Villefranche-le-Conflent, although stock is nominally allocated to Béziers where overhauls are carried out.

Cette ligne de Villefranche-le-Conflent à La Tour-de-Carol a été ouverte entre 1910 et 1929 et fut électrifiée à 850 V continu par troisième rail dès le début. La ligne traverse des montagnes sauvages avec des rayons de courbes très bas, des pentes très accentuées et plusieurs ponts spectaculaires. Le trafic marchandises cessa en 1974 et la ligne a été menacée de fermeture pendant longtemps. Cependant, des efforts pour promouvoir le tourisme semblent avoir porté leurs fruits. Tout le matériel fut modernisé en 1962–8 et peint dans la livrée rouge et jaune. Depuis 1983, le matériel a subi une plus grande modernisation et a été peint en jaune. Le dépôt est à Villefranche-le-Conflent, mais le matériel est affecté à Béziers où toutes les révisions ont lieu.

POWER CARS/MOTRICES   ZBD

Formerly Midi E ABDe 2–9/11–3/15–8. Cars marked * were built as trailers, these were converted to motor cars in 1912–21. They were originally Midi ABDe 14/11/3/5–8 respectively. EABDe 5 replaced an accident victim. The internal layout of these cars differs from the others which were built as motor cars.

Ce sont les voitures ex-Midi E ABDe 2–9/11–3/15–8. Les voitures marquées * furent transformées à partir des remorques Midi ABDe 14/11/3/5–8 en 1912–21. L'intérieur de ces dernières est différent de celui des motrices.

Built/Construction: 1908–09.
Builder-Mech. Parts/Constructeur-Partie mécanique: Carde & Cie.
Builder-Elec. Parts/Constructeur-Partie électrique: Sprague–Thomson.
Wheel Arrangement/Disposition des Essieux: BoBo.
Traction Motors/Moteurs de traction: 4 x 66 kW.
Accommodation/Places: –/40.   **Weight/Masse:** 32 (28*) tonnes.
Length/Longeur: 14.904 (14.384*) m.   **Max. Speed/Vitesse max.:** 55 km/ h.

| Z 102 | Z 104 | Z 106 | Z 108 | Z 111 * | Z 115 * | Z 116 * | Z 118* |
| Z 103 | Z 105 * | Z 107 | Z 109 | Z 113 * | Z 116 * | | |

MOTORED VANS/FOURGONS MOTEURS   ZD

The last survivors of ten motored vans built for freight use. Originally Midi E.De 8–9, then SNCF Z 208–9, later Z 201–2. Now used on snowplough duties.

Les derniers survivants de dix fourgons moteurs. A l'origine ils furent les Midi E.De 8–9, puis les Z 208/9 de la SNCF, et maintenant les Z 201/2. Ils sont utilisés maintenant comme chasse neige.

Built/Construction: 1908–09.
Builder-Mech. Parts/Constructeur-Partie mécanique: Carde & Cie/SACM.
Builder-Elec. Parts/Constructeur-Partie électrique: Sprague–Thomson.
Wheel Arrangement/Disposition des Essieux: BoBo.

Traction Motors/Moteurs de traction: 4 x 66 kW.
Accommodation/Places: None/aucun **Weight/Masse:** 27 tonnes.
Length/Longeur: 11.284 m. **Max. Speed/Vitesse max.:** 25 km/h.

Z 201 |Z 202

TRAILERS/REMORQUES ZRB

Three types of trailer car are in use:

  The surviving original cars not converted to motors (ex Midi ABDe 1–4).
* Open-top cars, originally roofed (ex Midi Be 30–4).
† Cars second-hand from the CF Economiques du Nord in 1936.

Il existe trois types de remorque:

  Les voitures d'origine (Midi ABDe 1–4) qui ne furent pas transformées en motrices.
* Des voitures ouvertes ex Midi Be 30–4 (avec toit à l'origine)
† Voitures ex CFEconomiques du Nord, achetées en 1936.
Built/Construction: 1908–09, 1912*, 1910–12†.
Builders/Constructeurs: Carde & Cie. (Decauvillet†).
Wheel Arrangement/Disposition des Essieux: 22.
Accommodation/Places: –/44 (–/59*, –/46†). **Weight/Masse:** 14.5 (10*, 13†) tonnes.
Length/Longeur: 14.384 (10.50*, 13.37†) m. **Max. Speed/Vitesse max.:** 55 km/h.

| ZR 20001 | ZR 20003 | ZR 20023 * | ZR 20031 * | ZR 20033 * | ZR 20036 † | ZR 20038 |
| ZR 20002 | ZR 20004 | ZR 20030 † | ZR 20032 * | ZR 20034 * | ZR 20037 † | ZR 20039 |

SNCF LIGNE DE SAVOIE

This line, opened in 1901, is one of the steepest adhesion railways in the world. Electrified from opening at 750 V dc third rail, it extends from St. Gervais les Bains to Vallorcine, where a connection is made with the Swiss Martigny–Châtelard Railway. Some through operation exists between the two railways. Six two-car units are to be ordered for through working with MC, see our "Swiss Railways" book.

The original stock was unusual since all vehicles were powered and multiple working fitted (including wagons!). However freight operations ceased in 1970, the remaining wagons being in departmental use until withdrawn in 1986. Modern stock introduced in 1958 included trailer cars. The depot is at St. Gervais-les-Bains.

Cette ligne, de St Gervais-les-Bains à Vallorcine (Suisse), qui a été ouverte en 1901, est la plus raide du monde à être exploitée en adhérence. Electrifiée dès l'ouverture, la ligne est raccordée à Vallorcine avec la Martigny–Châtelard. Il existe quelques voitures directs entre les deux lignes mais l'intention est de commander six rames de deux voitures pour assurer un service St.Garvais–Martigny vers 1996 (voir notre livre "Chemins de Fer Suisses").

La matériel d'origine fut très original parce que tous les véhicules avaient des bogies moteurs et pouvaient être exploités en UM y compris les wagons fret! Cependant, le service fret cessa en 1970 et les wagons restants ont été radiés en 1986. Le dépôt est à St Gervais.

MOTORED VANS/FOURGONS MOTEURS ZD

These surviving motored vans with one driving cab are retained for departmental and snow clearance work. Z 205 is fitted with rotating blades to remove snow from between the rails.

Ces fourgons survivants ont une cabine de conduite et sont utilisés comme chasse neige et pour des trains de travaux. Le Z 205 est équipé comme chasse neige rotatif.

Built/Construction: 1901–09.
Builder-Mech. Parts/Constructeur-Partie mécanique: Horme & Buire.
Builder-Elec. Parts/Constructeur-Partie électrique: .
Wheel Arrangement/Disposition des Essieux: Bo.
Weight/Masse: 23 tonnes.
Length/Longeur: 10.15 m. **Max. Speed/Vitesse max.:** 35 km/h.

Z 205 |Z 208

POWER CARS/MOTRICES   ZABD

Built/Construction: 1958.
Builder-Mech. Parts/Constructeur-Partie mécanique: Decauville.
Builder-Elec. Parts/Constructeur-Partie électrique:TCO.
Wheel Arrangement/Disposition des Essieux: BoBo.
Accommodation/Places: 8/34.   **Weight/Masse:** 40 tonnes.
Length/Longeur: 18.20 m.   **Max. Speed/Vitesse max.:** 70 km/h.

Z 601 |Z 602 |Z 603 |Z 604 |Z 605 |Z 606 |Z 607 |Z 608

Name/Nom: Z 601 CHAMONIX-MONT BLANC.

ROTARY SNOWPLOUGH/CHASSE NEIGE ROTATIF   1Bo

Built/Construction: 1958.
Builder-Mech. Parts/Constructeur-Partie mécanique: SNCF.
Wheel Arrangement/Disposition des Essieux: 1Bo.
Weight/Masse: 33 tonnes.
Length/Longeur: 9.015 m.   **Max. Speed/Vitesse max.:** 40 km/h.

Z 691

TRAILERS/REMORQUES   ZRAB (22)

Intermediate trailers for Z 601–8./Des remorques intermédiaires pour les Z 601–9.

Built/Construction: 1958.
Builder-Mech. Parts/Constructeur-Partie mécanique: Decauville.
Wheel Arrangement/Disposition des Essieux: 22.
Accommodation/Places: 24F/35.   **Weight/Masse:** 20 tonnes.
Length/Longeur: 18.20 m.   **Max. Speed/Vitesse max.:** 70 km/h.

ZR 20601 |ZR 20602 |ZR 20603 |ZR 20604

CHEMIN DE FER DU BLANC–ARGENT.

This line, owned by the SNCF is operated by the above company. Formerly running between the towns in its title, it now operates a passenger service only between Salbris to Luçay le Mâle. The passenger stock has been modernised, but freight traffic ceased in 1989. . The depot and workshops are located in Romorantin.

Cette ligne, qui appartient à la SNCF, est exploitée par cie du Blanc à Argent. De la ligne de Le Blanc à Argent, il ne subsiste qu'un service voyageurs entre Salbris et Luçay-le-Mâle. Le matériel voyageurs a été modernisé mais le service marchandises a cessé en 1989. Le dépôt et les ateliers sont à Romorantin.

DIESEL LOCOS/LOCOMOTIVES DIESELS   C

Formerly steam locos 25/28, built by Blanc Misseron in 1901.
Transformée à partir des locomotives à vapeur 25/28, construites par Blanc–Misseron en 1901.

Rebuilt/Construction: 1953.
Builder/Constructeur: Périgueux Works/Ateliers de Périgueux.
Engine/Moteur: Willème 517F8 (132 kW).   **Transmission:** Mechanical/mécanique.
Weight/Masse: 17 tonnes.   **Length/Longeur:** 8.45 m.
Wheel Dia./Diamètre des roues: 1050 mm.   **Max. Speed/Vitesse max.:** 30 km/h.

T 13 |T 14

RAILCARS/AUTORAILS
CLASS/SERIE X 200   XBD

The last survivor of 6 cars (X 201–206) transferred from the Réseau Breton in 1968. Reserve car.

Le dernier survivant de 6 autorails (X 201–206) qui furent transférés après la fermeture de Réseau Breton en 1968. Le X 205 sert comme voiture de réserve.

Built/Construction: 1948.
Engine/Moteur: Willème 517F8 (132 kW).
Accommodation/Places: –/51 1T.
Length/Longeur: 19.12 m.
Wheel Arrangement/Disposition des Essieux: 1AA1.
Livery/Livrée: Cream and red/crème et rouge.

Builder/Constructeur: De Dion Bouton.
Transmission: Mechanical/mécanique.
Weight/Masse: 18 tonnes.
Max. Speed/Vitesse max.: 70 km/h.

X 205

CLASS/SERIE X 210   XBD

X 211/2 came from the PO Corrèze in 1967. All four cars were refurbished in 1983–4 and fitted with new engines,when X 213/4 were renumbered from X 223/1 respectively.

Les X 211/2 ont été transférés du PO Corrèze en 1967. Les quatre autorails ont été modernisés en 1993/4 avec de nouveaux moteurs. Les anciens numéros de X 213/4 étaient X 223/1.

Built/Construction: 1950–51.
Builder/Constructeur: Verney.
Engine/Moteur: Poyaud 6L520S1 (185 kW).
Accommodation/Places: –/54 1T.
Length/Longeur: 18.535 m.
Wheel Arrangement/Disposition des Essieux: B2.
Livery/Livrée: Cream and brown/crème et brun.

Transmission: Mechanical/mécanique.
Weight/Masse: 21 tonnes.
Max. Speed/Vitesse max.: 85 km/h.

X 211 |X 212 |X 213 |X 214

CLASS/SERIE X 220   XBD

The last survivor in original condition of 4 cars (X 221–4) purchased new in 1950–1. Two others have been refurbished (see X 211–4). In reserve.

Le dernier survivant de quatre autorails (X 221–4) qui furent achetés en 1950/1. Les X 221/3 on été modernisés (voir plus haut). Voiture de réserve.

Built/Construction: 1951.
Engine/Moteur: Willème 517F6 (103 kW).
Accommodation/Places: –/53 1T.
Length/Longeur: 18.535 m.
Wheel Arrangement/Disposition des Essieux: B2.
Livery/Livrée: Cream and red/crème et rouge.

Builder/Constructeur: Verney.
Transmission: Mechanical/mécanique.
Weight/Masse: 18 tonnes.
Max. Speed/Vitesse max.: 80 km/h.

X 224

CLASS/SERIE X 240   XBD

Delivered as part of the modernisation programme for passenger stock.
Les X 241/2 ont été livreés dans le cadre d'un programme de modernisation.

Built/Construction: 1983.
Builder/Constructeur: CFD Montmirail/Socofer, Tours.
Engine/Moteur: Poyaud 6L520CS2 (175 kW).
Accommodation/Places: –/54 1T.
Length/Longeur: 18.27 m.
Wheel Arrangement/Disposition des Essieux: B2.
Livery/Livrée: Cream and brown/crème et brun.

Transmission: Hydraulic/hydraulique.
Weight/Masse: 25 tonnes.
Max. Speed/Vitesse max.: 85 km/h.

X 241   ROMORANTIN-LANTHENAY |X 242   VALENÇAY

CLASS/SERIE XR 700   XRBD

All refurbished 1983–4./Toutes ces remorques ont été modernisées en 1983/4.

Built/Construction: 1951.
Accommodation/Places: –/39 1T.
Length/Longeur: 12.975 m.
Wheel Arrangement/Disposition des Essieux: 22.
Livery/Livrée: Cream and brown/crème et brun.

Builder/Constructeur: Verney.
Weight/Masse: 9.5 tonnes.
Max. Speed/Vitesse max.: 85 km/h.

(* Ex PO Corrèze. 1967).

XR 701* |XR 702 |XR 703

▲BB 66491. Reims. 11.15 to/pour Amiens. 16/07/90.   *G.B. Wise*

▼BB 66710 + 66709. Dunkerque. 3600 tonne iron ore train/Un train de minerais de fer de 3600 tonnes. 22/06/89.   *David Haydock*

130

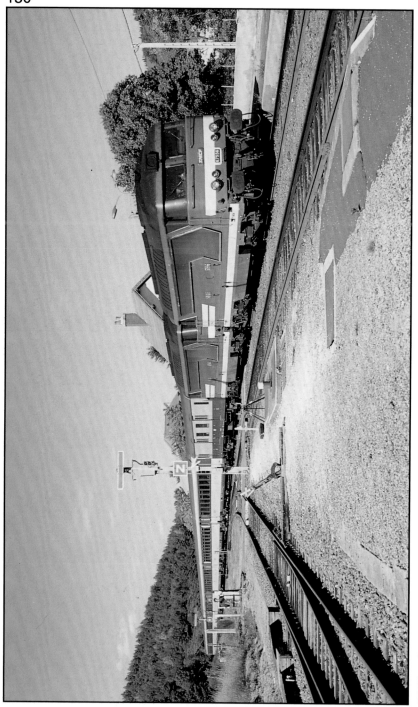

67556 + 67540 arriving at La Bastide–St. Laurent les Bains with the southbound 'Cevenol' from Paris Gare de Lyon to Nice in September 1990. Here the train will cross its northbound equivalent.
Gordon Wiseman

67556 + 67540 arrivent à La Bastide–St. Laurent les Bains avec le 'Cevenol' de Paris à Nice en Septembre 1990. Ici le train va croiser son équivalent vers le nord.
Gordon Wiseman

▲68523. Les Noues. Surveilliers–Le Bourget freight./Train de marchandises Survilliers–Le Bourget. 30/05/91   *David Haydock*

▼72080 'MULHOUSE'. Express Laon–Paris Nord. Aulnay-sous-Bois. 26/4/91.   *Peter Fox*

▲T 2010/09. Besançon. 12.00 Strasbourg–Lyon. 01/08/88. *G.B. Wise*

▼2 x X 2800. A Dijon–Morez train crossing the N5 road at Le Vaudioux./Un train Dijon–Morez
traverse la route N5 au Vaudioux. *Gordon Wiseman*

▲XR 8602 + X 4383. La Villette depot./Dépôt de La Villette. Livery/Livrée: 'A'. 05/08/89.
Adrian Norton

▼XR 8356+X 4366 refurbished/modernisé. Charleville-Mézières. Service to/à Givet. Livery/Livrée: white and blue/blanc et bleu 'Champagne-Ardennes'
David Haydock

▲RGP X 2722/XR 7722 refurbished/modernisée. Metz. Livery/livrée: white and red/blanc et rouge. (now in yellow/maintenant en jaune) 23/04/87. *C.R. Appleby*

▼X 94755. Lille Fives depot./Dépôt de Lille Fives. 18/04/85. *David Haydock*

▲ Y 5159. Thionville. 23/04/87. C.R. Appleby
▼ Y 8286 + Y 7207. Lens depot./Dépôt de Lens. 28/04/87. David Haydock

▲Z 5143. Toulouse Matabiau station./Gare de Toulouse Matabiau. 25/06/90.   *S.C. Falcus*
▼Z 6127. Aulnay-sous-Bois. 26/04/91.   *Peter Fox*

▲Z 6498. Paris St. Lazare. 31/01/89.   *Paul Russenberger*

▼Z 7105. Vias station./Gare de Vias. 16.42 Narbonne–Nîmes local/omnibus. Livery/Livrée: 'M'.
24/04/91.   *Peter Fox*

▲Z 7367. Avignon. 06/06/91. Livery: white and yellow 'TER Languedoc-Rousillon'./Livrée: blanc et jaune 'TER Languedoc-Rousillon'. *Peter Fox*

▼Z 9612. Annecy. 15/04/89. Livery/Livrée 'Z'. *T.N. Hall*

20510/09. Orry-la-Ville-Coye. The northern terminus of RER line D./Le terminus nord de la ligne RER 'D'. 30/05/91.

▲**SNCF Ligne de Cerdagne.** Z 104. Villefranche-le-Conflent.   *Paul Russenberger*
▼**SNCF Ligne de Savioe.** Class/série Z 600. St. Gervais. 02/86.   *David Haydock*

▲**CFTA**. X 97151 + X 97153. Paimpol. Train to/pour Guingamp. 08/90   *David Haydock*

▼X 2416. Carhaix. 08/90.   *David Haydock*

Chemins de Fer Corses. BB 405. Ponte Lecchia. Mixed freight Ajaccio–Bastia./Marchandises Ajaccio–Bastia.

Peter Fox

▲Chemins de Fer Corses. X 5001 + 212. Bastia. 11.10 arrival from Ajaccio./Arrivée à 11.10 d'Ajaccio. 09/09/88. *Doreen Fox*

▼Chemins de Fer de la Provence. X 304. Lingostière. 16.55 shuttle/navette Colomars–Nice. 01/09/89 *Peter Fox*

▲Nord 140C313. Preserved at Reims station./Présérvée à Gare de Reims. 01/08/88.   *G.B. Wise*
▼141TD740. Narbonne. Railtour ex-Port Bou./Train spécial de Port Bou. 28/07/87.   *Peter Fox*

CHEMINS DE FER CORSES (CORSICA)

The SNCF took over operation of this system on 01/01/83 after the last of a series of concessionary companies gave up. The main line runs from Bastia to Ajaccio with a branch from Ponte Leccia to Calvi. The central section of the main line is particularly scenic. There is a depot and workshop at Casamozza, and a depot at Bastia.

La SNCF a commencé l'exploitation du réseau en 1983. La ligne principale est de Bastia à Ajaccio avec une branche de Ponte Leccia à Calvi. La partie centrale de la ligne est très spectaculaire. Il y a un dépôt et atelier à Casamozza et un dépôt à Bastia.

DIESEL LOCOMOTIVES/*LOCOMOTIVES DIESEL*

114   B2

Built: 1958 using bogies from Billard A150D No. 114 (built 1938). Works from Calvi and is nicknamed the "Submarine".

Construction: 1958 en utilisant les bogies du Billard A150D No. 114. Utilisée à partir de Calvi et surnommée «le sous-marin».

Builder/Constructeur: Bastia depot.
Engine/Moteur: 75 kW.
Transmission: Mechanical/mécanique.

114

CLASS/*SERIE* BB 400   BB

Built/Construction: 1966. 404 was formerly Chemins de Fer de la Provence 403, and carries no number./La 404 est l'ex 403 des CF de Provence et ne porte pas de numéro.
Builder/Constructeur: CFD Montmirail.
Engine/Moteur: 310 kW.
Transmission: Mechanical/mécanique.

404 |405

RAILCARS/*AUTORAILS*

TRAILERS/*REMORQUES*   XRBD

Rebuilt: 1977 by/par Garnero. Ex Billard A210D.
Wheel Arrangement/Disposition des Essieux: 22.
Accommodation/Places: –/44 1T.   **Length/Longeur:** 19.80 m.

R 104 |R 105

113   XRBDx

The only survivor of a batch of six (111–6), this car was modernised in 1966, and converted to a driving trailer to run with 204 in 1987.

La dernière survivante de six remorques (111–116), cette voiture fut modernisée en 1966 et transformée en remorque pilote pour utiliser avec la 204 en 1987.

Built/Construction: 1938.
Builder/Constructeur: Billard. Type A 150 D.
Wheel Arrangement/Disposition des Essieux: 22.
Accommodation/Places: –/37 1T.   **Weight/Masse:**   tonnes.
Length/Longeur: 14.50 m.   **Max. Speed/Vitesse max.:** 75 km/h.
113

RENAULT ABH 8   XBD

Originally a batch of eight. Seating is 2+1 except refurbished vehicles which are 2+2 and 202 which is 3+0!

Sept de ces autorails restent d'une série de huit. La disposition des places est 2+1 sauf les voitures modernisées – 2+2) et la 202 (3+0!)

Built/Construction: 1949–50.
Engine/Moteur: Renault (195 kW).
Transmission: Mechanical/mécanique.
Accommodation/Places: –/28 1T, (40S 1T r, 24S 1T *)
Wheel Arrangement/Disposition des Essieux: B2.
Length/Longeur: 19.50 m.   **Max. Speed/Vitesse max.:** 60 km/h.

m Fitted for working with driving trailer./Equipé pour l'exploitation avec remorque pilote.
r Refurbished./Modernisé.
(U) Stored unserviceable./Garée hors service.

201 r |202 *m |203 (U) |204 m |205 (U) |206 r |207 r

TRAILERS/REMORQUES   XRBD

Ex Tarn 1966 (Seine et Marne 1966*). Rebodied except 212./Nouvelle caisse, sauf la 212.

Built/Construction: 1938/49.
Builder/Constructeur: Billard. Type A80D.
Wheel Arrangement/Disposition des Essieux: 22.
Accommodation/Places: –/28 1T (27S 1T†, 30S 1T*).
Length/Longeur: 11.50 m.

2 (U) |4 (U) |7 |210 |211 † |212 *

VANS/FOURGONS   XRD

Ex PO Corrèze.

Built/Construction: 1938/49.
Builder/Constructeur: Billard. Type A80D.
Wheel Arrangement/Disposition des Essieux: 22.
Length/Longeur: 11.50 m.

242 § |243 §

BILLARD A150D

503 (ex Seine et Marne 1966) and 513 (ex Tarn 1966) are departmental units for the Civil and Mechanical Engineering Depts respectively, and have new Deutz 75 kW engines. 502 is a grounded body.

503 et 513 sont des autorails réservés aux trains de service et ont des nouveau moteurs Deutz de 75 kW. La 502 n'est qu'une caisse par terre!

Built/Construction: 1938/48.
Builder/Constructeur: Billard. Type A150D6.
Wheel Arrangement/Disposition des Essieux: B2.

502 (U) |503 (D) |504 (U) |514 (D)

526   DRIVING TRAILER/REMORQUE PILOTE

Converted from Billard type A150D6. Ex tramways d'Ille et Villaine and Réseau Breton. Works with 202 between Calvi and Ile Rousse.

Transformée à partir du Billard type A150D6. Ex tramways d'Ille et Villaine et Réseau Breton. Utilisée avec le 202 entre Calvi et Ile Rousse.

Built/Construction: 1947.
Builder/Constructeur: Billard. Type A150D6.
Wheel Arrangement/Disposition des Essieux: 22.

526

CLASS/SERIE X 2000   XB

Originally numbered X 1201–5./Numérotées X 1201–5 à l'origine.

Built/Construction: 1975–76.
Engine/Moteur: 2 x 123 kW.
Wheel Arrangement/Disposition des Essieux: BB.
Accommodation/Places: –/48 1T.
Length/Longeur: 15.90 m.

Builder/Constructeur: CFD Montmirail.
Transmission: Hydraulic/hydraulique.
Weight/Masse: tonnes.
Max. Speed/Vitesse max.: 85 km/h.

X 2001 |X 2002 |X 2003 |X 2004 |X 2005

CLASS/SERIE X 5000   XB

A longer and more powerful version of X 2000.
Une version plus longue et puissante que les X 2000.

Built/Construction: 1981–2.
Engine/Moteur: 2 x 179 kW.
Wheel Arrangement/Disposition des Essieux: BB.
Accommodation/Places: –/48 1T.
Length/Longeur: 16.50 m.

Builder/Constructeur: CFD Montmirail.
Transmission: Hydraulic/hydraulique.
Weight/Masse: tonnes.
Max. Speed/Vitesse max.: 85 km/h.

X 5001 |X 5002

CLASS/SERIE X 97050   XBD

New railcars for the Bastia–Ajaccio service. Multiple working fitted.
De nouveaux autorails pour la service Bastia–Ajaccio. Couplables en UM.

Built/Construction: 1989–90.
Builder/Constructeur: Soulé.
Engine/Moteur: 2 x 6 cyl SACM (177 kW) at/à 2250 rpm/tpm.
Transmission: Hydraulic/hydraulique.
Wheel Arrangement/Disposition des Essieux: BB.
Accommodation/Places: –/44 1T.
Weight/Masse: 35.6 tonnes.
Length/Longeur: 18.28 m.
Max. Speed/Vitesse max.: 90 km/h.

X 97051 |X 97053 |X 97054 |X 97055
X 97052 |

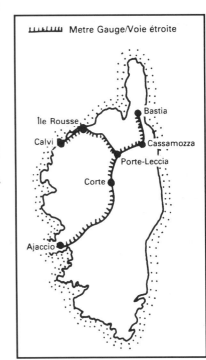

Metre Gauge/Voie étroite

CLASS/SERIE XR 9700   XRBDx

New driving trailers to work with Class X 97050.
De nouvelles remorques pilotes utilisées avec les X 97050.

Built/Construction: 1989/90.
Builder/Constructeur: Soulé.
Wheel Arrangement/Disposition des Essieux: 22.
Accommodation/Places: –/54 1T.
Weight/Masse: 22.4 tonnes.
Length/Longeur: 18.28 m.
Max. Speed/Vitesse max.: 90 km/h.

XR 9701 |XR 9703 |XR 9704 |XR 9705
XR 9702 |

PRIVATE RAILWAYS
CHEMINS DE FER PRIVÉS

The following gives details of French private railways (other than preserved lines).
Voici de détails de certains réseaux privés français (mis à part les lignes musées).

CHEMINS DE FER DE LA PROVENCE

This is the only non-SNCF adhesion non-preserved passenger railway left in France. It runs from Nice Gare du Sud to Digne, a distance of 151 km, and is the last remnant of the Chemins de Fer du Sud whose network included lines from Nice to Vence, Grasse, Draguignan & Meyrargues and from Saint Raphael to Toulon via St. Tropez. Depots are at Nice and Digne, with steam locos based at Puget-Théniers. There is a works at Lingostière (L).

Renumbering of the railcars commenced in 1986, but had still not been completed three years later!

La CP est le seul chemin de fer privé en France qui transports des voyageurs mis à part les lignes à crémaillères et lignes musées. La ligne de Nice (Gare du Sud) à Digne, une distance de 181 km, est le dernier vestige des Chemins de Fer du Sud dont le réseau comportait les lignes de Nice à Vence, Grasse, Draguignan et Mayrargues ainsi que St Raphael–Toulon via St. Tropez. Des dépôts sont à Nice et Digne, et les machines à vapaur sont basées à Puget-Théniers. Il y a des ateliers à Lingostière (L).

La renumérotation des autorails a débuté en 1986 mais n'était toujours pas terminée trois ans plus tard.

Gauge/Ecartement: 1000 mm.

DIESEL LOCOMOTIVES/*LOCOMOTIVES DIESEL*

51   D
Built/Construction: 1934.
Engine/Moteur: One 150 kW.

Builder/Constructeur: CFD Montmirail.
Transmission: Mechanical/mécanique.

51

62   BB
Built/Construction: 1951.
Engine/Moteur: One 450 kW.

Builder/Constructeur: Brissonneau & Lotz.
Transmission: Electric/électrique.

62

CLASS/*SERIE* BB 400   BB
Built/Construction: 1938/48*. BB 401 was ex PO Corrèze in 1971.
Builder/Constructeur: CFD Montmirail.
Engine/Moteur: One 310 kW.   **Transmission:** Mechanical/mécanique.

† Under repair at Lingostière./En réparation à Lingostière.

BB 401* |BB 402†

RAILCARS/*AUTORAILS*
CLASS/*SERIE* X 200   XD

The only survivor of this class. Now in departmental service.
Le dernier survivant de la série. Maintenant un autorail de service.

Built/Construction: 1937.
Engine/Moteur: 172 kW.
Wheel Arrangement/Disposition des Essieux: B2.

Builder/Constructeur: Billard. Type A 150 D.
Transmission: Mechanical/mécanique.

CLASS/SERIE X 300   XB

Built/Construction: 1972*/77†.
Engine/Moteur: Two x 123 kW.
Wheel Arrangement/Disposition des Essieux: BoBo.
AccommodationPlaces: –/48 1T.
Builder/Constructeur: CFD Montmirail.
Transmission: Mechanical/mécanique.
Weight/Masse: tonnes.

* Series 1 with flat ends/Première sous-série aux faces frontales plates.
† Series 2 with angled ends./Deuxième sous-série aux faces frontales à angles.

X 301 (SY 01) *	X 303 (SY 03) *	X 305 (SY 05) †	X 306 (SY 06) †
X 302 (SY 02) *	X 304 (SY 04) *		

CLASS/SERIE X 320   XB

The survivors of twelve cars (ZZ 1–12) built 1935–45. ZZ 21/2 were formerly ZZ 1/2. All are to be refurbished, with X 320/3/8 being converted to driving trailers. Voith hydraulic transmission will be fitted.

Les survivants d'une série de 12 autorails (ZZ 1–12) construites en 1935–45. Les ZZ21/2 sont lex ex ZZ1/2. Tous seront modernisés, mais les X 320/3/8 seront transformés en remorques pilotes. Les autorails recevront une transmission hydraulique Voith.

Built/Construction: 1935–36.
Builder/Constructeur: Renault. Type ABH 1 (ABH 5*).
Engine/Moteur: Two Renault 123 kW.
Transmission: Mechanical/mécanique.
Wheel Arrangement/Disposition des Essieux: BoBo.
AccommodationPlaces: –/44 1T (56S 1Lt).
Weight/Masse: tonnes.

X 320 (ZZ 10) *	X 322 (ZZ 22) Digne	X 326 (ZZ 6) †	X 328 (ZZ 8) *
X 321 (ZZ 21) L(U)	X 323 (ZZ 3) L(U)		

CLASS/SERIE X 350   XBD + Bx

A new two-car unit built for the "Alpazur" service, but now used for commuters.

Un nouvel autorail à deux caisses, construit pour le service «Alpazur», mais utilisés maintenant pour des trains de navetteurs.

Built/Construction: 1984.
Engine/Moteur: Two Renault 123 kW.
Wheel Arrangement/Disposition des Essieux: BoBo + 22.
AccommodationPlaces: –/56 1T + 65S 1L.
Builder/Constructeur: Soulé/Garnéro.
Transmission: Electric/électrique.
Weight/Masse: tonnes.

X 351 XR 1351

CLASS/SERIE XR1330   TRAILERS/REMORQUES

Built/Construction: 1937–58.
Wheel Arrangement/Disposition des Essieux: 22.
AccommodationPlaces: –/32 1T.
Builder/Constructeur: Billard. Type R 210.
Weight/Masse: tonnes.

* Rebodied by Garnéro./Nouvelle caisse construite par Garnéro.
s In departmental use./Autorail de service.
r To be rebodied./A recevoir une nouvelle caisse.
t ex CF du Tarn 1964.
v ex Vivarais 1969.

XR 1331	(RL 1) *	XR 1333	(RL 3) st	XR 1335	(RL 5) *	XR 1337	(RL 7) sr
XR 1332	(RL 2) (U)	XR 1334	(RL 4) *t	XR 1336	(RL 6) *v		

CLASS/SERIE XR1340   HAULED STOCK/VOITURES

Built/Construction: 19 .
AccommodationPlaces: –/52 1T.
Wheel Arrangement/Disposition des Essieux: 22.
Builder/Constructeur: Garnéro.
Weight/Masse: tonnes.

XR 1341	(AT 1)	XR 1342	(AT 2)	XR 1343	(AT 3)	XR 1344	(AT 4)

PRESERVED STEAM LOCOMOTIVES
LOCOMOTIVES À VAPEUR PRESERVÉE

No. No.	Type Type	Builder Constructeur	Date Date	
E 211†	1BCh4vt	Henschel	1923	ex CP (Portugal)
E 327*	2Cn4t	Fives-Lille	1909	ex Réseau Breton

* Preserved by/Présérvées par FACS (Fédération des Amis des Chemins de Fer Secondaires).
† Preserved by/Présérvées par Groupe d'Étude des Chemins de Fer de la Provence.

CHEMIN DE FER DE LA RHUNE

This rack line is the last remnant of the once extensive Voies Ferrées Départementales du Midi metre gauge system. Running from St. Ignace to La Rhune, it has been isolated from other railways since the closure of the line to St. Ignace in 1936. The line climbs into the Pyrénées giving views of the Basque Coast. Electrified since opening in 1924 at 3000 V 50 Hz three-phase, the original locos are still in use together with others from the similar closed line at Luchon. The line can be reached by bus from St. Jean de Luz.

Cette ligne à crémaillère est le dernier vestige du réseau à voie métrique des Voies Ferrées Départementales du Midi. Depuis la fermature en 1936 de la ligne jusqu'à St Ignace, la ligne de St Ignace à La Rhune est isolée des autres chemins de fer. La ligne grimpe dans le Pyrénées avec un panorama sur la côte basque. Les locomotives, qui datent de l'électrification à 3000 V 50 Hz triphasé en 1924, sont toujours en service avec d'autres provenant d'une ligne farmée à Luchon. On peut atteindre la ligne en autocar à partir de St. Jean-de-Luz.

Gauge/Ecartement: 1000 mm.

4 WHEEL RACK LOCOS
LOCOMOTIVES À CRÉMAILLÈRE À DEUX ESSIEUX

Built/Construction: 1912–15.
Builder-Mech. Parts/Constructeur-Partie méchanique: SLM.
Builder-Elec. Parts/Constructeur-Partie électrique: Brown Boveri.
Weight/Masse: 12 tonnes. **Length/Longeur:** 5050 mm.
Power/Puissance: 240 kW. **Max. Speed/Vitesse max.:** 8.5 km/h.

* ex Luchon–Superbagnères 1966.

1	2	3 *	4 *	5 *

CHEMIN DE FER DE CHAMONIX
AU MONTENVERS

This rack line, opened 1908–09 climbs into amazing mountain and glacier scenery. The 5 km line was electrified in 1954 at 11 kV ac 50 Hz. However diesel traction is used for works trains and in emergency and also for extra trains at peak periods.

Cette ligne à crémaillère, qui fut ouverte en 1909, grimpe dans un décor superbe de montagnes et glaciers. La ligne de 5 km fut électrifiée en 11 kV 50 Hz monophasé en 1954. Cependant les locomotives diesel sont utilisées pour des trains de service, en cas d'urgence et pour des trains supplémentaires pendant les périodes de grandes affluences.

Gauge/Ecartement: 1000 mm.

DIESEL LOCOS/LOCOMOTIVES DIESEL   1B

These locos work with articulated coaches 61–63.
Ces locomotives sont utilisées avec les voitures articulées 61–63.

Built/Construction: 1967/72*.
Engine/Moteur: Poyaud A12-150 Se of 485 kW or 520 kW*.
Transmission: Hydraulic/hydraulique.
Builder/Constructeur: SLM.
Driving Wheel Dia: 790 mm.
Max. Speed/Vitesse max.: 21 km/h.

Weight/Masse: 23.3 tonnes.
Length/Longeur: 7.50 m.

31 |32 * |33 *

ELECTRIC RAILCARS/AUTOMOTRICES   BoBo

These railcars have driving cabs at the lower end only. They normally work coupled to trailers 51–56.

Ces automotrices n'ont des cabines qu'a l'extremité inférieure. Elles sont normalement utilisées avec les remorques 51–56.

Built/Construction: 1954/60*/79†.
Builder-Mech. Parts/Constructeur-Partie méchanique: SLM.
Builder-Elec. Parts/Constructeur-Partie électrique: TCO.
Wheel Arrangement/Disposition des Essieux: BoBo.
Weight/Masse: 29.5 tonnes.
Power/Puissance: 475 kW.
AccommodationPlaces: –/84 (–/80*†).

Length/Longeur: 15.37 (15.94*†) m.
Max. Speed/Vitesse max.: 20 km/h.

41 |42 |43 |44 |45 * |46 †

PRESERVED STEAM LOCOMOTIVES
LOCOMOTIVES À VAPEUR PRÉSERVÉE

Three of the eight steam locomotives used on the line before electrification still survive at Chamonix:

Trois des huit locomotives à vapeur qui furent utilisées sur la ligne avant l'electrfication sont toujours à Chamonix:

No.	Type	Builder	Date	
No.	Type	Constructeur	Date	
6	B1zzh2t	SLM	1923	(Preserved/présérvée)
7	B1zzh2t	SLM	1926	(stored/garée)
8	B1zzh2t	SLM	1927	(for spares/pour pièces détachées)

TRAMWAY DU MONT BLANC

This rack line in the Savoy Alps was opened in 1909–14 between St. Gervais les Bains and Glacier Bionnassay, but never achieved its intended terminus closer to Mont Blanc. The 12 km line was electrified in 1957 at 11 kV ac 50 Hz. The depot is located at St. Gervais.

Cette ligne à crémaillère, longue de 12 km, dans les Alpes savoyardes fut ouverte entre 1909 et 1914 entre St. Gervais-les-Bains et Glacier Bionnassey mais n'a jamais atteint sont terminus prévu plus près du Mont Blanc. La ligne fut électrifiée en 1957 en 11 kV 50 Hz monophasé. Le dépôt est situé à St Gervais.

Gauge/Ecartement: 1000 mm.

RACK RAILCARS
AUTOMOTRICES À CREMAILLERE

These cars have driving cabs at the lower end only. They normally work with a trailer coupled at the upper end. the cars do not carry any numbers, but are identifiable by their different liveries.

Ces voitures n'ont des cabines qu'à l'extremité. Elles sont normalement utilisées avec une remorque attachée à l'extremité supérieure. Les automotrices n'ont pas de numéro mais peuvent être identifiées par leurs livrées différentes.

Built/Construction: 1956.
Builder-Mech. Parts/Constructeur-Partie méchanique: SLM/Decauville.
Builder-Elec. Parts/Constructeur-Partie électrique: TCO.
Wheel Arrangement/Disposition des Essieux: BoBo.

Weight/Masse: 12 tonnes.
One hour Rating: 475 kW.

Length/Longeur: 15.37 m.
Max. Speed/Vitesse max.: 20 km/h.

blue/yellow.	bleu/jaune.
yellow/blue.	jaune/bleu.
orange/cream	crème/orange.

Three of the six steam locomotives used on the line before electrification still survive:

Trois des six locomotives à vapeur qui furent utilisées avant l'électrification de la ligne existent toujours:

| No. | Type | Builder | Date | Location |
No.	Type	Constructeur	Date	
2	Bzn2t	SLM	1906	Evires (Preserved/présérvée)
3	Bzn2t	SLM	1909	St. Gervais (stored in depot/garée dans le dépôt)
4	Bzn2t	SLM	1909	St. Gervais (stored in depot/garée dans le dépôt)

RÉGIE DÉPARTMENTALE DES TRANSPORTS DES BOUCHES-DU-RHÔNE

This railway operates a number of freight-only lines between Marseille and Avignon.
Cette compagnie exploite plusieurs lignes de marchandises entre Marseille et Avignon:

Pas-des-Lanciers–Bel Air.
Arles–Fontvieille.
Tarascon–St Rémy-de-Provence.
Barbantane–Plan d'Orgon.

Gauge/Ecartement: 1435 mm.

CLASS/SERIE 50   Bo

Built/Construction: 1957–62.
Engine/Moteur:
Weight/Masse: 35 tonnes.

Builder/Constructeur: CEM/Fauvet Girel.
Transmission: Electric/électrique.
Length/Longeur:

| 51 | 52 | 53 | 54 | 55 | 56 | 57 |

CLASS/SERIE 300   Bo

Built/Construction: 1958–60.
Engine/Moteur:
Weight/Masse: 35 tonnes.

Builder/Constructeur: CEM/Fauvet Girel.
Transmission: Electric/électrique.
Length/Longeur:

| 301 | 302 |

CLASS/SERIE 1200   BoBo

These locos are similar to the SNCF Class BB 63500.
Semblables aux BB 63500 de la SNCF.

Built/Construction: 1964–68.
Engine/Moteur: MGO V12SH (605 kW)
Weight/Masse: 64 tonnes.
Wheel Dia./Diamètre des roues: 1050 mm.

Builder/Constructeur: Brissonneau & Lotz.
Transmission: Electric/électrique.
Length/Longeur: 14.68 m.
Max. Speed/Vitesse max.: 80 km/h.

| 1201 | 1202 | 1203 | 1204 |

CLASS/SERIE 1400   BoBo

Built/Construction: 1978.
Engine/Moteur:

Builder/Constructeur: Moyse.
Transmission: Electric/électrique.

1401

VOIES FERRÉES DES LANDES

This railway operates six freight only branches off the SNCF Bordeaux–Dax line totalling 67 km):

Cette compagnie exploite six lignes de marchandises, d'une longueur totale de 67 km, confluentes à la ligne SNCF Bordeaux–Dax.

Ychoux–Parentis (11 km).
Ychoux–Zone Industrielle (3 km).
Labouheyre–Mimizan Bel Air (30 km).
Laluque–Boos (4 km).
Laluque–Tartas (14 km).
Dax–Candale (5 km).

Gauge/Ecartement: 1435 mm.

CLASS/SERIE BB 01   BB

Built/Construction: 1977 (1955*).   **Builder/Constructeur:** CFD.
Engine/Moteur: **Transmission:** Mechanical/mécanique.

* Purchased 1979 from CFD./Achetée en 1979 du CFD.

BB 01 | BB 207*

CLASS/SERIE Y 01   B

Similar to SNCF Class Y 7400. Purchased 1974 from CFD.
Semblables aux Y 7400 de la SNCF. Achetés du CFD en 1974.

Built/Construction: 1967.
Builder/Constructeur: De Dietrich.
Engine/Moteur: Poyaud 6PYT (150 kW).   **Transmission:** Mechanical/mécanique.
Weight/Masse: 32 tonnes.   **Length/Longeur:** ι 34 m.
Wheel Dia./Dia. des roues: 1050 mm.   **Max. Speed/Vitesse max.:** 60 km/h.

Y 01 | Y 02

CLASS/SERIE BB 71000   BB

Purchased from SNCF./Achetés de la SNCF.

Built/Construction: 1965–6.
Engine/Moteur: Poyaud V12 (615 kW).
Weight/Masse: 55 tonnes.
Wheel Dia./Dia. des roues: 860 mm.

Builder/Constructeur: Fives/Lille/CFD.
Transmission: Mechanical/mécanique.
Length/Longeur: 11.85 m.
Max. Speed/Vitesse max.: 80 km/h.

BB 71003 | BB 71011 | BB 71015

CFTA (SOCIÉTE GÉNÉRALE DE CHEMIN DE FER ET DE TRANSPORTS AUTOMOBILES

This is a light railway organisation which owns or leases the following lines:
Cette société exploite les lignes suivantes dont certaines pour le compte de la SNCF.

Guingamp–Carhaix/Paimpol (89 km).
Gray–Is sur Tille–Poinçon Beneuvre. Gray–Chalindrey/Fresne St. Mammes. (143 km).
Châtillon–Troyes/Villars Sartenoge/Ep Soufflet. Ste. Colombe–Nuits-sous-Ravières. (149 km).
Clamecy–Cercy la Tour/Nevers/Corbigny/Entrains, Tamnay–Château Chinon. (208 km).
Longueville–Provins/Villiers St. Georges, Mezy–Montimirail (49 km)
Cézanne–Anglure/Cézanne–Esternay/Cézanne–Connantre (48 km).

Gauge/Ecartement: 1435 mm.

The CFTA also has a 40% share in the Chemins de Fer de la Provence. See p. 148.
Le CFTA possède 40% du capital des Chemins de Fer de la Provence. Voir le page 148.

CFTA has made do over the years with second hand locomotives. It has recently taken delivery of a batch of surplus diesels from the Houillères du Bassin du Nord et du Pas de Calais (HBNPC) and for its lines in Britanny has acquired its first newly built stock for many years in the shape of three four-wheeled diesel railcars.

La CFTA a toujours exploité ces lignes avec du matériel d'occasion. Cependant récemment, la société a acheté un grand nombre de diesels du Houillères du Bassin du Nord et du Pas de Calais (HBNPC) et a reçu trois autorails à deux essieux flambant neuf pour ses lignes en Bretagne.

Full details of the CFTA traction fleet are not known and the authors would be grateful for any further information. The following lists certain of their locomotives:

On n'a pas de détails complete de parc CFTA et les auteurs seraient contents de recevoir des renseignements supplémentaires. Voici une liste non-complète de leur matériel:

BB 551	Built CFD Montmirail. Was located at St. Dizier. Future uncertain.
	Construit CFD Montmirail. Elle fut utilisée à St Dizier. Avenir incertain.
BB 4032	Built GE USA 1946 and ex USATC
BB 4036	Built GE USA 1946 and ex USATC

CLASS/SERIE BB 4500   BB

Purchased from HBNPC. For details see SNCF BB 63000.
Achetés de la HBNPC. Pour détails voir SNCF BB 63000.

Built/Construction: 196 .   **Builder/Constructeur:** Brissoneau & Lotz.
Livery/Livrée: Blue with red lining/Bleu avec bandes rouge.

BB 4501	Chaumont	BB 4510	Is sur Tille	BB 4519	
BB 4502		BB 4511	Is sur Tille	BB 4520	
BB 4503	Chalindrey	BB 4512		BB 4521	
BB 4504	Chalindrey	BB 4513		BB 4522	
BB 4505		BB 4514		BB 4523	
BB 4506		BB 4515		BB 4524	
BB 4507		BB 4516		BB 4525	
BB 4508		BB 4517		BB 4526	
BB 4509		BB 4518			

CLASS/SERIE BB 4800   BB

Purchased from HBNPC. For details see SNCF BB 63500.
Achetés de la HBNPC. Pour détails voir SNCF BB 63500.

Built/Construction: 196 .   **Builder/Constructeur:** Brissoneau & Lotz.
Livery/Livrée: Blue with red lining/Bleu avec bandes rouge.

BB 4801	Cézanne	BB 4803	Chatillon	BB 4805	
BB 4802	Cézanne	BB 4804	Chatillon		

CLASS/SERIE X 97150   XBD

New railcars for Guingamp–Carhaix and Guingamp–Paimpol. Known as type 'A2E' (*autorails à 2 essieux*).

Des autorails neufs connus sous le nom A2E (autorail à 2 essieux) pour les services Guingamp–Carnaix et Guingamp–Paimpol.

Built/Construction: 1990.   **Builder/Constructeur:** Soulé.
Engine/Moteur: Cummins (210 kW).   **Transmission:** Hydraulic/hydraulique.
Wheel Arrangement/Disposition des Essieux: AA.
AccommodationPlaces: –/38 1T.   **Weight/Masse:** 26.5 tonnes.
Length/Longeur: 15.57 m .   **Max. Speed/Vitesse max.:** 90 km/h.
Livery/Livrée: White and green (Bretagne)./Blanc avec bande verte (Région Bretagne).

X 97151	X 97152	X 97153

CLASSES/SERIE X 2400 & XR 7800

Used on same service as X 97150. Details as SNCF class page 87.
Utilisé sur les mêmes services que les X 97150. Détails comme la même SNCF, page 87.
Livery/Livrée: White and green (Bretagne)./Blanc avec bande verte (Région Bretagne).

X 2416 | X 2429 | XR 8292
X 2429 is kept at Carhaix for spare parts.
X 2429 gardé à Carhaix pour pieçès detachées.

CHEMIN DE FER DE LA MURE

This metre gauge line originally extended from St Georges de Commiers to Corps with several short branches. Most of the system was electrified from 1903, but closures commenced in 1936, and all passenger services ceased in 1950. The section to La Mure survived as a coal carrier. During recent years tourist trains have commenced, and this is now the sole traffic with the closure of the colliery. The second generation of electric locomotives are the principle motive power, but there is an assortment of other stock from various sources.

Cette ligne à voie métrique allait à l'origine de St Georges de Commiers à Corps, avec plusieurs antennes. La plupart du réseau fut électrifiée à partir de 1903 mais des fermatures ont commencé en 1936 et le système a perdu tous ses services voyageurs en 1950. La section St Georges–La Mure a survécu grâce au trafic de charbon. Depuis quelques années le réseau exploite des trains pour touristes, et ceci constitue le seul trafic maintenant avec la fermeture de la mine. La plupart des trains est remorquée par les locomotives électriques de 1933, mais il existe un assortiment d'autre matériel.

Gauge/Ecartement: 1000 mm.

ELECTRIC LOCOS/LOCOMOTIVES ELECTRIQUES BoBo

Built/Construction: 1933.   **System/Système:** 2400 V dc/continu.
Builder-Mech. Parts/Constructeur-Partie mécanique: Ateliers du Nord de la France.
Builder-Elec. Parts/Constructeur-Partie électrique: Sécheron (Switzerland/Suisse).
Power/Puissance: 677 kW.   **Weight/Masse:** 60 tonnes.
Max. T.E./E.T. max.: kN.   **Length/Longeur:** 12.00 m.
Wheel Dia./Dia. des roues: 1060 mm.   **Max. Speed/Vitesse max.:** 40 km/h.

T6 | T7 | T8 | T9 | T10

Other Stock/Autre matériel:

A1	Electric Railcar/automotrice (Chantiers de la Buire, 1927)
A3	Electric Railcar/automotrice (Chantiers de la Buire, 1927)
A5	Electric Railcar/automotrice (Chantiers de la Buire, 1927)
1	Diesel OHL vehicle/draisine diesel (Berliet, 1931).
1	Electric Railcar/automotrice (SWS/BBC, 1916 ex NStCM (Switzerland/Suisse).
3	Electric Railcar/automotrice (SWS/BBC, 1913 ex ASD (Switzerland/Suisse).
5	Electric Railcar/automotrice (SWS/BBC, 1916 ex NStCM (Switzerland/Suisse).
12	Electric Railcar/automotrice (SWS/BBC, 1913 ex ASD (Switzerland/Suisse).
182	Electric Loco./Locomotive électrique (SLM/SAAS, 1928 ex RhB (Switzerland/Suisse).
T2	Diesel Loco./Locomotive diesel (Brissonneau & Lotz, 1951 ex Voies Ferrées de Dauphiné.
T4	Diesel Loco./Locomotive diesel (Brissonneau & Lotz, 1951 ex Voies Ferrées de Dauphiné.

PRESERVED LOCOMOTIVES
LOCOMOTIVES PRESERVEES

The current status of the motive power is indicated as follows:

M   Museum, on display (not active).
MA   Museum, active.
MR   Museum, under repair.
MS   Museum, stored.
P   Plinthed.
S   Stored.
T   In traffic. Reserved for NRM.

L'état actuel du matériel est indiqué comme suit:

M   Machine en musée ou sur ligne musée, en exposition mais pas en service.
MA   Machine en musée ou sur ligne musée, en service.
MR   Machine en musée ou sur ligne musée, en réparation.
MS   Machine en musée ou sur ligne musée, garée hors service.
P   Machine préservée sur socle.
S   Machine garée hors service.
T   En service. Réservé pour NRM.

Steam Locomotives/Locomotives à vapeur.

The system for describing steam locomotives used here is the one which is in general use in Germany. Firstly, letters and numbers are used to describe the wheel arrangement as follows:

Driven axles are denoted by letters where A=1, B=2, C=3 etc.
Non-driven axles are denoted by numbers.

This is then followed by 'h' for superheated locos (from the German 'heizdampf'), or 'n' for saturated locos (from the German 'nassdampf').

The number of cylinders follow, then codes for various features, i.e.

v   compound.
z   rack locomotive with 1 pinion.
zz rack locomotive with 2 pinions.
t   tank locomotive.

e.g.: 1D1h2t is a superheated 2–8–2 tank locomotive with 2 cylinders.

La classification des locomotives à vapeur utilisée ici suit le système allemand. D'abord des chiffres et des lettres sont employés selon la disposition des essieux comme suit:

Une lettre correspond au nombre d'essieux moteurs – A=1, B=2, C=3 etc.
Un chiffre correspond au nombre d'essieux porteurs.

Cette classification est suivie de la lettre 'h'pour les locomotives surchauffées ('h' de l'allemand 'heizdampf'), ou 'n' pour une locomotive saturée ('n' de l'Allemand 'nassdampf').

Ces lettres sont suivies du nombres de cylindres et, si necessaire, d'un code:

v   compound.
z   machine à crémaillère à 1 pignon.
zz machine à crémaillère à 2 pignons.
t   locomotive-tender.

Par example: 1D1h2t est une locomotive-tender 141 surchauffée à 2 cylindres.

Number / Numero	Details / Classification	Built / Date	Status / Etat	Location / Lieu
5 "SEZANNE"	1A1n2	1847	M	NRM Mulhouse (CF Montereau–Troyes).
6 "L'AIGLE"	1A1n2	1846	M	NRM Mulhouse (CF Avignon–Marseille).
33 "ST.PIERRE"	1A1n2	1843	M	NRM Mulhouse (CF Paris–Rouen).
80 "LE CONTINENT"	2An2	1852	M	NRM Mulhouse (CF Paris–Strasbourg).
NORD 701	2AAn4v	1885	M	NRM Mulhouse.
ÉTAT 2029"PARTHENAY"	1Bn2	1882	MS	NRM Mulhouse (SNCF 120A36).
PO 340	1B1n2	1882	M	NRM Mulhouse (SNCF 121A340).

PLM C 145	2Bn4v	1902	M	NRM Mulhouse (SNCF 220A85).
NORD 2.670	2B1h4v	1903	M	NRM Mulhouse (SNCF 221A30).
PLM 1423	Cn2	1854	M	NRM Mulhouse (SNCF 030A1).
NORD 3486	Cn2	1890	MS	Villeneuve St. Georges (NRM).
030C815	Cn2	1878	MS	NRM Mulhouse.
030C841	Cn2	1883	M	Delson, Canada.
030TA628	Cn2t	1874	MS	NRM Mulhouse.
030TB2	Cn2t	1870	P	NRM Mulhouse.
030TB130	Cn2t	1900	MA	Neuf Brisach CFTR.
030TB134	Cn2t	1900	MR	Neuf Brisach CFTR.
030TU13	Cn2t	1943	P	Caen (USATC 6102).
030TU22	Cn2t	1943	M	Longueville (USATC 4383).
MIDI 312 "L'ADOUR"	C2n2t	1856	M	NRM Mulhouse (SNCF 032TA312).
130B348	1Ch2	1862	MA	Longueville.
130B439	1Ch2	1882	P	Capdenac.
130B476	1Ch2	1883	MA	Chinon. TVT.
EST 32.031	1C1h2t	1925	M	NRM Mulhouse (SNCF 131TB31).
MIDI 1314	2Cn4v	1902	M	NRM Mulhouse (SNCF 230B614).
230B114	2Ch4v	1908	M	NRM Mulhouse.
230C531	2Cn4v	1905	MS	Villeneuve St. Georges.
230D9	2Ch4v	1908	M	NRM Mulhouse.
230D116	2Ch4v	1911	MA	Nene Valley Railway, Wansford, GB.
230G352	2Ch4v	1922	MR	Chinon. TVT.
230G353	2Ch2	1922	T	SNCF Noisy Le Sec.
PO 4546	2C1n4v	1908	M	NRM Mulhouse (SNCF 231A546).
NORD 3.1192	2C1h4v	1936	M	NRM Mulhouse (SNCF 231E22).
231C78	2C1h4v	1930	MS	Montargis (NRM).
231E41	2C1h4v	1937	P	St.Pierre des Corps.
231G558	2C1h4v	1921	A	Sotteville.
231H8	2C1h4v	1912	MS	NRM Mulhouse.
231K8	2C1h4v	1912	MA	FACS, La Chapelle.
231K22	2C1h4v	1914	M	Carnforth, GB.
231K82	2C1h4v	1920	MS	St.Étienne.
NORD 3.1102	2C2h4v	1911	M	NRM Mulhouse.
232U1	2C2h4v	1949	M	NRM Mulhouse.
PLM 4A51	Dn2	1878	M	Miramas (SNCF 040A51).
PLM 4B9	Dn4v	1892	M	Carnoules (SNCF 040B9).
NORD 4853	Dn2	1880	M	Longueville.
040TA137	Dn2t	1922	MA	Mortagne-sur-Sevre.
040TA141	Dn2t	1923	MR	Vigy.
140A259	1Dh2	1928	MS	Villeneuve St. Georges (NRM).
140A908	1Dh2	1892	MS	NRM Mulhouse.
140C22	1Dh2	1916	P	Vierzon-Chaillot. (No tender).
140C27	1Dh2	1916	MA	Conflans Jarny, CITEV.
140C38	1Dh2	1919	P	Caen.
140C231	1Dh2	1916	MA	Longueville.
140C287	1Dh2	1917	MR	L'Arbresle.
140C313	1Dh2	1917	P	Reims.
140C314	1Dh2	1917	MA	St Quentin.
140C344	1Dh2	1917	M	NRM Mulhouse.
141C100	1D1h2	1922	MA	Connerré.
141F282	1D1h4v	1925	M	NRM Mulhouse.
141R73	1D1h2	1945	M	Bressingham, GB.
141R420	1D1h2	1946	MA	Clermont Ferrand.
141R568	1D1h2	1945	MA	Conflans Jarny. CITEV.
141R840	1D1h2	1946	MR	Cosne-sur-Loire.
141R1108	1D1h2	1946	MR	Breil sur Roya.
141R1126	1D1h2	1947	MA	Toulouse.
141R1187	1D1h2	1947	M	NRM Mulhouse.
141R1199	1D1h2	1947	M	Vitré.
141R1207	1D1h2	1947	MA	Montargis.
141R1244	1D1h2	1947	MA	Brugg (Switzerland/Suisse).
141R1298	1D1h2	1947	M	Miramas.
141R1332	1D1h2	1947	S	Jarnac.
PO 5452	1D1h2t	1922	M	NRM Mulhouse (SNCF 141TA452).

141TB407	1D1h2t	1913	M	Longueville.
141TB424	1D1h2t	1913	MA	Neuf Brisach. CFTR.
141TC19	1D1h2t	1922	M	Chinon. TVT.
141TC51	1D1h2t	1935	M	NRM Mulhouse.
141TD740	1D1h3t	1931	MA	Toulouse St Jory.
241A1	2D1h4v	1925	M	NRM Mulhouse.
241A65	2D1h4v	1931	M	St. Sulpice (Switzerland/Suisse).
241P9	2D1h4v	1947	M	Guîtres.
241P16	2D1h4v	1947	M	NRM Mulhouse.
241P17	2D1h4v	1947	P	Le Creusot.
241P30	2D1h4v	1949	P	Vallorbe (Switzerland/Suisse).
242AT6	2D2h4v	1949	M	NRM Mulhouse (SNCF 242TA6).
150A065	1Eh4v	1912	MS	Longueau (NRM).
150P13	1E1h4v	1940	M	NRM Mulhouse.

Diesel & Electric Locomotives and Tractors
Locomotives électriques et diesel, et locotracteurs.

BB 36	BoBoe	1924	MS	NRM.
BB 824	BoBoe	19	MR	Paris.
BB 915	BoBoe	1936	S	Reserved.
BB 1282	BoBoe	1900	M	NRM Mulhouse.
BB 1501	BoBoe	1922	MS	Nîmes (NRM).
BB 1632	BoBoe	1925	MS	Nîmes (NRM).
2CC2 3402	2CoCo2e	1929	MS	Montluçon (NRM).
1ABBA1 3603	1ABoBoA1e	1927	M	NRM Mulhouse.
BB 4110	BoBoe	1929	MR	Toulouse St. Jory.
BB 4175	BoBoe	1932	MS	Béziers (NRM).
Midi E 4162	BoBoe	1932	M	Miramas (SNCF BB 4177).
2D2 5516	2Do2e	1934	M	NRM Mulhouse.
2D2 5525	2Do2e	1935	MA	Montrouge.
CC 7107	CoCoe	1953	T	.
BB 9004	BoBoe	1954	M	NRM Mulhouse.
2D2 9134	2Do2e	1951	MR	St. Etienne.
2D2 9135	2Do2e	1951	MA	Reserved for NRM, Paris Charolais.
CC 14018	CoCoe	1959	M	NRM Mulhouse.
CC 20001	CoCoe	1958	MS	Montluçon (NRM).
BB 60032	BoBode	1938	M	NRM Mulhouse.
C 61002	Cde	1950	MA	St. Jean du Gard TVC.
C 61032	Cde	1952	MA	Chinon. TVT.
C 61041	Cde	1952	MA	Fourmies.
C 61042	Cde	1952	MA	Mortagne-sur-Sevre.
C 61046	Cde	1953	MS	Le Havre Musée des Arts & Techniques.
TC 61107	Cde	1951	MS	Le Havre Musée des Arts & Techniques.
A1AA1A 62029	A1AA1Ade	1946	MA	Neuf Brisach.
A1AA1A 62036	A1AA1Ade	1947	MA	Chinon. TVT.
A1AA1A 62073	A1AA1Ade	1947	MA	Chinon. TVT.
CC 65001	CoCode	1956	MS	Sotteville (NRM).
CC 65002	CoCode	1956	MS	Assoc. de conservation de materiel ferroviaire de l'Ouest (Nantes).
CC 65003	CoCode	1956	MS	Nantes.
CC 65004	CoCode	1956	MA	CFT de la Seudre.
CC 65005	CoCode	1956	MA	Courpière, AGRIVAP.
CC 65006	CoCode	1957	MS	Chinon. TVT.
CC 65012	CoCode	1957	MS	Chinon. TVT.
CC 65501	CoCode	1955	T	.
BB 71010	BBdm	1965	MA	Le Bouveret, Switzerland.
BB 71017	BBdm	1965	MA	Saujon. CFT de la Seudre.
Y 2291	Bdm	1959	MA	NRM Mulhouse.
Y 2402	Bdm	1962	MA	Neuf Brisach.
Y 6013	Bde	1954	M	Miramas.
Y 6563	Bde	1957	MA	CFV3V. Mariembourg, Belgium/Belgique.
YBD 12004	Bdm	1932	MA	Sabres. CFT des Landes de Gascogne.
YBE 15053	Bdm	1936	MA	L'Arbresle.
Y 51125	Bdhm	1954	MA	Sabres. CFT des Landes de Gascogne.

| Y 51135 | Bdhm | 1954 | MA | Chinon. TVT. |
| Y 51147 | Bdhm | 1955 | MA | Chinon. TVT. |

Diesel Railcars/**Autorails.**

X 2401	BBdm	1951	?	?.
X 2402	BBdm	1951	MA	Etival.
X 2403	BBdm	1951	MA	Miramas.
X 2423	BBdm	1952	MA	Alençon.
X 2425	BBdm	1952	MA	Brive, Regiorail.
X 2426	BBdm	1952	MA	CFT du Cotentin.
X 2431	BBdm	1952	MA	Boulogne, Train à Petite Vitesse des Morins.
X 2448	BBdm	1956	MA	Train Touristique de la Scarpe St. Amand-les-Eaux.
X 2468	BBdm	1955	MA	Toulouse St. Jory, CFTMP.
X 2475	BBdm	1956	MA	St. Étienne.
X 2709	B2dm	1954	MA	Brive. Regiorail.
XR 7716	22	1954	MA	Brive. Regiorail.
X 2716	B2dm	1955	MA	Montargis, AATY.
XR 7762	22	1955	MA	Montargis, AATY.
X 2719	B2dm	1955	MA	Breil sur Roya, Rail Voyages et Tourisme.
XR 7708	22	1955	MA	Breil sur Roya, Rail Voyages et Tourisme.
X 3601	B2dm	1948	MA	Chinon. TVT.
X 3623	B2dm	1949	MA	St.Quentin.
X 3710	1AA1dm	1949	MA	Sentheim.
X 3801	B2dm	1951	MA	Elbeuf Ville. CF Forêt de la Londe.
X 3810	B2dm	1951	MA	Sabres. CFT des Landes de Gascogne.
X 3814	B2dm	1952	MA	Toucy, AATY.
X 3817	B2dm	?	MA	CFT de la Selune.
X 3818	B2dm	?	MA	Tamnay (Nièvre),TMMB.
X 3823	B2dm	?	MA	Elbeuf Ville. CF Forêt de la Londe.
X 3824	B2dm	?	M	Miramas.
X 3825	B2dm	?	MA	CFT du Cotentin.
X 3835	B2dm	?	?	?.
X 3837	B2dm	?	MA	CFT de la Canner.
X 3838	B2dm	?	MA	Stenay–Mouzon.
X 3845	B2dm	?	MA	Narbonne. Autorail Touristique du Minervois.
X 3846	B2dm	?	MA	Narbonne. Autorail Touristique du Minervois.
X 3850	B2dm	?	MA	Attigny ATVA.
X 3858	B2dm	?	MA	Neuf Brisach.
X 3865	B2dm	?	MA	RVT Viaduc (Aubenas (07).
X 3866	B2dm	?	MA	St. Quentin. CFT du Vermandois.
X 3867	BBdm	?	MA	Vitréon.
X 3871	B2dm	?	MA	Toucy. AATY.
X 3876	B2dm	?	MA	Tamnay. TMMB.
X 3890	B2dm	?	MA	Loudéac. CF du Centre Bretagne.
X 3897	B2dm	?	MA	Attigny. CFTSA.
X 3898	B2dm	?	MA	CFV3V. Mariembourg, Belgium/Belgique.
X 3907	B2dm	?	MA	Caen? CFT de la Suisse Normande.
X 3926	B2dm	?	MA	Saujon. CFT de la Seudre.
X 3934	B2dm	?	MA	Ambert, AGRIVAP.
X 3937	B2dm	?	P	Rambouillet. (Clubroom).
X 3939	B2dm	?	MA	L'Arbresle.
X 3943	B2dm	?	?	? Association de Ceyzèriat.
X 3944	B2dm	?	MA	Tournemire. CF Causse et Rougier.
X 3953	B2dm	?	MA	Connerrée. CFV de la Sarthe.
X 3959	B2dm	?	MR	L'Arbresle.
X 3968	B2dm	?	MA	Espalion. CFT de l'Aveyron.
X 3971	B2dm	?	MA	Elbeuf Ville. CF Forêt de la Londe.
X 3976	B2dm	?	MA	Guitres. CFT Guîtres–Marcenais.
X 3989	B2dm	?	M?	Annonay. Modélistes et Amis du Rail Vivarois.
X 3998	B2dm	?	MA	CFV3V. Mariembourg, Belgium/Belgique.
X 4001	B2dm	?	MA	Anduze or Conflans Jarny (CITEV).

X 4013	B2dm	?	P	Sancerre. (Cher).
X 4025	B2dm	?	MA	Besançon ABFC (AT3DJ042).
X 4028	B2dm	?	MA	Narbonne. Autorail Touristique du Minervois.
X 4039	B2dm	?	MA	Dijon ABFC (AT3DJ043).
X 4046	B2dm	1962	M	Denain. Cercle d'Études Ferroviaires du Nord.
X 4051	B2dm	1961	MA	Besançon.
X 4203	Bo2de	1959	MS	NRM Brive.
X 4204	Bo2de	1959	MA	Belfort.
X 4206	Bo2de	1959	MA	Conflans-Jarny. CITEV.
X 4208	Bo2de	1959	MA	AGRIVAP (Ambert).
X 5506	1A2dm	1950	MA	Chinon. TVT.
X 58??	?	?	MA	Tamnay. TMMB.
X 5815	1A2dm	1953	MA	L' Arbnesle.
X 5822	1A2dm	1953	MA	Sabres. CFT des Landes de Gascogne.
X 5830	1A2dm	1954	MA	St.Quentin.
X 5845	1A2dm	1954	MA	Miramas.
X 5852	1A2dm	1954	MA	Sentheim.
X 9152	AAdm	19??		Miramas.
PO ZZEty 23859	B2dm	1934	M	NRM Mulhouse (SNCF X 2211).
État ZZB2Ef 23901	A1pm	1921	M	NRM Mulhouse.
État ZZy 24091	B2dm	1937	M	NRM Mulhouse (SNCF X 3421).
État ZZy 24408		1935	M	NRM Mulhouse (SNCF XB 1008).
X 52103	BoBode	1945	MR	Bordeaux NRM.
Est ZZABSC Ety 54005		1936	MS	NRM Mulhouse (SNCF XM 5005).
PLM LZZBE 39	Bdm	1928	MA	La Barque.

Electric Units/**Automotrices**

Z 209	Bo	1901	T	Reserved for NRM.
Z 1208	A1AA1A	1914	M	NRM Mulhouse.
Z 1567	BoBo	1930	MS	Le Mans NRM.
Z 1572	BoBo	1930	MS	PSL for St. Mande Museum.
Z 3713	BoBoBo	1938	MA	Elbeuf Ville. CF Forêt de la Londe.
Z 3714	BoBoBo	1938	MS	Le Mans NRM.
Z 4001	Bo2	1904	MS	Brive NRM.
Z 4156	BoBo		MS	NRM.
Z 4909	BoBo	1913	MS	Brive NRM.
Z 4313	BoBo	1927	MS	NRM.
État ZABEyf 23001	Bo2	1902	MS	NRM Mulhouse.
Z 216	Boe	1908	M	La Mure.
Z 450	Boe	1908	M	La Mure (Snowplough).
Z 10003	Boe	1901	M	La Mure.
Z 10004	Boe	1902	M	La Mure.
Z 10212	Boe	1901	M	La Mure.
Z 10316	Boe	1908	M	La Mure.
Z 10422	Boe	1908	M	La Mure.

Additional Abbreviations/**abbréviations supplémentaires**

AATY	Association des Autorails touristique de l'Yonne.
AJECTA	Association des Jeunes pour l'exploitation et la Conservation des Trains d'Autrefois.
AGRIVAP	Les Amis du Musée de la Machine Agricole et à Vapeur.
CFT	Chemin de Fer Touristique (Tourist railway).
CFTMP	Chemin de Fer Touristique Midi-Pyrénées.
CFTR	Chemin de Fer Touristique du Rhin.
CFTSA	Chemin de Fer Touristique du Sud des Ardennes.
CFV3V	Chemin de Fer à Vapeur des Trois Vallées, Mariembourg, Belgium/Belgique.
CITEV	Compagnie Internationale des Trains Express à Vapeur.
FACS	Fédération des Amis des Chemins de Fer Secondaires.
NRM	Musée National du Chemin de Fer.
TMMB	Train Musée Morvan Bazois.
TVC	Trains à Vapeur des Cevennes.
TVT	Trains à Vapeur de Touraine.

The nameplate of SYBIC 26006./Le nom de SYBIC 26006. Dijon Perrigny. 15/07/90.　　　　*Éric Dunkling*

CAP D'AGDE
LANGUEDOC, SOUTH OF FRANCE
HOLIDAY VILLA TO LET

New holiday villa (37 m²) to let close to sandy beach (Plage Richelieu), shops, Aqualand etc. Sleeps 4 (one double bed in a separate bedroom and two single beds). Shower room, cooker, fridge. Satellite TV for English-speaking channels. Parking space. Patio with separate patio table and chairs.

For details telephone 0742-671129 (office) or write to publishers address for details.

SNCF SELF-PROPELLED DEPARTMENTAL STOCK.
MATÉRIEL MOTEUR DE SERVICE DE LA SNCF

Very little exists as such, as traffic locos are normally used. Several Picassos exist as inspection saloons and other DMUs will be found in departmental use. Details of these are included with the respective classes.

Ce matériel inclut les Picassos mentionées plus haut ainsi que 7 chasse-neige autonome. Voici de brefs détails.

SNOWPLOUGHS/CHASSE-NEIGE

The SNCF has several rotary snowploughs. Brief details of those known are as follows:
La SNCF a plusieurs chasse-neige rotatifs. Ci-dessous sont des détails brefs des chasse-neige à notre connaisance.

CN 1	Beilhack/65	1972	Chambéry.
CN 2	Beilhack/64	1972	Chambéry.
CN 3	Beilhack/91	1981	Dôle.
CN 4	Beilhack	1987	St. Gervais les Bains. (1000 mm).
CN 5	ex BB 4119	1928	Toulouse
CN 6	ex BB 4123	1928	Toulouse
CNS	ex BB 60021		Aurillac

Snowplough/Chasse neige CNS (UIC 974 7 082) ex BB 60021. Aurillac depot/Dépôt de Aurillac. 17/09/89
Eric Dunkling

EX-SNCF LOCOMOTIVES IN INDUSTRY
LOCOMOTIVES EX SNCF
EN UTILISATION INDUSTRIELLE

Many SNCF locomotives have been sold to industrial concerns for further use. In many cases they still carry their SNCF numbers. The following is just a brief survey and further news and observations are welcomed.

Beaucoup de locomotives SNCF ont été vendues pour utilisation industrielle. Dans certains cas elles gardent leurs numéros d'origine. Voici une liste brève – d'autres observations seraient les bienvenues.

DIESEL LOCOS/LOCOMOTIVES DIESEL

C 61019	RATP T 104
C 61025	RATP T 105
C 61011	RATP T 106
C 61024	RATP T 107
C 61006	RATP T 108
C 610	RATP T 130
C 610	RATP T 131
C 61037	Sermaize les Bains.
CC 65505	Société Drouard
CC 65507	Desquenne et Giral
CC 65510	Travaux du Sud Ouest
CC 65522	Travaux du Sud Ouest
BB 66691	L'Entreprise Déhé No. 269
BB 66692	L'Entreprise Déhé No. 270
BB 71001	Port de Rouen
BB 71019	Kronenbourg Brewery, Strasbourg or Lyon.
BB 71020	Transport Briguier, La Chapelle St. Ersin
BB 71022	Kronenbourg Brewery, Strasbourg or Lyon.
CC 80001	Desquenne et Giral

TRACTORS/LOCOTRACTEURS

Y 2106	Coop Agricole de la Charente, Angouleme, Zone Industrielle No.3 (ex Reseau 6!)
Y 22	Socemi Fillod. (AT1 DJ 033)
Y 2335	St. Jean de Maurienne
Y 6234	Meccoli.
Y 6240	Agricher
Y 6249	Cereal Coop.
Y 51122	Chambre de Commerce et d'Industrie d'Avignon-Courtine
Y 51129	Magazins Generaux de Toulouse, Haut Garonne
Y 51130	Cooperative du Mans, Le Mans
Y 51206	L'Entreprise Déhé
Y 51207	La Cellulose du Rhone et de l'Aquitaine, Tarascon
Y 51219	Cooperative Agricole des Charentis, Charmont
Y 51228	Entreprise de Travaux Ferroviaires, Vecchietti, Italy/Italie

DB Class 211s in France:/Série 211 du DB en France:

211 111	AT3 PSL 192	Desquenne et Gival, near/près de Mantes.
211 114	AT3 PSL 193	Desquenne et Gival, near/près de Mantes.
211 154	AT3 PSL 194	Desquenne et Gival, near/près de Mantes.
211 238	AT3 PSL 195	Desquenne et Gival, near/près de Mantes.

MUSEUMS AND MUSEUM LINES

There are now many museums and museum lines in France. After a very slow start the number of museum lines has mushroomed in recent years. They range from the purely tourist/ childrens railway where in some cases narrow gauge diesel locomotives run disguised as steam locomotives, garden railways, to fully-fledged preserved branch lines.

This review concentrates on the main centres and ignores garden railways and small diesels with steam outlines!.

One of the most interesting developments in recent years has been the preserving of diesel railcars with over 40 Picassos saved. Many of these are used on branch lines but some are used by groups for long distance runs over SNCF scenic lines etc.

After much thought on how to present the information the places are listed in "Départment" order. Unless otherwise shown all are standard gauge.

02. AISNE

St. Quentin. 02104. CFT du Vermandois.

St. Quentin–Gauchy–Origny St. Benoîte (Aisne). 22 km. Operates steam and diesel trains on certain sundays and holidays in summer.
2 steam, 3 diesel railcars.

06. ALPES-MARITIME

Nice. 06000. Chemins de Fer de la Provence.

Steam trains operate over part of this private metre gauge railway on most sundays May to October.

07. ARDECHE.

Tournon. 07300. Chemins de Fer du Vivarais.

Once part of a much larger system the line today runs for 33 km from Tournon to Lamastre. A daily service operates from mid May to end August, saturdays and sundays in September, and sundays in October. Tournon is across the river from Tain L'Hermitage.
9 steam, 3 diesel, 5 diesel railcars.

08. ARDENNES.

Attigny. 08   . CFT du Sud des Ardennes.

Attigny–Challerange and Amagne–Lucquy. 40 km. A tourist operation in both directions from Attigny on sundays May–September.

11. AUDE.

Narbonne. 11100. Autorail Touristique du Minervois.

Narbonne (rue Paul Vieu) to Bize 20 km. A Picasso operation on most saturdays, sundays and holidays in the summer.

13. BOUCHES DU RHÔNE.

Miramas. 13140. Old SNCF Depot Workshop and yard.

The stock is kept under cover in the old repair shop or out in the open around the turntable.
6 steam, 1 electric, 1 diesel, 5 diesel railcars.

17. CHARENTE MARITIME.

Saujon. 17600. CFT De La Seudre.

Saujon–La Tremblade 21 km. Operates wednesday and sundays July–September.
3 steam, 3 diesel, 1 diesel railcar.

21. CÔTE D'OR.

Bligny sur Ouche. 21360. CFT de la Valée de l'Ouche. 600 mm.

Bligny–Oucherotte/Pré-Magnin, 4 km. sundays and holidays May–September.
2 steam, 4 diesel.

30. GARD.

St. Jean du Gard. 30270. Train à Vapeur des Cevennes.

St. Jean Du Gard–Anduze 13 km. Uses locos and stock belonging to Compagnie Internationale des Trains Express à Vapeur (CITEV). Daily operation in July and August, until first week in September then thursdays, saturdays and sundays only in September and sundays only in October. Steam trains operate most days but avoid monday and saturday!. On weekdays buses run from Alès and Nîmes.
3 steam, 4 diesel railcars.

33. GIRONDE.

Guîtres. 33230. Train Touristique Guîtres–Marcenais.

This 12 km line operates sundays May–October and TThSSuO in the peak summer weeks. The nearest SNCF station is Coutras (5 km).
4 steam, 2 diesel railcars.

37. INDRE ET LOIRE.

Marcilly sur Maulne. 37330. Musée Vivant, CF de Marcilly. 600 mm.

This small railway has more than 10 locomotives including 3 steam. 2 of the steam locos are from Poland and are former "Feldbahn" tank engines, one of which has a supplementary tender.

37500 Chinon. Trains à vapeur de Touraine. TVT.

Chinon–Richelieu, 21 km. Operates saturdays and sundays May–September.
4 steam, 8 diesel, 3 diesel railcars.
Most stock believed to be at Richlieu.

38. ISÈRE.

St. Georges de Commiers. 38450. Chemin de Fer de La Mure. (1000 mm).

St. Georges de Commiers–La Mure 30 km. Until quite recently this electrified mineral line operated occasional passenger trains over its spectacular line. Now the tourist train is more the mainstay of the line. Operates daily May–September then SSuO and holidays until mid November. The line climbs high into the alps along mountain ledges giving views over dammed valleys. If you have not been make sure you include a visit on your next holiday!. St. Georges de Commiers is near Grenoble and SNCF trains call there. First train on the museum line is usuall 09.45. Reservations are necessary at busy times.
2 diesel, 6 electric, 5 electric railcars.

40. LANDES.

Sabres. 40300. CFT des Landes de Gascogne.

Sabres–Marquèze, 4 km. Operates daily June–September with a train every 40 minutes 10.30–17.20 except for the lunch break.

43. HAUTE LOIRE.

Dunières. 43220. CF du Velay. (1000 mm).

Dunières–St. Agrève 37 km. This is another part of the old Vivarais system but unfortunately has not operated for years now. The precise reason is not known but the locos and stock are rotting away in several locations. Future unknown.
4 steam, 2 diesel, 10 diesel railcars.

45. LOIRET.

Pithiviers. 45300. Musée de Transports de Pithiviers. MTP. (600 mm).

Pithiviers–Bellébat, 4 km. This system was once part of a large sugar beet network and the line is noteworthy as being the first preserved railway in France with operations having started about 1966. Operates sundays May–October and also saturdays in July and August. Nearest SNCF station is Étampes.
13 steam, 2 diesel, 2 diesel railcars.

50. MANCHE.

TRAINS TOURISTIQUES DU COTENTIN.

Two extremities of the same line, Carentan–Carteret.

Barneville-Carteret. 50270. Trains Touristique de la Côte des Isles.

Carteret–Port Bail 9 km. Operates sundays and holidays from may to september.

Carentan 50500. Trains Touristique des Marais.

Carentan–Baupte 10 km. Operates tuesdays and thursdays in summer.

Pontaubault 50300. CF de la la Vallée de la Selune.

Pontaubault–Parigny–St. Hilaire du Harcourt 24 km.
Operating days unknown.

54. MEURTHE & MOSELLE.

Conflans Jarny. 54800.

CITEV has acquired part of the wagon works as a workshop and maintains some of its rolling stock here in the winter months. Otherwise stock is at St. Jean du Gard.

57. MOSELLE

Abreschviller. 57560. CF Forestier D'Abreschviller. (700 mm).

Abreschviller–Grand Soldat 6 km. As the name implies this is a forest railway dating back to 1884 which closed in 1966. The beauty of the line was realised and by 1968 a tourist service was started. Operates saturdays and sundays May to end of September and daily in July and August. Sarrebourg SNCF station is 12 km away from where buses operate.
4 steam, 1 diesel.

Vigy, 57640. CFT Vallée de la Canner.

Vigy–Hombourg–Budanges, 12 km. Operates sundays and holidays May–early October. The line closed to freight traffic in 1976 and the tourist trains started in 1985.
4 steam, 1 diesel, 1 diesel railcar.

59. NORD.

Denain. 59220. Train Touristique du Hainaut.

Denain Mines–Arenberg, 8 km. A Picasso runs over the old mining line on certian weekends in the summer. There is a museum at Denain.
4 steam, 3 diesel, 1 BE, 1 diesel railcar.

63. PUY DE DÔME.

Ambert. 63600. Train Touristique Livradois–Forez. Les Amis du musée de la machine agricole et à vapeur (AGRIVAP).

Ambert–Courpière 37 km. saturdays, sundays and holidays in July and August.
1 steam, 2 diesel, 1 diesel railcar.

64 PYRÉNÉES ATLANTIQUE.

Saint Ignace. 64310. CF à Crémaillere de La Rhune. (1000 mm).

St. Ignace–La Rhune 4 km. Not a preserved line but included for its interest as it is generally unknown. A spectacular line climbing from 169 m to 887 m and is close to the Spanish frontier. Daily July–September, saturdays, sundays and holidays May–October.

Artouste. 64440. Train Touristique D'Artouste. (500 mm).

La Sagette–Lac d'Artouste, 9 km. This is another of those rather unknown lines. Situated 2000 metres up in the Pyrénées it is no wonder!. However the journey to this outpost is well worthwhile. The Artouste dam dates back to the CF du Midi electrification schemes and the need for a power supply. This 500 mm gauge railway was built for moving construction supplies. Today it serves a completely different purpose offering marvellous views if the weather is clear. Take warm clothing with you just in case!. Operates daily June–September.

67. BAS.

Ottrot. 67530. Train Folklorique de Rosheim–Ottrot.

Ottrot–Rosheim 8 km. 1 steam. Operation uncertain.

68. HAUT RHIN.

Mulhouse. 68200. National Railway Museum.

Open daily except at Christmas and New Year. A splendid collection of locomotives and rolling stock.
35 steam, 6 electric, 2 diesel, 1 electric railcar, 1 diesel railcar.

Neuf Brisach. 68600. CFT du Rhin.

Volgelsheim (Port Rhenan)–Marckolsheim 16 km. An industrial line along the river operating from May to September on saturdays, sundays and holidays. Colmar is 12 km away.
6 steam, 8 diesel, 1 diesel railcar.

Sentheim. 68700. CFT de la Vallée de la Doller.

Sentheim–Cernay 14 km. Operates Sundays and holidays June–September, with daily trains in July and August (except mondays and tuesdays). Steam trains only on sundays/holidays.
4 steam, 3 diesel, 4 diesel railcar, 1 electric railcar.

69. RHONE.

L'Arbresle. 69 . Train Touristique des Monts du Lyonnais.

L'Arbresle–Sainte Foy L'Argentière, 21 km. A new operation to the west of Lyon using locos and stock formerly on the CFT du Breda which has closed. Operates sundays June–September.
3 steam, 2 diesel, 2 diesel railcars.

72. SARTHE.

Connerré. 72160. CFT de la Sarthe.

Connerré-Beillé–Bonnétable. 18 km. sundays in July and August. Railcar in the morning, steam in the afternoon.
2 steam, 1 diesel, 5 diesel railcars.

74. HAUTE SAVOIE.

Chamonix. 74400 CF Chamonix au Montenvers. (1000 mm, Rack).

Chamonix–Montenvers, 6 km. Not a museum line but included for completeness. Daily service from mid May to end September/October.

Le Fayet 74190. Tramway du Mont Blanc (1000 mm, Rack).

Fayet–Bionnassay glacier, 12 km. Once again a line included for completeness. Operates daily June–September.

Évian les Bains. 74500. Rive Bleue Express.

An international line. Actually based in Switzerland but included here as one end of the line is in France. Le Bouveret (Switzerland)–Évian, 22 km. Operates saturdays (diesel) and sundays (steam) July–September. The steam is Swiss whilst the diesel is ex SNCF 71010!,

77. SEINE & MARNE.

Longueville. 77650. AJECTA Museum.

This society has taken over the old SNCF roundhouse for use as a museum and workshop.
9 steam, 3 diesel, 1 diesel railcar.

Grez sur Loing. 77880. Tacots des Lacs (600 mm).

A bit more than a garden railway. This 2.5 km line operates every sunday and holiday throughout the summer — weather permitting.
5 steam, 3 diesel.

80. SOMME.

Le Crotoy. 80550. CF de la baie de Somme (1000 mm).

Le Crotoy–Noyelles, St. Valery, and Cayeux. 27 km sundays and Holidays May–September with TWFO operation in July and August on the St. Valéry–Noyelles/Le Crotoy sections; Cayeux–St. Valéry and Noyelles saturdays and sundays/holidays only July and August.
9 steam, 5 diesel, 5 diesel railcars.

Froissy, 80340?. Le Petit train de la Haute Somme (600 mm).

Froissy–Dompierre, 7 km, Operates sundays and holidays May–September with additional operating days on wednesdays and saturdays mid July–end August.
9 steam, 10 diesel.

81. TARN.

Saint Lieux lès Lavaur. 81500. CFT du Tarn. (500 mm).

A 3 km line operting from May to October on sundays and holidays with additional runs on mondays and saturdays in July and August. Steam usually only on sundays and holidays.
3 steam, 12 diesel, 2 BE.

85. VENDÉE.

Mortagne sur Sèvre. 85290. Train a vapeur du Puy du Fou.

Mortagne–Les Epesses and Les Herbiers, 21 km. Saturdays and sundays June–September. Usually ex SNCF 040TA137 in use.
2 steam.

89. YONNE.

Toucy. 89130. CFT de la Puisaye.

Toucy–Montagis. 81 km. Operates Sundays only June–September.
4 diesel railcars.

91. ESSONNE.

Evry. 91000. CF de Saint Eutrope. 600 mm.

Whilst garden railways are not included, this park railway had been as it is in the Paris area and has a good collection of rolling stock. Operates 2.5 km of line on wednesdays, saturdays, and sundays/holidays May to November. Steam normally only on sundays/holidays.
7 steam, 9 diesel, 1 diesel railcar.

94. VAL DE MARNE.

Sainte Mandé. 94160. Musée des Transports Urbans (60, av. de Sainte Marie).

A collection of trams and buses as well as metro cars. Various gauges are represented and steam locos are not forgotten.
5 steam, 26 trams, 4 electric railcars.

95. VAL D'OISE.

Valmondois. 95760. Musée de Transports de la Vallée du Sausseron. (1000 mm).

Valamondois–Bois–Thibaud, 1 km. A short line operating each sunday May to November with steam on the first and third sundays of the month!.
7 steam, 3 diesel.

Museum lines and tourist operations are still developing in France, all the more so as SNCF is closing branch lines. Many of these lines are in scenic areas and more operations can be expected. In the planning stages are:

Alençon–Pré en Pail (Orne), Elbeuf–La Moulineaux (Seine Maritime), Louvigny–Thury Harcourt (Calvados), Molsheim–Romansviller (Bas Rhin), and St. Omer–Lumbres (Pas de Calais) and no doubt there are more.

However some lines have closed. CFT du Breda has moved from Pontcharra to L'Arbresle whilst there is still no news of the CFT Meyzieu starting up again yet this line had 6 steam and 3 diesel.

Not to be forgotten are the preservation groups that are allowed to run their locos over SNCF tracks. Perhaps two main ones come to mind. 231G558 at Sotteville and 141R420 at Clermont Ferrand. SNCF should not be forgotten as well as it still owns and operates 230G353. Then there are the wonderful locos in Mulhouse Museum – it is a real pity that these are not operational! Finally 1991 should see the debut of two new main lines locomotives 141R1126 at Toulouse and 231K8 (La Chapelle?).

LES MUSÉES ET LIGNES MUSÉES

Il y a maintenant beaucoup de musées et lignes musées en France et chaque année on voit de nouvelles ouvertures. Récemment, on a sauvé beaucoup d'autorails du chalumeau, surtout des 'Picassos'. La plupart de ceux-ci sont utilisés sur des petites lignes mais parfois il y a des parcours sur les lignes pittoresques de la SNCF. Voici notre liste de lignes musées département par département. Sauf indications contraires, toutes sont à voie normale.

02. AISNE

St. Quentin. 02104. CFT du Vermetois.

St. Quentin–Gauchy–Origny St. Benoîte (Aisne). 22 km. On exploite des trains à vapeur et diesel certains dimanches et jours fériés en été.
2 vapeur, 3 autorails.

06. ALPES-MARITIME

Nice. 06000. Chemins de Fer de la Provence (1000 mm).

Il y a une service de trains à vapeur sur cette ligne privée les dimanches de mai à Octobre.

07. ARDECHE.

Tournon. 07300. Chemins de Fer du Vivarais (1000 mm).

A l'origine, un gret réseau ce qui reste est une ligne de 33 km de Tournon à Lamastre. Le service est tous les jours de la mi-mai à la fin Août, les samedis et dimanches en septembre et les dimanches en octobre. Tournon est d'autre côté du Rhône que Tain L'Hermitage (SNCF).
9 vapeur, 3 diesel, 5 autorails.

08. ARDENNES.

Attigny. 08   . CFT du Sud des Ardennes.

Attigny–Challerange et Amagne–Lucquy. 40 km. Exploitation touristique dans les deux sens à partir d'Attigny. Dimanches de mai à septembre.

11. AUDE.

Narbonne. 11100. Autorail Touristique du Minervois.

Narbonne (rue Paul Vieu) à Bize 20 km. On exploite un 'Picasso' la plupart des samedis, dimanches et jours fériés en été.

13. BOUCHES DU RHÔNE.

Miramas. 13140. Old SNCF Depot Workshop et yard.

Le materiel se trouve soit dans l'ancien atelier soit à l'extérieur autour du pont tournant.
6 vapeur, 1 électrique, 1 diesel, 5 autorails.

17. CHARENTE MARITIME.

Saujon. 17600. CFT De La Seudre.

Saujon–La Tremblade 21 km. Exploitation les mercredi et dimanches de juillet à septembre.
3 vapeur, 3 diesel, 1 autorail.

21. CÔTE D'OR.

Bligny sur Ouche. 21360. CFT de la Valée de l'Ouche. 600 mm.

Bligny–Oucherotte/Pré-Magnin, 4 km. dimanches et jours fériés mai à septembre.
2 vapeur, 4 diesel.

30. GARD.

St. Jean du Gard. 30270. Train à Vapeur des Cevennes.

St. Jean Du Gard–Anduze 13 km. Sur cette ligne, on utilise le matériel de la CITEV (Compagnie Internationale des Trains Express à Vapeur). Les trains sont assurés tous les jours en juillet et août. les jeudis, samedis et dimanches en septembre septembre et les dimanches en

octobre. Pas de vapeur les lundis et samedis! Des services d'autocars de Alès et Nîmes sont assurés sauf les dimanches.
3 vapeur, 4 autorails.

33. GIRONDE.

Guîtres. 33230. Train Touristique Guîtres–Marcenais.

Cette ligne, longue de 12 km, est exploitée les dimanches de mai à octobre plus les mardis, jeudis et samedis les semaines d'été. La gare SNCF la plus proche est à Coutras (5 km).
4 vapeur, 2 autorails.

37. INDRE ET LOIRE.

Marcilly sur Maulne. 37330. Musée Vivant, CF de Marcilly. 600 mm.

Cette petite ligne a plus de 10 locomotives y compris 3 vapeur. 2 des machines à vapeur sont du "Feldbahn" en Pologne.

37500 Chinon. Trains à vapeur de Touraine. TVT.

Chinon–Richelieu, 21 km. Exploité les samedis et dimanches de fin mai au début septembre.
4 vapeur, 8 diesel, 3 autorails.
On présume que la plupart du matériel est à Richelieu.

38. ISÈRE.

St. Georges de Commiers. 38450. Chemin de Fer de La Mure. (1000 mm).

St. Georges de Commiers–La Mure 30 km. Vois plus haut dans les lignes privées.
2 diesel, 6 électrique, 5 automotrices.

40. LANDES.

Sabres. 40300. CFT des Letes de Gascogne.

Sabres–Marquèze, 4 km. Exploité tous les jours de juin à septembre avec un train toutes les 40 minutes 10.30–17.20 sauf 12.00–14.00.

43. HAUTE LOIRE.

Dunières. 43220. CFT du Velay. (1000 mm).

Dunières–St. Agrève 37 km. Encore une partie de l'ancien réseau Vivarais. Malheureusement, la ligne n'a pas été exploitée depuis quelques années et son avenir est incertain. Le matériel est garé en plusieurs endroits.
4 vapeur, 2 diesel, 10 autorails.

45. LOIRET.

Pithiviers. 45300. Musée de Transports de Pithiviers. MTP. (600 mm).

Pithiviers–Bellébat, 4 km. La première ligne en France à être sauvée par des amateurs. L'exploitation de cette ligne, qui faisait partie d'un réseau pour transporter des betteraves à sucre, a commencé en 1966. Exploitée les dimanches de mai à octobre. La gare SNCF la plus proche est Étampes.
13 vapeur, 2 diesel, 2 autorails.

50. MANCHE.

TRAINS TOURISTIQUES DU COTENTIN.

Deux extremitiés de la même ligne, Carentan–Carteret.

Barneville-Carteret. 50270. Trains Touristique de la Côte des Isles.

Carteret–Port Bail 9 km. Exploitée les dimanches et fêtes de mai à septembre.

Carentan 50500. Trains Touristique des Marais.

Carentan–Baupte 10 km. Exploitée les mardis et jeudis en été.

172

Pontaubault 50300. CF de la la Vallée de la Selune.

Pontaubault–Parigny–St. Hilaire du Harcouet 24 km.
Jours d'exploitation non connus.

54. MEURTHE & MOSELLE.

Conflans Jarny. 54800.

La CITEV (voir 30 GARD) utilise une partie des ateliers SNCF et y entretient une partie de son matériel en hiver. Le solde du matériel est à St. Jear du Gard.

57. MOSELLE

Abreschviller. 57560. CF Forestier D'Abreschviller. (700 mm).

Abreschviller–Gret Soldat 6 km. Cette ligne forestière pittoresque fut ouverte en 1884 mais fermée en 1966. Un service touristique commença en 1968. Exploité les samedis et dimanches de mai à septembre et tous les jours en juillet et août. Un service d'autocars est assuré de la gare de Sarrebourg (12 km).
4 vapeur, 1 diesel.

Vigny, 57640. CFT Vallée de la Canner.

Vigny–Hombourg–Bundange, 12 km. Exploité les dimanches et jours fériés de mai au debut d'octobre. La ligne fut fermée aux marchandises en 1976 et a été réouverte aux trains touristiques en 1985.
4 vapeur, 1 diesel, 1 autorail.

59. NORD.

Denain. 59220. Train Touristique du Hainaut.

Denain Mines–Arenberg, 8 km. Un 'Picasso' assure une navette sur cette ancienne ligne minière certains weekends de l'été. Il existe un musée à Denain.
4 vapeur, 3 diesel, 1 BE, 1 autorail.

63. PUY DE DÔME.

Ambert. 63600. Train Touristique Livradois–Forez. Les Amis du musée de la machine agricole et à vapeur (AGRIVAP).

Ambert–Courpière 37 km. Exploitée les samedis, dimanches et jours fériés en juillet et août.
1 vapeur, 2 diesel, 1 autorail.

64 PYRÉNÉES ATLANTIQUE.

Saint Ignace. 64310. CF à Crémaillere de La Rhune. (1000 mm).

St. Ignace–La Rhune 4 km. Voir plus haut. Cette ligne est pres de la frontière de l'Espagne. Exploitée tous les jours de juillet à septembre, et les samedis, dimanches et jours fériés de mai à octobre.

Artouste. 64   . Train Touristique D'Artouste. (500 mm).

La Sagette–Lac d'Artouste, 9 km. Une ligne méconnue, située à 2000 m d'altitude! Cependant cette ligne «mente un détour». Cette ligne fut construite par le CF du Midi pour transporter les matiériaux destinées au barrage d'Artouste qui alimenté le Midi en électricité. Maintenant, c'est une ligne touristique qui donne des panoramas merveilleux si le temps permet! Prenez les vêtements chaudes...... Exploité tous les jours de juin à septembre.

67. BAS.

Ottrot. 67530. Train Folklorique de Rosheim–Ottrot.

Ottrot–Rosheim 8 km. 1 vapeur. Jours d'exploitation non connus.

68. HAUT RHIN.

Mulhouse. 68200. Musée National du Chemin de Fer.

Ouvert tous les jours sauf a Noel et au Nouvel An. Une superbe collection de locomotives et matériel remorqué.
35 vapeur, 6 électrique, 2 diesel, 1 automotrice, 1 autorail.

Neuf Brisach. 68600. CFT du Rhin.

Volgelsheim (Port Rhenan)–Marckolsheim 16 km. Une ligne industrielle qui longe la rivière. Exploitée de mai à septembre les samedis, dimanches et jours fériés. Colmar est à 12 km.
6 vapeur, 8 diesel, 1 autorail.

Sentheim. 68700. CFT de la Vallée de la Doller.

Sentheim–Cernay 14 km. Exploité les dimanches et fêtes de juin à septembre, et tous les jours sauf lundis et mardis en juillet et août. Vapeur seulement les dimanches et fêtes.
4 vapeur, 3 diesel, 4 autorail, 1 automotrice.

69. RHONE.

L'Arbresle. 69 . Train Touristique des Monts du Lyonnais.

L'Arbresle–Sainte Foy L'Argentière, 21 km. Une nouvelle ligne a l'ouest de Lyon qui exploite le matériel du CFT du Breda qui est fermé. Exploité les dimanches de juin à septembre.
3 vapeur, 2 diesel, 2 autorails.

72. SARTHE.

Connerré. 72160. CFT de la Sarthe.

Connerré-Beillé–Bonnétable. 18 km. Exploitée les dimanches en juillet et août. Un autorail le matin et vapeur l'après-midi.
2 vapeur, 1 diesel, 5 autorails.

74. HAUTE SAVOIE.

Chamonix. 74400 CF Chamonix au Montenvers. (1000 mm, Rack).

Chamonix–Montenvers, 6 km. Voir plus haut. Exploitée tous les jours de mi-mai au fin de septembre.

Le Fayet 74190. Tramway du Mont Blanc (1000 mm, Rack).

Fayet–Bionnassay glacier, 12 km. Voir plus haut. Exploitée tous les jours de juin à septembre.

Évian les Bains. 74500. Rive Bleue Express.

Une ligne internationale. La base est en Suisse mais la ligne se termine à Évian. Le Bouveret (Suisse)–Évian, 22 km. Exploité les samedis (diesel) et les dimanches (vapeur) de juillet à septembre. La machine à vapeur est Suisse tandis que le diesel est BB 71010 ex-SNCF.

77. SEINE & MARNE.

Longueville. 77650. Musée d'AJECTA.

Cette association loue l'ancienne rotonde SNCF et l'utilise comme musée et atelier.
9 vapeur, 3 diesel, 1 autorail.

Grez sur Loing. 77880. Tacots des Lacs (600 mm).

Un peu plus d'un réseau de jardin! Cette ligne de 2.5 km est exploitée les dimanches et fêtes en été.
5 vapeur, 3 diesel.

80. SOMME.

Le Crotoy. 80550. CF de la baie de Somme (1000 mm).

Crotoy–Noyelles, St. Valery, et Cayeux. 27 km dimanches et fêtes de mai à septembre plus les mardis, mercredis et vendredis en juillet et août sur les sections St. Valery–Noyelles/Le Croytoy. Exploitée les samedis et dimanches et fêtes en juillet et août sur Cayeux–St. Valery et Noyelles.
9 vapeur, 5 diesel, 5 autorails.

Froissy, 80340?. Le Petit train de la Haute Somme (600 mm).

Froissy–Dompierre, 7 km, Exploité dimanches et jours fériés de mai à septembre et des mercredis et samedis du mi juillet à la fin août.
9 vapeur, 10 diesel.

81. TARN.

Saint Lieux lès Lavaur. 81500. CFT du Tarn. (500 mm).

Une ligne de 3 km line qui est exploitée des dimanches et jours fêtes de mai à octobre et les lundis et samedis en juillet et août. Vapeur seulement les dimanches et fêtes.
3 vapeur, 12 diesel, 2 BE.

85. VENDÉE.

Mortagne sur Sèvre. 85290. Train a vapeur du Puy du Fou.

Mortagne–Les Epesses–Les Herbiers, 21 km. Fridays, samedis et dimanches de juin à septembre. La 040TA137 ex SNCF est normalement en service.
2 vapeur.

89. YONNE.

Toucy. 89130. CFT de la Puisaye.

Toucy–Montagis. 81 km. Exploitée les dimanches de juin à septembre.
4 autorails.

91. ESSONNE.

Evry. 91000. CF de Saint Eutrope. 600 mm.

Bien que les chemins de fer de jardins ne sont pas inclus dans ce livre, ce réseau (2.5 km) dans un parc pres de Paris est inclu grâce à son excellente collection de matériel. Exploitée les mercredis, samedis, dimanches et fêtes de mai à novembre. vapeur seulement les dimanches et fêtes.
7 vapeur, 9 diesel, 1 autorail.

94. VAL DE MARNE.

Sainte Meté. 94160. Musée des Transports Urbans (60, av. de Sainte Marie).

Une collection de tramways et bus ainsi que de voitures de métro et des locomotives à vapeur.
5 vapeur, 26 tramways, 4 automotrices.

95. VAL D'OISE.

Valmondois. 95760. Musée de Transports de la Vallée du Sausseron. (1000 mm).

Valamondois–Bois–Thibaud, 1 km. Une petite ligne exploitée les dimanches de mai à novembre. Vapeur les premieres et troisième dimanches du mois.
7 vapeur, 3 diesel.

Avec la fermeture de beaucoup de lignes secondaires par la SNCF, le nombree de réseaux touristiques augments très rapidement. Beaucoup de ces lignes sont dans des régions pittoresques. Quelques lignes en voie de développement sont:

Alençon–Pré en Pail (Orne), Elbeuf–La Moulineaux (Seine Maritime), Louvigny–Thury Harcourt (Calvados), Molsheim–Romansviller (Bas Rhin), et St. Omer–Lumbres (Pas de Calais). Sans doûte il y en aura d'autres.

Cependant, quelque lignes est fermé. Le CFT du Breda a été transférré de Pontcharra à L'Arbresle. Il parait que le CFT Meyzieu est perdu de ban.

Il ne faut pas oublier les locomotives préservées qui peuvent être exploitées sur les voies SNCF. deux machine à vapeur sont particulièrement célèbre – La 231G558 de Sotteville et la 141R420 de Clermont Ferrand. En plus, la SNCF a son propre 230G353. Quel dommage que les locomotives au musée de Mulhouse ne soient pas exploitables! Enfin, il faut mentionner que les 141R1126 de Toulouse et la 231K8 doivent être mises en service pendant 1991.

BUILDERS/CONSTRUCTEURS

The following builder codes are used in this publication:
Les codes suivants sont utilisés pour les constructeurs:

ANF	Ateliers Construction du Nord de la France, Blanc Misseron.
Alsthom	Société Générale de Constructions Electriques et Mécaniques Alsthom.
Baldwin	Baldwin Locomotive Works, Philadelphia, PA, USA.
BDR	Baudet Donnon Roussel.
Billard	Anciens Établissements Billard & Cie., Tours.
Brissonneau & Lotz	SA des Établissements Brissonneau & Lotz, Aytré.
Brown Boveri	Brown Boveri & Cie.
CAFL	Compagnie des Ateliers et Forges de la Loire, St. Chamond.
CEM	Compagnie Electro-Mecanique, Le Havre, Le Bourget & Nancy.
CFD	Compagnie des Chemins de Fer Départementaux.
CGC	Compagnie Générale de Constructions Batignolles, Paris, Chatillon & Nantes.
CIMT	Compagnie Industrielle de Matériel de Transport, Marly les Valenciennes.
Carde & Cie	Carde & Compagnie, Bordeaux.
Carel & Fouché	Établissements Carel & Fouché SA, Le Mans.
De Dietrich	De Dietrich & Cie., Reichshoffen.
De Dion	Société des Automobiles De Dion, Puteaux, Paris.
Decauville	Société Nouvelle Decauville-Aîné, Corbeil.
Études	Société d'Études pour l'Electrification des Chemins de Fer.
Fauvet Girel	Établissements Fauvet-Girel, Suresnes, Arras & Lille.
Fives-Lille	Compagnie de Fives-Lille pour Constructions Méchaniques et Entreprises, Fives, Lille.
Francorail-MTE	Consortium of various french builders. Un consortium de plusieurs constructeurs français.
Jeumont	Forges et Ateliers de Constructions Électriques de Jeumont.
Lilloise	Société Lilloise de Matériel de Chemins de Fer, Aulnoy-sous-Bois, Seine St. Denis.
MTE	Société de Matériel de Traction Électrique.
Moyse	Établissements Gaston Moyse, La Courneuve.
Oerlikon	Société Oerlikon, Switzerland/Suisse.
Renault	Regie Nationale des Usines Renault, Billancourt.
SACM	Société Alsacienne des Constructions Mécaniques.
SEMT	Société des Études des Machines Thermiques, Chantiers de l'Atlantique, St. Denis.
SLM	Schweizerische Lokomotiv- und Maschinenfabrik, Winterthur, Switzerland/Suisse.
Saurer	Saurer, Arbon, Switzerland/Suisse.
Schneider	Société des Forges et Acieries du Creusot, Usines Schneider, Le Creusot.
Siemens	Siemens AG, Berlin, Nürnberg & Erlangen, Germany/Allemagne.
Soulé	Soulé Fer et Froide, Bagnères de Bigorre.
Sprague–Thomson	Société Parisienne de Matériel Roulant, Paris.
Séchéron	SA des Ateliers de Séchéron, Genève, Switzerland/Suisse.
TCO	Traction CEM-Oerlikon.

SNCF DEPOTS/DÉPÔTS DE LA SNCF

The following depot codes are used in this book:
Les codes suivants sont utilisé dans ce livres pour les dépôts titulaires.

AC	Achères		NB	Nantes Blottereau
AV	Avignon		NP	North Pole (London BR)
BD	Bordeaux		NV	Nevers
BZ	Béziers		PA	Paris Les Ardoines
CA	Caen		PC	Paris Châtillon
CB	Chambéry		PE	Paris Sud Est
CF	Clermont Ferrand		PJ	Paris Les Jonchérolles
CY	Chalindrey		PL	Paris La Chapelle
DP	Dijon Perrigny		PO	Paris Sud Ouest
DV	Dijon Ville		PS	Paris St. Lazare
FF	Forest (Bruxelles SNCB)		PV	Paris La Villette
HE	Hendaye		RS	Rennes
LA	Les Aubrais		SA	Saintes
LE	Lens		SB	Strasbourg
LG	Limoges		SG	St. Gervais les Bains
LM	Le Mans		SO	Sotteville
LN	Longueau		TA	Tarbes
LP	Le Landy (Paris)		TL	Toulouse
LV	Lyon Vaise		TP	Tours St. Pierre
MB	Marseille Blancarde		TV	Thionville
MN	Mohon		VE	Vénissieux
MR	Montrouge		VF	Villefranche le Conflent
MY	Massy (RATP)		VG	Villeneuve St. Georges
MZ	Metz Sablon			

OTHER ABBREVIATIONS/*AUTRES ABRÉVIATIONS*

(D)	Departmental use./Matériel de service.
(S)	Stored servicable./Garé en bon état.
(U)	Stored unservicable./Réparation diférée.

PLATFORM 5 EUROPEAN RAILWAY HANDBOOKS

Each title in this series lists all locomotives and multiple units/railcars of the country concerned, giving details of number carried, braking/heating facilities and depot allocation (where applicable) for each vehicle. Also includes technical information for each class of vehicle and many illustrations including at least 16 pages in colour. The following are available at August 1991:

French Railways/Chemins de Fer Français	£9.95
Swiss Railways/Chemins de Fer Suisses	£9.95
DB/German Federal Railway 2nd edition	£6.95
OBB/Austrian Federal Railways 2nd edition	£6.95
Benelux Locomotives & Coaching Stock 2nd edition	£6.95

Available from the address on title page. Please add 10% (UK), 20% (overseas) for postage & packing. For a complete updated list of titles available, please send a stamped self-addressed envelope to the same address.

Back Cover: Refurbished Renault railcar of the Corsican Railways No. 207 is seen with the 18.00 Calvi–Ile Rousse at Tennis Club on 11th September 1988. This shuttle service is marketed as 'Trains-tramways de la Balagne'.
Peter Fox

Dos de Couverture: L'autorail Renault mordernisé 207 des Chemins de Fer Corses assure le train 66 Calvi–Ile Rousse à Tennis Club. Cette navette est connue sons le nom de «Trains-tramways de la Balagne».
Peter Fox